Advance Praise

"This book is essential reading for anyone seeking to help individuals, families, or communities heal the ongoing wounds of the colonial enterprise. Makungu Akinyela clearly and compellingly shares the wisdom gained in his journey to become the scholar–activist–healer these pages reveal him to be. I marvel at his ability to combine intellectual theory, personal history, and practical guidance in a way that keeps me engaged page by page."

—**Gene Combs, MD,** coauthor of *Narrative Therapy: The Social Construction of Preferred Realities*

"Dr. Makungu Akinyela's *Testimony Therapy: Decolonizing Mental Health for Black Therapists and Clients* offers modern-day Western psychology a crucial and overdue challenge to the field's Eurocentric, noncontextualized, individualist, and colonizing foundations. Akinyela highlights how traditional Western psychological frameworks are not only culturally biased but have historically served as 'architects of adjustment' by preserving the status quo, while denying any social responsibility for perpetuating harmful sociopolitical knowledges. Mainstream Western psychology is further implicated in supporting the neoliberal agenda that defines distress, suffering, and trauma as privatized within the individual and viewed as phenomenon of a 'mismanaged life' rather than acknowledging relational, cultural, structural, and socioeconomic oppression. Dr. Akinyela's African-centered approach to narrative therapy and relational interviewing pushes us forward. This book will dramatically change how you practice therapy."

—**Stephen Madigan, PhD,** training director, Vancouver School of Narrative Therapy, author of three editions of *Narrative Therapy*

"Makungu Akinyela's *Testimony Therapy* is the book every Black person wishes their therapist had. In wonderfully legible prose, Akinyela explains why mental health care must be decolonized and exactly how to do it. Rife with examples and case studies, *Testimony Therapy* shows therapists how to help their African American clients draw on their cultural strengths to move forward with hope.

Akinyela offers concrete suggestions for working with African Americans that look, feel, and sound *Black*. While intended for clinicians, *Testimony Therapy* is also a text of self-empowerment, as it shows individuals how to do their own structured reflections about their lives, challenges, and futures. I cannot wait to gift this book to so many people in my life!"

—**Monica A. Coleman, PhD,** John and Patricia Cochran Scholar of Inclusive Excellence Professor of Africana Studies, University of Delaware, author of *Bipolar Faith: A Black Woman's Journey with Depression and Faith*

"This outstanding book introduces testimony therapy, a pioneering approach that utilizes African American cultural practices of testifying and empowerment through storytelling. It makes a strong case for decolonizing mental health by positioning this narrative therapy within Black historical traditions. Through clinical and supervisory examples, therapists will learn to help clients overcome adversity and oppression by nurturing hopefulness, cultural authenticity, and strong racial identities. It should be required reading in all programs training mental health professionals."

—**Nancy Boyd-Franklin, PhD,** Distinguished Professor Emerita, Rutgers University, author of *Black Families in Therapy: Understanding the African American Experience*

TESTIMONY THERAPY

TESTIMONY THERAPY

Decolonizing Mental Health

for Black Therapists

and Clients

MAKUNGU M. AKINYELA, PhD

Norton Professional Books

An Imprint of W. W. Norton & Company
Independent Publishers Since 1923

Note to Readers: This book is intended as a general information resource for professionals practicing in the field of psychotherapy and mental health. It is not a substitute for appropriate training or clinical supervision. Standards of clinical practice and protocol vary in different practice settings and change over time. No technique or recommendation is guaranteed to be safe or effective in all circumstances, and neither the publisher nor the author(s) can guarantee the complete accuracy, efficacy, or appropriateness of any particular recommendation in every respect or in all settings or circumstances.

All case subjects described and all transcripts presented in this book are composites. Any URLs displayed in this book link or refer to websites that existed as of press time. The publisher is not responsible for, and should not be deemed to endorse or recommend, any website other material other than its own or any content that it did not create. The author, also, is not responsible for any third-party material.

Copyright © 2026 by Makungu M. Akinyela

All rights reserved
Printed in the United States of America
First Edition

For information about permission to reproduce selections from this book, write to Permissions, W. W. Norton & Company, Inc., 500 Fifth Avenue, New York, NY 10110

For information about special discounts for bulk purchases, please contact
W. W. Norton Special Sales at specialsales@wwnorton.com or 800-233-4830

Manufacturing by Versa Press
Production manager: Gwen Cullen

ISBN: 978-1-324-08241-5 (Paperback)

W. W. Norton & Company, Inc., 500 Fifth Avenue, New York, NY 10110
www.wwnorton.com

W. W. Norton & Company Ltd., 15 Carlisle Street, London W1D 3BS

Authorized EU representative: EAS, Mustamäe tee 50, 10621 Tallinn, Estonia

1 2 3 4 5 6 7 8 9 0

This book is dedicated first to my ancestor parents, Cary B. Tyler and Carolyn Tyler, my first teachers in the art of resistance to oppression. I also want to dedicate this book to my friend and wife Chinganji, who is my constant companion and inspiration.

Contents

Acknowledgments ix

Introduction xi

CHAPTER 1: What Is Decolonization/Coloniality? 1

CHAPTER 2: A Cultural Understanding of Mental Health 18

CHAPTER 3: Testimony Therapy: An African-Centered Theory 33

CHAPTER 4: Testimony Therapy in Practice 56

CHAPTER 5: Supervision and Testimony Therapy 97

CHAPTER 6: Repaying and Repairing Our Souls 116

CHAPTER 7: A Hundred Flowers Blooming: The Future of Decolonization 133

Conclusion 161

References 167

Index 173

Acknowledgments

This book would not have been possible without the consistent encouragement and determination of my wife Chinganji. She has been my promoter, my first line reader, and discussant throughout the preparation. I am also aware that I stand on the shoulders of so many others. I am grateful to the encouragement over the years of my mentor Dr. Nancy Boyd-Franklin, author of *Black Families in Therapy*, who was the first to make me feel that my ideas on decolonizing mental health were significant. Nancy is also the one who challenged me to think beyond the Eurocentric idea of "post-colonialist" therapy to the self-determining idea of decolonizing therapy. I am likewise grateful for the mentorship and friendship of Dr. Antonia Darder, who introduced me to the work of Paulo Freire and critical pedagogy, and through hours of discussions helped me integrate this perspective into my clinical thinking.

The first conversations about testimony therapy as a critique of and a deepening of narrative ideas was had with my friends and colleagues, Vanessa Jackson and Vanessa Mahmoud, the two Black women who were my coworkers in organizing the first International Narrative therapy and community work conference held in the United States. The conference was held in Atlanta, Georgia in 2002, sponsored by Michael White and the Dulwich Centre of Adelaide, Australia. Conversations with the two Vanessas were powerful in helping be shape the basic ideas of testimony therapy.

I am thankful for being introduced to the international narrative therapy community by Dr. Stephen Madigan of the Vancouver School for Narrative Therapy. After meeting him in Atlanta, Georgia at a family therapy conference,

Stephen invited me to his Therapeutic Conversations Conference in Toronto, Canada and introduced me to my friends from New Zealand, Kiwi Tomasese and Charles Waldegrave. Tomasese and Waldegrave are two of the developers of Just Therapy, which is grounded in the history and culture of Māori and Pacific island peoples. This introduction led to decades of support and conversations with some amazing thinkers in the narrative tradition across many cultures, including Jill Freedman and Gene Combs of the Evanston Family Therapy Center in Chicago. I would be remiss in these recognitions if I did not acknowledge the amazing encouragement and support of my friends Cheryl White and David Denborough, the guiding lights of the Dulwich Centre since the untimely death of Michael White.

Finally, my eternal thanks go to my Aboriginal sisters, the late Auntie Barbara Wingard of the Dulwich Centre, and Tileah M. Drahm, as well as my other indigenous and Aboriginal friends, who I have met through the international narrative training work of the Dulwich Centre. All of these people and many more have contributed greatly to the work of decolonizing not only mental health, but decolonizing our lives as we move toward self-determination, cultural democracy, and liberation.

Introduction

I have been writing this book for over 20 years! A book about my observations, theoretical meanderings, and applied practices working as a psychotherapist in Black communities in the United States. Almost 40 years ago, I made an intentional choice to pursue marriage and family therapy as my chosen mental health discipline because, as a young social justice activist grounded in an African-centered worldview, I saw family therapy as the closest reflection of how I believed Black people experience our lives and our emotions. Family therapy was a way of practicing mental health that allowed me and my clients to acknowledge that the clients existed in relationship to others in their lives, whether there was only an individual, a couple, or a family in the room. That relational lens fit my African-centered, communitarian view of the Black lived experience.

I began my training in the mid-1980s, when many of the early developers of family therapy were still engaging in vigorous debates about their ideas and approaches to the work. Since its establishment in the 1950s, family therapy has made several significant transitions. From early systems models to structural, strategic models through second-order cybernetics and the resultant focus on constructivist, discursive therapies, the change over six decades has been significant. For the most part, this has been a transition centered in Western, Eurocentric cultural ideas and concepts as imagined in Europe and its former settler colonies such as Australia, Canada, and the United States. The questions and issues of families of color were rarely posed or reflected on up until the 1980s and the emergence of multiculturalism as a subject. Even then, therapy with Black people has largely been a footnote, a chapter, or a single nonessential course in programs to train family therapists and other counseling professionals.

Over the past 25 years I have been particularly drawn to what seem like the more inclusive ideas of narrative therapy, but even within this progressive stream of family therapy, there have been few significantly recognized books specifically striving to outline narrative ideas and practices for working with Black families in therapy.

If you're reading this, you're probably interested in family therapy like I am, and if you've been in the field for any length of time, you are probably feeling the new rumbles and murmurings among family therapists questioning whether the title *family therapy* is even appropriate in the 21st century, with all the changes and challenges of this postmodern era. A leading shaper of family therapy, Karl Tomm (2017), wrote in the *Journal of Systemic Therapy*, "the title family therapy might be limiting what has become a huge range of ideas, practices, and contexts for our work. It is not just families we work with, nor is it even exclusively a question of doing therapy anymore" (p. 21). After some reflection, I had to admit that there may be some truth to what Tomm said, but on the other hand, for Black people in America and other parts of the African diaspora, *family* has never meant the same thing it has traditionally meant in the Western sense. Family in the experience of African-descendant people continues to be a much broader relational and communitarian term, going far beyond what those early Eurocentric family therapy pioneers imagined. I really appreciate and think about the idea of family described by the Black American sociologist Andrew Billingsley (1994), who said that Black families in America are

> *an intimate association of persons of Black descent who are related to one another by a variety of means, including blood, marriage, formal adoption, informal adoption, or by appropriation; sustained by a history of common residence in America; and deeply embedded in a network of social structures both internal to and external to itself. Numerous interlocking elements come together, forming an extraordinarily resilient institution. (p. 28)*

As I think about that and about the people who have come to me in therapy and their experience of family, as well as how I have experienced family in my life, this idea of family-in-community is extremely important. This *intimate association* exists in a community that connects individuals through a network of institutions and organizations which grow out of a collective heritage and unite them in a unique cultural and historical life experience.

That unique cultural and historical life experience, though it is often dismissed, is important to the mental health of Black people and the Black community. This is why I have written this book. These are the things that drew me to thinking about mental health and the impact of living Black lives in the context of a society dominated by the ideas, history, culture, and significance of white culture. With these thoughts about recent changes and challenges in mind, I wanted to write a book that filled the social, cultural, and political spaces too often unexplored as they relate to therapy provided for Black families and individuals. I wanted to write about the significance of a therapy derived from the cultural and historical context of 400 years of enslavement, racial segregation, structural racist policies, coloniality, and Black resistance to them. I wanted to write a book about decolonizing mental health through narrative practices centered in the culture, history, and knowledge of Black people liberating themselves for themselves. I wrote this book because I believe that Black therapy for and by Black people matters.

The therapy that I have practiced and shaped and thought about over the past 25 years I named testimony therapy. If you've been around Black people and Black culture, you probably know what we mean when we talk about *giving a testimony* or *testifying*. For those of you who don't know, it has nothing to do with legal matters or the court system. For Black people, to testify is to tell your story. Specifically, it's to tell the story that you want told about you, your legacy story. It's what you want left behind so that others will remember you.

The telling of the story is very important when we talk about testimony. This means that for testimony, the notion of orality is very important. Testimony comes out of the African oral tradition of Black people, which you'll learn a lot more about as you read this book. Because testimony therapy is a storytelling therapy, it should also be considered a narrative therapy, another important idea in this book. Narrative therapy ideas have been a significant part of the story of testimony therapy for almost 30 years.

I was first made aware of narrative therapy in 1996 when I met Canadian therapist Stephen Madigan at a professional conference in Atlanta, Georgia, in the United States. As I sat in Stephen's workshop, I became intrigued by his work and how similar it seemed to my own approach to therapy. He focused on the importance of discourse and the social construction of ideas and the importance of privileging the client's experience in the therapeutic relationship. I was fascinated and eager to learn more about this work that I witnessed, and I was pleased to be invited by Stephen to come to Toronto the next spring to attend a conference he hosted called Therapeutic Conversations and present my own work. At that conference I was introduced to Charles Waldegrave and Kiwi Tamasese, two therapists from New Zealand who practiced their own brand of therapy, Just Therapy, which was very much derivative of the Māori, Samoan, and Pākehā (a Māori-language word that means European New Zealander) culture and history of New Zealand (Waldegrave et al., 2003). These therapists insisted that I should plan to attend the Narrative Therapy and Community Work conference in Adelaide, Australia the following November. It was at this conference where I first met Michael White, Cheryl White, and David Denborough of the Dulwich Centre. This series of unexpected meetings across cultures, histories, and experiences was the beginning of a long and beneficial relationship and dialogue between myself as a practitioner of testimony therapy and my friends and colleagues who work through narrative approaches to therapy.

Since those early meetings, much of my writing and speaking on the subject has focused on demonstrating both the similarities and differences between narrative and testimony approaches to therapy, and the reasons that this explication of sameness and difference is so important.

At subsequent conferences and international gatherings, I have continued to meet and dialogue with colleagues from the international community. This has given me the opportunity to discuss and share therapeutic experiences and the meaning of *narrative* from various cultural contexts and understandings. What has become abundantly clear to me is that while we all agree that people's lives are indeed constituted through the stories we tell, and that stories are socially constructed, how those stories are told, how they are understood, and the metaphors that define our stories are culturally mediated. I mean by this that socially constructed ideas, which can be and are shared across our many cultures, generally find their specific meanings for our various communities through the lens of the histories and cultures in which we are shaped.

Testimony therapy as a culturally definitive idea and practice began to take shape in my conversations with the international narrative therapy community. These conversations pushed me to think more deeply about the importance of culture in mental health work and the impact of histories of colonialism and slavery on Black families and the families of other colonized people. In 2002, the *International Journal of Narrative Therapy and Community Work* published my article "De-colonizing Our Lives" (Akinyela, 2002), where I called for decolonizing the therapeutic lives of non-European peoples. In this article I argued for the need for decentering European cultural norms and metaphors from the therapeutic practices of non-European peoples. This article was an early attempt to articulate the need to create collective stories of cultural independence for the collective communities of indigenous descendants of Africa, Asia, North and South America, and the Caribbean and Pacific Islands. The article was a call for respect for the cultural ideas and healing practices of non-European-descendant peoples. This respect would first need to begin among the people themselves; hence the call for decolonizing our lives. Systemic racism has often created a sense of inferiority among peoples of color about our own cultural practices and ideas, and an inordinate sense of gratitude toward therapeutic ideas and practices that are grounded in European-descendant cultures, with an overwhelming sense that those cultures are superior.

The good news is that I have not been the only one thinking about these things. In communities of color around the world, "many flowers are blooming" in the therapeutic garden. Around the world, indigenous therapists are asserting the power of their own traditional ideas and meanings and applying them to therapeutic practices. I believe that this is evidence of cultural democracy in practice. Far beyond just multiculturalism, which tends to be simply the inclusion of cultures and ideas other than European ones in the arena created by Europeans, cultural democracy is decolonization in practice. As the peoples of Asia, Africa, the Americas, and the Islands reclaim their own voices and speak their own special truths about therapy and healing, we are finding that we have similar experiences, similar ideas, and even similar outcomes, which we can share with each other and with our Euro-descendant colleagues gladly. However, because we are now able to speak in our own voices, and our practices are mediated through our own traditional cultures, we also find that we can offer healing methods to our own communities that are received as familiar and authentic.

What follows in these pages is my own contribution to this beautiful flower garden of cultural, therapeutic decolonization and liberation.

This book makes three major assumptions:

1. Traditional Western approaches to family therapy are grounded in Eurocentric cultural ideas and practices that, when applied to the experiences of Black American families and other families of color, have the impact of continuing the psychological and cultural effects of colonizing control on those individuals.
2. Decolonizing family therapy practices for Black American people must be grounded in recognizing that coloniality has psychological, cultural, and social impacts on Black American people. Decolonizing therapeutic practice is grounded in intentional, culturally centered, liberatory methods aimed at challenging the structural and social realities that contribute to the relational and mental health problems affecting Black American families.
3. A narrative approach to Black American relationship therapy grounded in Black American culture, history, and knowledge rather than Eurocentric culture and knowledge is the first step in decolonizing and liberatory practice. This African-centered narrative practice posits that people understand and experience their lives through stories they tell about themselves. These stories are socially constructed and culturally mediated. For Black people, these stories exist in a political context of cultural hegemony and resistance to it.

Testimony Therapy: Decolonizing Mental Health for Black Therapists and Clients outlines my efforts over the past three decades to decolonize my own work as a therapist working primarily with Black people. This book begins by expanding on the idea of narrative therapy and challenging some of the cultural assumptions of the narrative approach. This cultural challenge is initially reflected in my use of the term *testimony therapy,* borrowed from the Black American cultural tradition of storytelling about oneself, which is referred to as *testifying.*

While all people experience their lives narratively, cultural community stories are mediated through meanings that cannot be generalized across cultures. The cultural meaning of story is experienced differently in communitarian, orally-based cultures like that of Black American people. This means that even the idea of family will be experienced differently between cultural communities. This has rarely been acknowledged in family therapy, including narrative theories of the past 60 years. Thus, both Black families who consult with therapists and Black therapists find themselves forced to fit into a colonizing dialogue that is often alien to and oppressive of their own indigenous cultural context. Additionally, both Black and non-Black therapists often find themselves confused, frustrated, and disappointed when Black clients are unresponsive or seemingly resistant to efforts to help them through traditional family therapy approaches.

This book illustrates that family and community are two critical ideas that give meaning to the story or testimony that Black Americans share about themselves to each other and to the world. This is even more clearly demonstrable currently as racist microaggressions and an apparent hardening of white nationalist and anti-Black sentiment are rising, along with marginalization of other nonwhite peoples in the United States.

When Billingsley's network of "numerous interlocking elements" and the communitarian context in which it exists is considered as *family,* we see that it both aligns with and stands culturally distinct from the new ideas about family therapy that are emerging. What is significant is that these are indigenous ideas coming from an indigenous source and not dependent on the expertise of nonindigenous thinkers. This book makes the strong point that in the Black American cultural context, family includes the various relationship possibilities of the kin network, and members of the kin network/family are influenced by the communitarian idea expressed in the South African concept of Ubuntu (personhood): "Umuntu ngumuntu ngabantu" or "a person is a person because of people." This idea is translated by the Kenyan religious philosopher John Mbiti (1969) as "I am because We are and because We are, therefore, I Am." This social/relational idea of the Black sense of personhood, as explained by Africana philosophers, is in contradistinction to the internal state psychology best defined by Descartes's philosophical idea, "I think, therefore I am." This African-centered relational idea of self has profound implications for how therapists approach the work they do with families and the people who engage each other in them.

Chapter 1 of this book answers the question, "Why is decolonization of mental health practice necessary?" The chapter introduces readers to the two most significant influencers of testimony therapy, the psychiatrist Frantz Fanon from Martinique and the Black American sociologist W. E. B. Du Bois. Using their concepts, such as Du Bois's *double consciousness* and Fanon's *alienation* and *zone of nonbeing*, I discuss the very real social, cultural, and mental health impact of coloniality on the lived experience of Black individuals.

I will be using fictionalized story examples based on a variety of people who have come to see me. While the characters in these stories are conglomerations of individuals I have met, the situations reflect issues that show how coloniality—as seen in social marginalization; daily experiences of microaggression; unequal economic, educational, and employment opportunities; and historical structural racism—impacts and disrupts relationships; creates experiences of self-doubt, internalized racism, and inferiority; and negatively impacts the mental health of Black communities.

In Chapter 2 you will learn that coloniality centers the culture, history, values, and knowledge of the colonizer in the everyday lived experience of the colonized, resulting in double consciousness and internalized racism, with no self-consciousness for the colonized. This often results in the inability of Black people to enjoy authentic self–other relationships with intimate others from their community. Most relationships with other Black people are mediated by the psychological and emotional presence of alienating white culture sitting at the center of all their significant experiences. This chapter describes the testimony approach of centering the culture, history, values, and knowledge of the Black American community in mental health practice. The chapter will demonstrate how intentionally privileging Black people's culture in therapeutic conversations and practice creates liberated spaces for therapy that seeks change not only in individuals but for the wider community. Because of internalized racism, decolonization requires that we move the center from the colonizer's culture to the culture of the colonized. These concepts are illustrated with stories and case examples demonstrating the importance of cultural understanding in the therapy room.

Chapter 3 is a discussion of the theory of testimony therapy with a closer and more detailed explanation of both the similarities and differences from narrative therapy. Here we explore the meaning of "giving testimony" in Black cultural tradition and the significance of call and response in a conversation for coconstructing a story. The chapter describes the importance of understanding Ubuntu, which is a communitarian-relational notion of the self. This concept challenges traditional Western ideas of individualistic internal state psychology. This difference can have radical implications for how we practice therapy. It means that all therapy is relational even if only one person is in the therapy session. This chapter also discusses the importance of distinguishing testimony's use of orality as the guiding metaphor of how we tell stories, rather than the use of literary metaphor, as is the practice of traditional narrative therapy. This is a significant difference that gets to the heart of the meaning of story in the culture of Black people and how stories are told with a focus on orality. Here we will discuss the importance for the therapist of listening to the rhythm and beat of a conversation and understanding the importance of the body as an instrument of telling the story in the therapy room. In this chapter you will learn the importance of the therapist's use of self and making the therapist's emotional experience of therapeutic conversations a tool for healing.

Following up on the previous detail of testimony therapy theory, Chapter 4 focuses on the practice of therapy and how it is applied in the therapy session. Using stories and case examples, this chapter introduces practices and techniques I have developed to help clients give their testimony. The chapter demonstrates practices such as the four healing questions, as well as using bridging questions to encourage deeper reflection. The chapter explains how the testimony therapist uses artifact exploration, which invites people to share significant material articles from everyday life to discover deeper meanings and ideas that may have been hidden to them. This chapter discusses the practice of creating knotted codes, which are short, open-ended stories, and guiding clients with questions to unknot the story and help clients discover solutions to problems that have troubled their lives. The chapter also explores the use of *problematizing questions* and the importance of the therapist's focusing on and demonstrating curiosity about the victorious moments that run counter to the doom-and-gloom, problem-saturated stories that clients may bring into a session.

In Chapter 5, we shift our focus from a therapy of decolonization to a decolonizing approach to supervision for new therapists. A critical focus of this chapter is the importance of determining who will take up the ethical challenge of refusing to be gatekeepers for the status quo and who will be caretakers committed to accepting their assigned roles in an oppressive society. Testimony approaches to clinical supervision, like testimony therapy, are collaborative, culturally centered, and intentionally focused on developing therapists who have a decolonizing view of mental health. This chapter explores how testimony theory and practices can be used with therapists in training and how supervisors can use communitarian approaches and orality as metaphor, Ubuntu, problematizing questions, and therapists' use of self to help rising therapists develop sound, ethical decolonizing practices.

Chapter 6 involves a discussion of the long-sought solution for repairing the effects of enslavement and racist discrimination of Black people in America: reparations. This chapter pays attention to the long history of this demand, which often is thought of as only a demand for financial repayment for unpaid slave labor, and refocuses our attention to the question of repairing the emotional and spiritual damage that oppression causes, using testimony therapy principles as a way to tell the wider story of the Black community's experience of oppression and resistance in organized truth and reconciliation circles (similar to the efforts in South Africa after the defeat of the racist apartheid government).

The concluding chapter speculates on what a liberated and decolonized future could look like. Through a series of dialogues and interviews with narrative therapy practitioners from other cultures, we put cultural democracy into practice and let the thousand blossoms bloom! Chapter 7 creates a vision for a society that honors the cultures of all its people and is committed to a cultural democracy. The chapter imagines what mental health practice can be like if the various cultural communities that make up our society are free to mine their own histories and cultural resources to discover healing practices and storying traditions which speak to their unique communities. The chapter emphasizes the importance of developing indigenous therapists from our various communities and the importance of these therapists taking healing practices beyond the therapy room into wider communities. The chapter provides several examples of culturally centered approaches to narrative practices that, like testimony, rely on the indigenous traditions of their cultural communities. This chapter demonstrates that there is a rising tide of culturally centered decolonizing therapy practice which portends a more liberated future for the practice of mental health, both in the United States and in the international community.

As I've indicated above, though all the case examples and dialogues presented throughout the book are from my own work with people who have come to me for support, none of the people, situations, or conversations described in the case examples represent specific individuals. They are all composites that I created to simulate clients, situations, and conversations that I might encounter and experience in the therapy room.

TESTIMONY THERAPY

CHAPTER 1

What Is Decolonization/Coloniality?

Occupation and resistance to occupation are the central forces shaping the identities of the peoples of the world today. From Palestine in the West Bank and Gaza to Australia and Canada, to the Pacific Islands and the South American continent, the ugly ghost of coloniality, or the brutal reality of colonialism, is at the center of the lived experience of millions of people. My own people, the Blacks in America, first suffered enslavement and then colonization, dispersal from the land, and ongoing genocidal practices for the past 150 years following enslavement.

The realities and experience of colonization and occupation are evident to us all: The imprisonment of thousands of children, men, and women and increasing laws to criminalize even the smallest aspects of our lives. The targeting of our young men as dangerous and thus justifiable targets of violence from the state and vigilante settler forces. Cordoning off large sectors of our population into designated living spaces that are pacified by permanent military occupation forces that practice terror and intimidation as normal policy in the name of policing. Creating educational systems that track our children in directions leading to prison rather than preparing them to support and help their people. The denial of resources such as health care, housing, food, water, and other elements needed for daily life. The resultant increase in disease, emotional stress, family dissolution, destruction of traditional cultural institutions, vulgar individualism, and internalized violence are all evidence of the reality of the state-sanctioned violence of occupation waged against us.

It does not matter what geographical region these occupied and colonized people live in. It does not matter which of the colonizing languages we speak. It does not matter whether we live in rural or urban environments or seasonally hot or cold climates; occupation looks, feels, and acts the same all over the world.

However, just as there is occupation, there is the inevitable response of resistance to that occupation. All over the world for the last 500 years, as the West has worked toward the subjugation and colonization of the rest of the world, we have resisted in many different ways and on many different levels. We have resisted loudly and quietly. We have resisted peacefully and violently. We have resisted individually and collectively.

Occupation and Cultural Domination

While this colonial occupation certainly imposes itself on our social, political, and economic lives, it also moves beyond that into our very cultures. Our everyday histories, social practices, myths, folkways, knowledges, and ideas of personhood and the meaning given to it are assaulted in small ways every day. And as they are assaulted, they are replaced with the idea of the superiority of Western knowledge, values, and cultural practices; even in our needs for sources of healing and repair for our people's fighting spirit.

This reality brings us to what I believe is a profound and powerful ethical question that we therapists who are from the occupied cultural communities must confront. What is our responsibility to resist not only the political, social, and economic occupation of our people and communities, but also the occupation of our culture, identities, and very thought processes through therapeutic ideas, practices, and traditions imported from our occupiers—even when they are well intentioned?

I raise this question fully convinced that all ideas, practices, and knowledge are socially constructed and culturally mediated. All ideas, practices, and knowledge are grounded in the history, mythology, metaphor, and philosophy of their source culture. If we can accept this as true, and if we are supporters of our people's right and need to resist occupation, then this should also include resistance to cultural domination, which is the ground of political domination.

Through the cultural, religious, and educational institutions supported by the colonizers, even those of us who are committed to the liberation of the humanity of our peoples have been seduced by cultural hegemony and a belief in the basic superiority of Western ideas and practices. This happens whether we use the pathology-diagnosis-based practices of psychoanalytic theory, or the individualizing assumptions of internal state psychology, or the so-called evidence-based assumptions of cognitive behavioral therapy, or even the narrative therapy assumptions that the stories people tell about their lives are always grounded in literary metaphors.

Ethics and Cultural Responsibility

Through cultural hegemony, colonialism convinces the oppressed that even the ideas and practices of therapy, and the myths and metaphors of the colonizer on which they are based, are superior to the traditions, memories, stories, and healing practices of the oppressed. This often means that therapists from colonized and formerly colonized peoples, using therapeutic practices grounded in the culture of the colonizer, unwittingly reinforce the cultural, colonial domination of the oppressed even as we seek to bring healing through our practice.

I'm not claiming that the practices of these familiar therapeutic approaches are never useful, but if we are to complete the challenge of decolonizing the lives of our occupied people, then should we not critically investigate, challenge, and unpack the cultural significance of these practices and their impact on the cultural lives and mental health of our community?

This book describes the perspective and practices of testimony therapy, which, like other discursive and so-called social constructionist therapies, assumes that people's perception of their lives and relationships consists of the stories they tell about themselves. Testimony therapy assumes that there is healing possibility in the telling, listening to, and enacting of stories. An important question that I pose to therapists impacted by coloniality (as well as our allies) is, shouldn't people impacted by coloniality who have had a Eurocentric,

Western worldview imposed on us be able to inquire about the storytelling traditions of our own cultures? If we were to ask our ancestors, what would they say is the meaning of story? What forms did storytelling take before colonization? What metaphors best described the contours, boundaries, and structure of the stories? Who were the traditional storytellers, and what was the traditional context of the stories told? What were the spiritual beliefs behind the telling, and what purpose did they play in the shaping of personal and community identity? Were stories ever a part of traditional healing practices, and what roles did people take on as they participated as healers or those seeking healing?

What I am raising here is that we therapists carry an ethical responsibility to critically reflect on the collective cultural knowledge, traditions, and storytelling practices of our people in order to create indigenous narrative practices that encourage a community spirit of national self-determination and liberation.

When we look to decolonize mental health, it means we take seriously the claim that for Black and other non-European-descended peoples living in Eurocentric social realities, this lived experience is dangerous and damaging to our mental health and relationships.

Even for those of us, like Blacks in America, who are citizens of our former colonizing entities and who theoretically enjoy the freedoms of Western democracies, coloniality and cultural hegemony, the imposition of Eurocentric values, beliefs, assumptions, perspectives, and most importantly racial white supremacy, impacts every aspect of our lived experience.

Throughout history, colonization has held a purpose—the exploitation and manipulation of the powerless poor for the political/economic, cultural, and military benefit of the powerful rich. Africa and the Black diaspora, including the Caribbean and the United States, has been exploited by Europe and the West for over 500 years since 1492. In the United States, past colonization looked like slavery and Jim Crow. Today colonization looks like systemic and structural racism.

Coloniality is the cultural, social, and psychological impact of colonialism on the oppressed. Coloniality results in internalized racial hatred, inordinate dependence on validation by the oppressor, and disrupted relationships between colonized peoples. Coloniality contributes to the experience of alienation and condemns the colonized to perpetually being in a zone of nonbeing, unrecognized as fully human.

Decolonization is the ongoing striving and struggle of the oppressed to be recognized as human and to be self-determining and politically, economically, socially, culturally, and psychologically free of the oppressive colonial system. Let's look at an example of what that struggle might look like for an individual Black person.

Clarissa

Clarissa, a Black woman in her early 50s, complains that her 15-year marriage with her husband is passionless, sexless, and lacks intellectual stimulation for her. Her husband, who works away from home several days a week, seems oblivious to Clarissa's complaints or even that there is a problem in the marriage. She has suggested several times that he come with her to speak with a counselor, but he consistently says he is too busy and that he doesn't see any problems in the marriage that they can't handle on their own.

Clarissa continues in therapy for herself to help her make some decisions about her relationship. This is her second marriage and her third significant relationship. Her first relationship was both physically and emotionally abusive and resulted in two children, though she never married. She escaped that relationship with the help of friends after several years. Her second relationship, though it resulted in marriage, was tumultuous and painful due to relentless infidelities by her husband, resulting finally in her contracting an STD, which was the last straw before she filed for divorce.

She had hoped after several years being single that this husband, whom she met in church, would be different . . . but here she is. She is feeling like a failure. After several sessions discussing these painful memories, Clarissa one day comes into session and declares, "I hate Black men!" She laughs as she says this but then continues, "All my life Black men have fucked me over. Even my daddy. He was abusive and didn't want to work. My mama took care of everything around the house, and she made the money. I just get tired of being another Black woman messed over by Black men! I mean, what's wrong with me that they treat me so bad? Is my hair too nappy? Am I too dark? I mean really... what's the problem? I hate Black men!"

Clarissa is experiencing marital problems exacerbated by the sexist attitudes and abusive behaviors of the men she has met in her life. This is an experience that many women in a patriarchal, heteronormative society experience. However, from Clarissa's perspective, the problem is not sexism or heteronormativity. She sees all her problems with the men in her life as ones grounded in the Blackness of the men. She sees these problems as the result of Blackness. It is an experience in which racialization impacts and colors every experience and is the answer to most problems. This worldview alienates Black people from relationship with other Black people.

The Fact of Our Blackness and Africana Critical Theory

Clarissa's story and the other stories you will find in this book of Black people seeking mental health support are all told through the lens of a decolonizing worldview. These stories represent experiences that are all too common among Black Americans. These are stories that are likely only heard when the storyteller feels that they are in a safe and welcoming space where they will not be pathologized, discounted, or misunderstood by a witnessing therapist who does not understand how common these experiences are for Black folk. Decolonizing mental health is first and foremost about placing the stories—the testimonies—that Black people share about their experience in the context of the coloniality and racialized oppression that we experience daily. The way that therapists hear and construct meaning along with the storytellers is essential to the practice of decolonizing mental health.

These stories of Black people navigating the world they live in remind us that we live daily with the *fact* of our Blackness and the knowledge that it alienates us from the centers of power and influence and significance in society. We live resentful of that knowledge and angry with ourselves and with the larger society. That knowledge is constantly with us; sometimes faintly at the margins of our thoughts, but frequently floating near the forefront of our minds, influencing us, nagging us, and causing self-doubt. But then there are those times when the *fact* of our Blackness sits heavily in the center of our consciousness and distorts all that we are as we interact with the world.

Black people are constantly aware of the *fact* of our Blackness in our hair, our speech, and our bodies and movement. Reminded of it in our dress and our hygiene and the choices of our style. Some manage this knowledge well; some find it unwieldy and destabilizing. Many find it overwhelming and debilitating, and all of us find different ways of living with the *fact* of our Blackness.

Coloniality is the emotional and psychological impact of living with the *fact* of our Blackness. Growing up in this social and cultural reality influences and shapes how our brains learn to deal with the world. It shapes how we relate to other Black people around us as well as other nonwhite people, and it certainly shapes the way we relate to white people. It shapes how we think about ourselves and how we give meaning to our existence. The fact of our Blackness and our constant awareness of it on varying levels is the most significant influence on daily living for Black people in America.

While Euro-Western theories of psychology and approaches to therapy might sometimes be useful when Black people come to us for mental health support, if there is no consideration or understanding of the central significance of coloniality in our lives and the negative disempowering impact of Euro-Western domination of Black people, then those colonizing Euro-Western approaches can only further contribute to alienation of Black people from ourselves, our relationships, and the larger society.

This is why it is important to decenter Euro-Western assumptions and practices and to center Africana knowledge, experiences, and cultural ways for engaging with Black people who come to us for mental health support. This is the work of decolonizing mental health.

I'm writing this fully aware that I am not the first person to think about these things. I stand on the shoulders of thinkers and activists who have struggled with the *fact* of our Blackness and ways of overcoming and healing the wounds imposed by colonizing white supremacy in our lives. Throughout the modern period, over the past 500-plus years (since 1492) that Europe has imposed its cultural, economic, and political will on us, Blacks have thought critically about the problems and solutions to colonization and white supremacy in our lived experience. This tradition of African-descendant thinkers and actors wrestling critically with our everyday realities has developed into an *Africana critical theory* (Rabaka, 2009) within the Black radical tradition.

Of course, for many of you who might have knowledge of Western intellectual traditions and philosophy, when I mention *critical theory*, your thoughts float immediately to 20th-century European philosophers like Theodor Adorno, Herbert Marcuse, and Jürgen Habermas and their Frankfurt School of critical theory. Certainly, you didn't think about any Black thinkers or philosophers. This is the hidden power of coloniality. It decenters and marginalizes all that is not white from our thoughts and references.

Critical theory is a social and philosophical approach that critiques and seeks to change society by analyzing the power structures and ideologies that sustain inequality and oppression. Coloniality would invite us to believe that only white men of the ruling class can have the capacity to think critically about inequality and oppression, and it prevents us from considering that people who might be oppressed could think about their own condition and develop ideas of liberation from their own knowledge and experience. Coloniality prevents us from centering our thought and practice in the African cultural tradition, yet African-descendant people have done this throughout the modern era. This is the tradition of Africana critical theory that we want to learn from, and where we want to base our decolonizing mental health practice.

Many activists, scholars, and intellectuals among us have identified this experience of living with the *fact* of our Blackness. Foremost among those, for me, have been W. E. B. Du Bois and Frantz Fanon. Du Bois (1903) calls it *double consciousness*. For Fanon (2008), it is the *white gaze* that entraps us in an "epidermal racial schema" of our bodies.

W. E. B. Du Bois and Double Consciousness

The brilliance of William Edward Burghardt Du Bois spanned both the 19th and 20th centuries. He is without doubt one of the most important intellects of his time. Du Bois, who was a historian, a sociologist, a philosopher, and an activist for the freedom of Black people before there was a name for it, grounded his thinking and research in Afrocentric methodology.

Through his research, Du Bois documented social relationships of Black people in both urban and rural living spaces, taking note of economic, religious, social, cultural, and other factors in the context of a white racist society that impacted their life chances. All these contexts of relationship, for Du Bois, resulted in an internal psychological experience that he names double consciousness. He writes,

> *It is a peculiar sensation, this double consciousness, this sense of always looking at one's self through the eyes of others, of measuring one's soul by the tape of a world that looks on in amused contempt and pity. One ever feels his two-ness,—an [white] American, a Negro [Black American]; two souls, two thoughts, two unreconciled strivings; two warring ideals in one dark body, whose dogged strength alone keeps it from being torn asunder. (1903, p. 2)*

This is a troubling and somehow beautiful description of living with the *fact* of our Blackness. It is a description that might elude you if you have not lived it, but if you are Black, you likely immediately and almost intuitively get it! You feel the conflict within yourself of loving and hating your existence all at the same time. What if therapists were to center this knowledge when considering all problems that people who identify as Black, or at least so-called nonwhite, bring to the therapy room?

What if we ask ourselves how this double consciousness might impact the way people experience themselves and others like them? How might it influence the way they communicate with their loved ones as their dissociated "white" soul sits in judgment of their every action, look, and way of being in the world, and their "Black" soul sometimes agrees with and sometimes rejects that judgment? What must be the experience of being in constant conflict with self as you live your life daily? This is the problem that Du Bois moves from the shadows and the margins and makes central and explicit with his theory of double consciousness. This is a powerful idea that we were never taught to consider in traditional Western therapeutic training.

Du Bois's double consciousness has been very significant in helping me center the knowledge and experience of Black people in the therapy room. Paying attention to how double consciousness might influence thinking and relationships is a powerful resource. In addition to the brilliant ideas of this ancestor, my work is most influenced by one of the greatest decolonizing Africana critical thinkers and mental health practitioners of the 20th century, Frantz Fanon. Because of his influence on my thought and practice, I want to end this chapter with a critical focus on Fanon's ideas about decolonization and mental health.

Reclaiming Frantz Fanon

Frantz Fanon, the Black psychiatrist from the small Francophone island of Martinique, is revered throughout the Black diaspora and the Third World as one of the great anticolonial intellectuals and activists of the 20th century. In a span of less than 10 years he authored four books and numerous papers, many of which were published posthumously after his death at the age of 36 in 1961. His most influential book, *The Wretched of the Earth* (Fanon, 2004), became known as "the bible" for revolutionary anticolonial activists around the Third World. It was particularly important to the thinking that shaped the Black Power Movement in the United States in the 1960s and '70s. Much of his writing focused on the clinical aspects, psychological implications, and cultural meanings he observed as Black people and their families struggled against white supremacy and colonial oppression.

Fanon grew up in an upper-middle-class family on the West Indian island of Martinique, which today is a department of the French Republic, and which was a colony of France at the time of his birth. By all accounts, Fanon was a precocious and active child and youth who joined the colonial French army to fight in France in World War II at 19. While he left his island home as an optimistic youth excited about visiting the "home country" of France, his experience as a colonial soldier soon hardened him and made him cynical about France and about his relationship to the country as a Black person. Fanon was seriously injured in combat and received the French Croix de Guerre for bravery. He came to realize that he was more willing to fight and give his life for French freedom from Nazi Germany than the French peasants who lived in the country. It was also during this time that he realized that he was looked on by white French citizens as a *nigger* before they recognized him as French.

After the war he first considered dentistry but later decided to enter medical school and specialize in psychiatry. He studied in the French city of Lyon, where he also began to write his first book, *Black Skin, White Masks*, which he initially hoped would be his medical school dissertation, but when it was rejected chose to write on a less controversial subject. It is in this book that I find Fanon's most groundbreaking ideas that inform how we can think about decolonizing mental health practice.

Fanon served a residency in psychiatry under the mentorship of François Tosquelles, a radical psychiatrist who helped Fanon focus on the relationship between culture and psychopathology, which enabled Fanon to make significant contributions to liberation psychology, though he remains best known for his political writings. After a short period of practicing psychiatry in France, Fanon was assigned to head the psychiatric hospital in Blida-Joinville in Algeria.

In Algeria, Fanon was able to practice and perfect his radical liberatory methods of psychiatric work, which included doing away with the practice of restraining patients with chains and straitjackets. He initiated sociotherapy practices focused on the patient's cultural context. He also created space in the hospital for family members of Algerian patients to visit, to create a more normal sense of lived experience for them. He instituted work programs to allow patients to exercise creativity and productivity, and he insisted that they be treated with respect and civility.

When the war to liberate Algeria began in 1954, Fanon secretly joined the FALN (Algerian National Liberation Front). By 1956, as the fighting increased, he resigned from his hospital position and committed himself totally to the fight for Algerian independence while making a total break with his identity as a colonial subject of France.

Understanding Fanon as a Mental Health Practitioner

For over half a century, Dr. Frantz Fanon has been remembered as a philosopher of revolution, a champion of decoloniality, and a founder of postcolonialism, but only rarely is his mental health work discussed, even though to the end of his life Fanon considered his psychotherapeutic work as his primary identity. However, despite his significance as a contributor to clinical practice, cultural issues, and family life, Fanon and his ideas have rarely, if ever, been included in thinking about and practicing psychotherapy or family therapy. This seems particularly important now when so much space seems to be taken up in writing and at therapeutic conferences on issues of cultural competency, cross-cultural counseling, and multicultural therapy. As significant as Fanon's contributions to mental health practice are, his ideas, techniques, and theories in this area are rarely discussed.

In his short life Fanon authored four books, all of which document his intense interest and concern for the impact of coloniality on the mental health of the colonized, but it is Fanon's first book, written when he was only 27 years old, that gives us powerful and useful concepts for thinking about the psychological impact of coloniality on the mental health of Black people who may consult with us in therapy today. For me the most significant of his ideas is the concept of "the white gaze," which reminds me of Du Bois's double consciousness, conceived of 50 years prior and in a different geographical and cultural context. Du Bois, an Anglophone Black American, and Fanon, a Francophone person from Martinique, both creatively described a similar experience of racial dissociation.

In a psychoanalytic self-analysis of his experience as a young medical student living in France, Fanon writes, "And then we were given the occasion to confront the white gaze. An unusual weight descended on us. The real world robbed us of our share. In the white world, the man of color encounters difficulties in elaborating his body schema. The image of one's body is solely negating. It's an image in the third person" (Fanon, 2008, p. 90). Elsewhere in the same chapter, Fanon reminds us that under the white gaze, "not only must the black man be black; he must be black in relation to the white man" (p. 90).

It is through the white gaze that we Black people are shaped and through which the meaning of "Blackness" in the Western world is defined. Our Blackness only has significance in the presence of a significant and assumed superior "whiteness." It has only been in the 500-year encounter with European expansion and domination in the assumed guise of "whiteness" that being Black has any real meaning. We must be Black in relation to the white man, and we experience our Blackness constantly from the perspective of defining whiteness.

Jordan Peele (2017) produced and directed a movie that struck a nerve among Black people, creating horror and immediate recognition at the same time. It was in fact a horror movie carrying a title that every Black person knew should be the reaction when you sense that you are in a terrifying situation: *Get Out!* It has been an Black inside joke for years that Black people would never in real life be caught in horror movie situations the way young white people in slasher flicks always seem to be. White folks, we joke, always seem to be oblivious to danger and in fact mindlessly run toward the screams, when we all know the average Black person would immediately get out and get away. But while the usual white slasher film is about crazed human or inhuman monsters chasing white kids around isolated woods, *Get Out!* is about the everyday horror of benign white racism that sneaks up on you when you least expect it.

At the heart of the story in *Get Out!*, the white antagonists are able to seduce and hypnotize their Black victims, who then fall into "the sunken place," where they are aware of the danger they are in yet can do nothing to stop what is happening to them, and no one else around them can see or recognize them or their humanity. Since that film's debut, this idea of "the sunken place" has become a popular way among Black people to describe people caught in the controlling gaze of whiteness and held powerless to do anything for themselves or their community.

Over 60 years before Peele would show us the horror of racism in *Get Out!*, Frantz Fanon in *Black Skin, White Masks* described what he called the *zone of nonbeing*. In the introduction he writes, "Running the risk of angering my black brothers, I shall say that a Black is not a man. There is a zone of nonbeing, an extraordinarily sterile and arid region, an incline stripped bare of every essential from which a genuine new departure can emerge" (2008, p. xii).

Fanon says this almost in passing in his introduction, but then in the book's seventh chapter, in a section called "The Black Man and Hegel," he tackles and flips on its head one of the foundational concepts of Western philosophy and consequently Western psychology, Hegel's so-called "master–slave" dialectic.

The main point of Hegel's philosophy is that human consciousness and self-awareness are achieved through mutual recognition between the self and the other after a struggle between self and other for dominance. It's all a metaphor about how we come to be aware as human beings.

Fanon looks at Hegel's philosophy and then argues that in the relationship between the colonizer (whites) and the colonized (Blacks), there is no mutual recognition, because in the world of whiteness the colonized are never considered truly human. They exist somewhere outside of humanity in the zone of nonbeing. In the colonizer/colonized relationship, the colonized are simply part of the background or scenery that makes up the world of the colonizer, like a tree, or a chair, or a pet, but rarely if ever a significant subject worthy of recognition.

Fanon's ideas on the zone of nonbeing could answer those nagging *how* and *why* questions that never seem to have good answers in conversations about race and racism in America. "How could one group of people hold another group of people in slavery for centuries, working and brutalizing them to the point of death?" "Why did the U.S. government allow Black citizens to be deprived of basic civil and human rights for over 75 years during the period of Jim Crow in America?" "How could over 4,000 Black men, women, and children be lynched in public by mobs of smiling white men, women, and children, often with photographs and the selling of souvenirs, with no legal repercussions?" "Why would a police officer rest his knee on the neck of a dying Black man pleading for his life and calling for his mother for 9 minutes and 29 seconds while the officer smiled in defiance at a Black crowd pleading for the man's life?" Fanon's answer would be, "a Black man is not a man." In the world of whiteness, Black human beings are not recognized as humans. We live in an in-between zone, a zone of nonbeing.

I want to suggest that even among Black people who have never explicitly stated or discussed these ideas, on some level most Black people are aware of this reality. It rests in our consciousness uneasily, like the *fact* of our Blackness, moving into our conscious awareness when traumatic events happen. Whether forcing us to confront our situation when we witness or experience overt racism, or pestering us like a mosquito buzzing around our heads when we endure vaguely irritating microaggressions with white people, living in Fanon's zone of nonbeing can make us feel crazy.

So, what is the impact of this experience of being Black in the context of whiteness? How does coloniality affect us in our everyday lives? Fanon argued that colonialism (systemic oppressive exploitation) created a sense of inferiority in the oppressed, centered in the reality of being limited in life chances by white supremacist racism.

Fanon did not believe that the colonized naturally considered themselves inferior to colonizing whites. He believed that we are *inferiorized* by the structural, social, and cultural limitations of living in a society created to benefit white people, which creates a treadmill effect, where we seem to always be running to get equal access to the benefits of white society yet always seeming to fall short. The constant chasing after success becomes an unconscious chasing after whiteness, while knowing that it can never be achieved. Fanon writes,

> *I start suffering from not being a white man insofar as the white man discriminates against me; turns me into a colonized subject; robs me of any value or originality; tells me I am a parasite in the world, that I should toe the line of the white world as quickly as possible, and that we are brute beasts; that we are a walking manure, a hideous forerunner of tender cane and silky cotton, that I have no place in the world. (2008, p. 78)*

Living in a world where we always feel two steps behind; witnessing the passing of laws that invalidate our right to equality and justice and being surrounded by media which constantly suggests that we just don't quite fit in is an inferiorizing experience. This is the basis of the racialized inferiority complex. It is an inferiority grounded in material and social reality that reminds us that no matter how educated, or skilled, or well-dressed we are, no matter how well we speak English or how polite we are, no matter how good our grades are in school or how long we have worked faithfully at our jobs, we never quite measure up. We are always going to be suspected of being a diversity, equity, and inclusion (DEI) hire or filling a racial quota requirement, and as long as we strive to overcome inferiority only in the context of the path to whiteness allowed to us, we meet frustration and exhaustion.

Fanon said that the treatment for this inferiority complex was to take a person through a process of conscientization focused on changing the racist social structure, that is, to confront the oppressive system. The solution to inferiorization is to refuse to accept either the conclusions or the solutions of white supremacist racism. The way out of the limiting situations of coloniality is not forced inclusion in a structurally oppressive system, but liberation and dismantling of the system itself for a new and liberated consciousness.

Culture and Resistance: Black Community Institutions as Cultural Organizing Spaces

For Fanon, mental health and psychotherapy must always be considered in cultural and social context. He argued that all mental disorders were social and relational circumstances (Fanon, 2008). He argued that when human beings are alienated from other humans, from nature, from familiar social institutions, and so on, they also become alienated psychologically from themselves. Alienation—psychological fracturing—is magnified in the oppressive conditions of colonial society.

This way of understanding Fanon and reclaiming his ideas for decolonizing mental health for Black people suggests five assumptions:

1. Coloniality for Blacks in America is still defined by the institutional violence of structural racism, which inhibits human growth, negates inherent potential, limits productive living, and causes death (Bulhan, 1985, p. 135).
2. This institutional violence produces a psychological outcome of alienation, double consciousness, and cultural inferiority among Blacks in America.
3. Alienation, double consciousness, and cultural inferiority disrupts supportive, interpersonal, and mutually beneficial social relationships among Blacks in America.
4. Decolonizing-focused relational psychotherapy inviting individuals, families, and communities to critically question experiences of double consciousness, alienation, and inferiority helps to negate the psychological impact of institutional violence and racist coloniality on oppressed people.
5. African-centered institution building and organized resistance demanding social justice detoxifies alienation, double consciousness, and cultural inferiority. This resistance does not necessitate violence on the part of the oppressed. What is necessary for detoxification is collective self-determining actions of resistance to oppression, which may include cultural resistance, political resistance, economic organizing, social institution building, and so on, all in the interest of becoming a people for themselves rather than simply being an oppressed people in themselves.

It's important to emphasize here that even decolonized mental health practices are not in themselves liberating. This is another lesson learned from the example of Frantz Fanon, who used his training as a psychotherapist to help restore the mental health of Algerian freedom fighters while working with the wider liberation movement in the service of social justice. When decolonizing mental health is understood as more than metaphor, and coloniality is understood as the social and political context that impacts the lived experience and mental health of Blacks in America, then providing therapy for our people has meaning beyond simply aiding people to accept their place in an oppressive society. The work of providing mental health care becomes a cultural resource for strengthening people's sense of cultural being and helping them to develop a *critical consciousness* (Freire, 2018), to move beyond social, cultural, and political limit perceptions. This work can set the minimum foundation for oppressed people to become people for themselves.

This chapter has described my ideas grounded in Africana critical theory of coloniality and why it is so important that we take on the task of decolonizing mental health. In the following chapters I will describe testimony therapy as a specific approach to decolonizing mental health practice that I have developed over the past two decades.

CHAPTER 2

A Cultural Understanding of Mental Health

Coloniality centers the culture, history, values, and knowledge of the colonizer in the everyday lived experience of the colonized, resulting in double consciousness and internalized racist inferiorization, with no self-consciousness for the colonized. This often results in the inability of Black people to enjoy authentic self–other relationships with intimate others from their community. Most relationships with other Black people are mediated by the psychological and emotional presence of alienating white culture sitting at the center of all their significant experiences.

The medical model, which is the primary way of thinking about mental health and mental illness in the West, assumes that emotional and mental instability is rooted in dysfunctions in the brain. The popular explanation, inspired by media bombardment and commercials to sell more drugs, is that when people experience mental problems it's because of a "chemical imbalance in the brain." It's then the work of the therapist to figure out how the brain is broken by referring to the latest edition of the *Diagnostic and Statistical Manual of Mental Disorders* (*DSM*) (2022), which has compiled over 300 disorders of the brain. The therapist can then apply "evidence-based" therapeutic practices that have been "scientifically proven" to be effective in treating these disorders. Of course, since these are dysfunctions rooted in a brain plagued with chemical imbalances, the most respected solution will be to prescribe a "proven" medication to restore balance to those chemicals. Unfortunately, sometimes those medications create imbalances in other parts of the brain or body (side effects), but certainly it's worth it to help the mentally ill person to fit back into "normal" society—a society that categorizes people into predetermined cubbyholes based on a social pyramid of race, class, gender, sexual orientation, and ideals of beauty, with the overarching assumption that being rich, white, and male deserves an automatic place at the top of the pile. Our job then as therapists is to help people realize their place in the pyramid so that they can learn to be comfortable there. Rarely are we expected to question the very structure and existence of the pyramid itself. The people who come to us are assumed to be the problems, with the solution being to learn and relearn how to fit into their proper place in the already smoothly running society. If a person who comes to us has trouble fitting in, then something is certainly wrong with their broken brain, and there is a disease name that will give meaning to their "abnormal" behavior. We professionals only need look it up in the *DSM*, and once we have identified (diagnosed) the disease, we can prescribe the right medicine or the properly researched and evidence-based therapeutic approach, which will certainly have the client behaving and thinking in the proper way about themselves and their place in society.

This system of mental health care would be unnerving even in a homogenous democratic society, but in a society rooted deeply in assumptions of racial, gender, class, and sexual hierarchy and privilege, this can be downright horrifying! This describes a society where words can literally make you crazy, where assumptions of cultural, intellectual, and moral superiority of one group over others can condemn whole communities to positions of inferiority and oppressive living conditions constantly struggling to be considered normal.

The same so-called scientific methods rooted in Western European rationalism of the Enlightenment period, which have given us mental disorders such as borderline personality disorder, excessively diagnosed in Black women, oppositional defiant disorder predominantly observed in Black and Brown children, and paranoid schizophrenia among Black men in unbelievable numbers, also gave us drapetomania (runaway slave disorder), dysaesthesia aethiopica (oppositional slave disorder), and Negritude (Negro skin coloration disorder).

Now you may have never heard of these scientifically researched diseases, but they all at one time were discussed, rationalized, and written up in scientific journals and contributed to the network of ideas, myths, assumptions, and justifications for the enslavement of Black people in America until, as a result of centuries of resistance to oppression by Black people, these "scientifically validated" diseases simply disappeared from the journals and medical books, only to return in future decades like unkillable movie monsters with new names and new justifications for control of powerless people. Think about how over a century ago, Western science was convinced that women's ovaries were the source of women's out-of-control "irrational" behavior, which made them hysterical, with the logical medical procedure to cure them being a hysterectomy. Think of the millions of men and women placed in mental hospitals, given electroshock, medicated, or banished from society because they were sexually attracted to someone of the same gender. Western science recognized homosexuality as a mental disorder and documented this in the *DSM* as late as 1973. Like the end of the racist slave control diseases, this mental disorder only disappeared from scientific journals because of massive resistance of LGBTQ+ people and their refusal to be defined by an oppressive social structure.

Western science and the so-called scientific method stand at the very core of the colonial oppression of Black people in America and throughout the Black diaspora. The very notion of the cultural, social, and mental inferiority of African-descendant people is grounded in so-called scientific racism, which was touted to prove, through research and reason, the inferiority of all so-called racial groups in relation to Europeans and the special inferiority of the "Negroid" racial group. For over 500 years, Western science has made itself the enemy and justified the oppression of Blacks, Asians, Latinx, and Native indigenous peoples around the world.

In his second book, *A Dying Colonialism*, documenting the social and cultural impact of the Algerian independence movement away from French colonialism, Frantz Fanon (1967) devoted an entire chapter to medicine and colonialism, describing the use of Western scientific knowledge in justifying and maintaining French colonialism up to and including the use of French doctors and psychiatrists in support of the torture and killing of Algerian freedom fighters. In a similar and yet somehow even more disturbing way, Harriet A. Washington (2006), in her book *Medical Apartheid: The Dark History of Medical Experimentation on Black Americans from Colonial Times to the Present*, narrates a horror story of the torture and use of Black bodies in medical experiments and testing that have contributed to so-called medical advances from gynecology (which was developed by experimenting on enslaved Black women without anesthesia who were purchased like lab rats for this purpose) to the scores of Black people purposely exposed to nuclear radiation to determine the effects on the human body.

Besides being, thankfully, documented in books by activist researchers and thinkers, these horror stories have been told and retold in the testimonies of Black people around kitchen tables, in churches and barbershops, in barbecue joints and fish fries, and in all the sacred and secular gathering places where Black people's culture and ways are preserved and expanded. This is the source of the much puzzled-over and maligned lack of trust of Black folk in medicine and especially psychology. Black people have learned that the relationship between medicine and the *fact* of our Blackness is fraught with danger and poor outcomes.

Those conversations in cultural gathering places link us to our ancestors' tradition of testifying (telling their story) and reaffirming the validity of their lives in the face of cruel enslavement. Gathered in sacred places in Southern backwoods and fields, enslaved people worshipped illegally in brush harbors, cleared spaces in the woods where chopped branches and small trees were bound together to create covering, allowing them to sing and pray and tell stories of victory away from the prying, inferiority-defining gaze of white men and women. In the brush harbor, the self-defining testimonies of enslaved people resisted the definitions and stories told about us by racist enslavers. In the brush harbor, we could tell our truth and give meaning to our lives as we experienced them.

It is the legacy of the brush harbor that grew after slavery in the barbershops and beauty parlors, where Black men and women shared stories about the horrors they and their relatives experienced living under the yoke of colonization. It was in these sacred spaces that elders taught young ones how to navigate and move safely in this dangerous land. Contrary to the racist, dehumanizing, Eurocentric public transcript (Scott, 1990) about Black people, they shared a hidden testimony that was liberating and self-defining about their experience in America. This is how our people developed what Nancy Boyd

Franklin (2003) calls *practical paranoia*—a paranoia about racist intentions based in experiences of racism and racial harm over centuries.

Sharing these stories and creating these sacred cultural institutions that reinforce Black traditions of community and identity is cultural resistance to coloniality. It is in the context of culture and community that Black people in America have been most successful in defending ourselves and maintaining our mental health despite our histories of racist alienation and oppression.

This last point is very important. Very often the story of Black people in America is presented as purely doom and gloom, in which we are depicted as perpetual victims who have been pushed around, shaped, and defined by oppression and made into mindless, cultureless, ill-formed imitations of white people. This image of the helpless, hopeless Black is used by racists to justify our continued oppression, and it is used by liberals to generate pity and white guilt, and often financial contributions to the latest liberal cause. But far from this narrative about the impact of coloniality on Black lives is the reality of Black resistance to oppression. We have fought and continue to fight to resist oppression and colonization. We have been shaped by white America into this oppressed image, yes, but equally true is that we have shaped and continue to Africanize American culture as we resist and fight back. This is the source of the solution to decolonizing mental health for Black people in America.

What Is Culture and How Is It Created?

So, what do I mean when I talk about culture? Is culture simply the food a group eats, or the way it dresses, or the music it plays? What exactly is culture and why is it important? This is an important question, because often in the doom-and-gloom story, the public transcript about Black people in America claims that our culture was destroyed by slavery, so as a result, we lack the cultural values or moral stamina to do well as a community. This has often been cited as a reason for the huge disparities in social, economic, health, educational, and other conditions in Black communities. Once again, it's the image of Black people as helpless victims of oppression who have no will to resist the constant onslaught of history. In this view, culture is a one-time package offer, a single collection of foods, clothes, music, religion, and customs that is passed down in whole form forever (unless you get enslaved and it's destroyed), and this culture is what makes you equal to all other human communities. This doom-and-gloom story makes Black people in America targets of both pity (because we were victims of slavery) and disdain, because we have not been strong enough to hold onto our culture to make ourselves equal to other humans.

But that's not how culture works! Food, clothing, dance, music, and religious practice are examples of expressions of culture, but these things change in all cultures over time. The collected and connected system of thought, worldview, values, beliefs, customs, habits, and assumptions shared by a group in the context of their collective historical and social experience as they contend with each other and with both human and nonhuman forces outside of the group is the engine that generates culture. Culture is the human psychological, physical, emotional, and spiritual response to everyday situations and conditions that a group encounters on its journey in the world. Within the group, cultural practices and customs are created as various subgroups contend for influence and dominance within the community. These contentions might be defined by gender, class, skin complexion, sexualities, spiritual traditions, and so on. As power is negotiated between group members, new ideas, traditions, customs, music, food, spiritualities, and other cultural expressions emerge. Culture is always shifting, changing, and growing. Like energy, culture cannot be destroyed; it can only change in response to historical and social conditions.

From this viewpoint, culture is constructed as the more powerful and the less powerful segments of society contend for positions of power and privilege between themselves. This means that any given culture is a complex of cultures between unequal class, gender, religious, language, sexual, and other elements within groups. In this way, culture is in a constant process of construction and reconstruction. This is the dialectic of culture, which suggests that there are no homogenous national cultures so much as systems of contending social groups within national groups or ethnicities. It is the interrelationship of these groups that continually produces and reproduces culture.

This then is an argument against notions of cultural purity and permanence. It is the nature of culture to adapt from and to outside influences. Culture is constructed in the constant process of dynamic change. The resulting material manifestations of cultural phenomena—for example, artistic, social, and political expressions—are behaviors of resistance and survival that assist and motivate cultural actors to make sense of and give meaning to their collective existence. At best we can only identify cultural historical moments in any civilization's process, as opposed to identifying classical paradigms that define a culture for all time.

From this perspective, rather than accepting the notion that Black people in the United States have been passive objects of a process of de-Africanization and Americanization, they can be understood as active subjects in the process of Africanizing the European culture they encountered and reshaping their own Black culture in response. Whatever religious, linguistic, familial, or sociopolitical form was thrust upon them has been appropriated, internalized, and Africanized into a new collective (though by no means consistent) ethos. There is no need to seek "pure" classical Black cultural forms to prove the Africanity of Black people in the United States. There have never been such unchanging forms even on the African continent.

Reclaiming Our Center

The hallmark of the modern era has been Europe centering Western knowledge, history, values, and culture as the standard for the rest of the world, creating the illusion that humanity has only experienced progress and development because of the superior culture of Europeans. Over 500 years, as Europe colonized the world, this supremacy has dominated the globe. The work of decolonizing our lives and mental health requires us to decenter European cultural values and concepts from our daily lived experience and center our own culture, history, knowledge, and values as the determining source of our practices and methods of healing. This is the mandate for an African-centered approach to mental health practice.

My grandmother used to joke about Black people's preference for all things white. She would laugh and say, "The white man's ice is always colder" when discussing why Black people preferred going to white establishments or professionals even when Black ones were more convenient and cost less. That is the power of the dominating Eurocentric worldview. The assumption is that the history, knowledge, culture, ways of being and doing, and even the ice produced by white people were superior to anything that could come from the minds or hands of Black people. It need not be said aloud, but it is the often unspoken assumption of everyday Black life.

But Europe's place at the center of world power has been an uneasy position. Even as Black and other colonized peoples around the world seem to submit and accept the domination of the West in our lives, ongoing resistance, remembrance, and reconstruction of our mother cultures are pushing against and moving the center. Particularly after the end of the American Civil War and into the 20th century, scholars and activists like W. E. B. Du Bois (1903), Ana Julia Cooper (1892), Carter G. Woodson, and Ida B. Wells (1970) challenged white supremacist assumptions and relied on ancestral Black wisdom and knowledge to study the problems and find solutions to Black life questions.

It was in a second wave of activist scholarship that a key question about Black culture and social reality was defined: What is the connection of Black culture in America to the cultures of Africa? Throughout the era of European domination, the story was told that Blacks had no history and consequently no culture. The logical assumption then was that even if enslavement was a bad thing in itself, it was through slavery that Blacks were introduced to civilization, so consequently slavery was a blessing and a benefit for Black people in America, who would have otherwise been born into abject savagery and barbarism. Growing out of this logic was the assumption that all the problems of Black people in America, from poverty to illiteracy, to family and other social conflicts, were the result of the natural racial inferiority of our Black ancestors. We Blacks in America were fortunate that we had been culturally cut off from this inferior ancestry, and now we were fortunate enough to be mentored into civilized life (over time) in the greatest society ever conceived, the United States of America.

Through this racist haze of miseducation, a young Black sociologist named E. Franklin Frazier (1939) challenged the very basis of these white supremacist assumptions designed to justify the historical and continuing domination of Black people in white America. Through historical and social reconstruction of enslavement data and study of current Black communities, Frazier argued that the problem was slavery itself, and after slavery the oppressive system of Jim Crow and the ongoing economic, social, and political marginalization of Black people in American society. He showed through his research that it was in the crucible of enslavement that the culture and customs of Black people were destroyed and that after slavery they had been left without the social supports and systems that a free people needed. Further, it was the ongoing systems of racial marginalization and oppression that continued to limit the life chances of Black people in American society. He believed that the deficits created by racist policies were the cause of the social problems of Black people. While he still accepted the argument that there was nothing of Black culture left in the everyday lived experience of Black people, Frazier's central challenge to white racist sociological assumptions about Black people was a radical one.

At about the same time, another scholar (ironically, a white man) was challenging Frazier's acceptance of the claim that Black people in America had no connection to the history and cultures of Africa. Melville Herskovits (1941), an anthropologist, proposed a radical theory of Black continuity and demonstrated, in his study of Black cultures in West and Central Africa, Brazil, the Caribbean, and the American South, a continuity of culture in terms of language, food preparation, musical styles, cosmologies and religious practices, family and social organization, and other areas.

This ignited an ongoing debate that has been central to Black social and cultural studies for over 80 years now: the deficit-pathological view posited by Frazier versus the continuity, strength-based assumption posited by Herskovits. This debate became critically important when Daniel Moynihan (1965), a white sociologist, was asked by President Lyndon B. Johnson to conduct a study on Black family life with a special view of the ongoing shift of millions of Black people from the rural South to the urban North. The question was why there were so many social problems in this new explosion of urban Black life. What was the source of the poverty, child truancy, alcohol and substance use, crime and violence, and general ghettoization of the growing Black urban population?

From this research, Moynihan, who was a student of Frazier, published *The Negro Family: The Case for National Action*, in which he argued that "the negro family is a tangle of pathology." Moynihan concluded that the destruction of Black people's culture during slavery and the racial discrimination since that time had facilitated the rise of a Black matriarchy, in which Black women held dominance and control of Black families, resulting in the demotion of Black men from normal places of male authority and influence in family life. This matriarchal control resulted in broken families, out-of-wedlock childbirths, juvenile delinquency among children without proper male role models, and millions of listless and directionless Black men who felt dismissed and displaced from their normal places in a nuclear family.

While this dominant pathological view of Black families and culture became the primary determinant of social policy throughout the remainder of the 20th century, up to and including the hyperracist policies of the Reagan presidency, which doubled down on the myth of the Black matriarchy with the even more demonizing myth of the Black welfare queen, the strength-based approach to understanding Black family life and culture was upheld and sharpened by a number of researchers and practitioners (Hill, 1999; Guttman, 1976; Billingsley, 1994; Sudarkasa, 1997; Nobles, 1985).

This scholarship laid the groundwork for what has developed into an African-centered focus on Black family and culture, which contributes to a decolonization of mental health practice in the interest of Black liberation. All of these efforts were finally sharpened with the initiation in 1968 of Africana (Black) studies as an academic discipline, as well as the organization of two Black professional organizations, the Association of Black Psychologists (ABPsi) and the National Association of Black Social Workers (NABSW), both founded that same year only months after the assassination of Dr. Martin Luther King Jr. on a Memphis, Tennessee hotel balcony. That year marked a defining moment in the destiny of Black people in America, when the long-simmering desire for self-determination and liberation from racist coloniality and Eurocentric domination crystallized into a decolonizing upsurge in every segment of Black life, including mental health.

What does it mean to shift our cultural center from the West (Europe) back to an African-centered cultural worldview, and how might this impact our practice and experience of mental health? A decolonizing mental health practice, rather than relying on historical narratives of Blacks in America, will ask curious questions and challenge old ideas to uncover older, more assertive stories of resistance and resilience flowing from the traditions, customs, metaphors, symbols, and knowledges of ancestors learned during the crucible of slavery, but also learned and taught by the parent and grandparent communities of our enslaved ancestors and those who created societies and ways of living even before our ancestors were ripped from our African homeland.

Decolonized mental health practice will challenge the ideas of colorblindness and sameness rooted in narratives that Black people's culture and worldview can only be a distorted version of white people's culture and worldview because slavery destroyed any relevant culture that might have been remembered from Africa. Decolonization would honor, privilege, and respect the cultural ways and knowledge of Black folk and utilize them as stepping stones to help individuals, family, and communities get back to healthy connections.

In our Eurocentric training, we therapists are taught to revere and accept as real the theories, worldviews, and conceptualizations of what it means to be human with little questioning. We may place ourselves in various camps of thought and philosophy. Whether it is the psychoanalytic/psychodynamic theory of Sigmund Freud, the behaviorism of Watson and Skinner, or the humanistic psychology of Rogers and Maslow, the uniting thread in these ideas is that they are grounded in the history, culture, and knowledges available to those old dead white men, with little other reference. We are taught to accept them as truth for all humans wherever they might be in the world. Our task then as therapists is to bend and fold the thinking and experiences of those descendants of Africa into the cultural expectations and theories of these "great thinkers" and to define clients as mentally ill when they do not fit in as expected.

As therapists we were taught to revere these great white theorists, and we could hardly imagine any ideas which might diverge from the cultural boundaries and assumptions of their thinking. We were culturally tied to the metaphors, myths, cosmologies, and philosophies behind these theories. At the same time, we were blinded to the value of the metaphors and stories of our own grandparents.

Decolonizing mental health practice makes room for the beliefs, practices, traditions, cosmologies, and worldviews of Black grandparents and ancestors. We can see this adaptation in cultural expressions like soul food and jazz, gospel music, and Ebonics (Williams, 1975), or so-called African American Vernacular English (AAVE). These retentions can be found in the way Black women stand and Black men walk, or in the call-and-response that can be heard in both churches and political rallies. It's maybe more obvious in Sunday church services or in the rhythm and beat of R&B or hip-hop music, or in the dance moves of young people at a party, or in the bright colors and asymmetrical fashion stylings of both Black men and women, especially on Saturday night and Sunday morning. These are the most obvious expressions of Africanisms in the everyday culture of Black people, even when they may not be noted or recognized in the lived moment as African. But for people who study culture, there are other, more subtle clues that one of the warring souls battling for dominance in Du Bois's double consciousness is an African soul.

One of the key challenges for us therapists indigenous to Black communities is to find ways of healing the negative effects of double consciousness and coloniality which are grounded in the culture of our own people and to recognize the impact of racial trauma and alienation on the Black lived experience. Culture and context are not marginal or secondary to the mental health of Black people in America, but is the central issue to be considered when people consult with us about mental health problems.

Testimony therapy, discussed in the following chapters, is therapy in the context of the history and culture of African descendants in the United States and relies on the meanings, metaphors, customs, and traditions that have developed in the daily lived experience of Black people since the first enslaved people arrived in North America in 1619. Contrary to the medical model of psychotherapy that currently dominates mental health practice in the United States, with an emphasis on empirically supported treatments (ESTs) and manuals, I assume the validity of the argument for common factors and the contextual model (Wampold & Imel, 2015; Duncan et al., 2010; Sprenkel et al., 2009) across models of psychotherapy. This means that although I describe particular practices and approaches that are helpful in therapy, I believe that what empowers therapeutic change is primarily grounded in the experiences and knowledge clients bring into the therapy room, the client's experience of the therapist's authenticity, and the sense of hopefulness for healing that the therapist is able to engender through the rituals of therapeutic practice. Testimony therapy, then, focuses on the historical and cultural context of Black lived experience to create a welcoming and familiar space for healing to happen.

In the chapters to follow, I highlight four important principles of this African-centered, decolonizing approach to mental health work. You will learn about the importance of storytelling and witnessing. In Black cultural tradition, a testimony is the story that individuals and communities prefer to be told about them. Storytelling is a very significant part of Black people's culture in the United States, and there are Black storytelling practices that are extremely relevant to therapeutic work. Perhaps most relevant is that these stories are socially constructed, and require not just a storyteller, but a witness to respond to the story as it's being told. In fact, it is this call-and-response interaction that makes the story and gives it meaning. In the United States, if you enter any Black church, you are likely to see this process in action. Those leading the ceremony are consistently joined by the witnesses, who sing, call out, and respond in a variety of ways to cocreate the rhythm and meaning of the stories that are being told. The idea of call and response, and teller and witness, is a good image to hold as we think about the relationship between therapist and client in decolonizing mental health practice. This focus on orality, social construction, and call and response is very important to testimony therapy ideas.

Second, I focus on the importance of interrogating meaning in these stories and interpretation as the story is being constructed. What does the experience say about the person or the community in the present moment? Again, interpretation is not a solitary endeavor. It is communal and requires problematizing questions between the storyteller and the witness.

The interpretation of texts and meaning, or hermeneutics, is a significant aspect of decolonizing therapeutic conversations (Parry & Doan, 1994). Rather than any one true meaning existing in relation to any situation, the meaning is crafted and created through interpretation. This makes space for the client and therapist (storyteller and witness) to collaborate on making new meanings from the events in the client's life.

In the West African cultural traditions out of which Black American culture is derived, there is a messenger between humans and gods. In some traditions it is Esu, in others Elegba (Gates, 2014), the deity who mediates divinations. He is the one through whom we find and make meaning. This messenger/trickster from African tradition is similar to the messenger god Hermes of Greek tradition. Of course, *Hermes* is the root of the word *hermeneutics*, which is the art of textual interpretation and giving meaning. In the Black tradition, divination or interpretation occurs through a dialogue, telling stories, and acknowledging that every story holds multiple meanings. A decolonizing therapy makes room for the therapist and client to engage in a joint process of divining meaning and creating alternative meanings for people's stories.

The trickster is also the guardian of the crossroads, another important concept in Black/African culture that can be found in blues and R&B songs, children's games, and everyday sayings. The crossroad is a sacred space (Thompson, 1984). The crossroads represent the space between the spirit world and the material world. It's also a space in which decisions are made. In every conversation and relational interaction, decisions are being made that will either invite a turn toward preferred meanings or lead individuals away from them. Thinking of a client in relationship (family, couple, community) as being at a crossroads, at a sacred place where decisions are made, helps me think through my role as a therapist. As therapists, we have responsibilities in cocreating the meanings that are formed in the conversations we share with our clients.

Stories Against the Grain

The consistently dominant story about Black people in America is a story of helplessness, pathology, and victimization. At the same time, in our sacred spaces, in the barbershops, beauty parlors, churches, and family gatherings, an alternative story is being told. Decolonizing mental health practice makes space for these alternative stories.

In his book *Domination and the Arts of Resistance*, John Scott (1990) describes in some detail the infra-politics of life for colonized people. He describes the ways in which they find means to resist and hold onto their humanity and dignity despite larger forces. These means of resistance are often pathologized by colonizing mental health practice, and oppressed people are labeled as *passive aggressive, resistant to change, personality disordered*, or any number of terms that reinforce the idea of the people being the problem. Decolonizing mental health practice makes the therapist curious and interested in the alternative stories that are revealed when we are aware of the infrapolitics of everyday life as means of reclaiming dignity rather than as signs of pathology. As a therapist, I want to create a safe cultural space that is familiar to my clients so that those often secret, rarely revealed alternative stories can be freely told.

Over the next few chapters, I share my own ideas about how we can codify the traditions of our Black ancestors and render them therapeutically useful in our mental health work. Much like our ancestors, we can use our own cultural experience and understanding to contradict the oppressive messages and influences that contribute to the sense of alienation and double consciousness we feel as we live the fact of our Blackness. Testimony therapy acknowledges the pioneering influence of Black predecessors in psychology and social sciences like Fanon, Amos Wilson (1993), Du Bois, and others. This therapy is grounded in the critical understanding that culture is never fixed or homogenous but is always changing and developing, and is the result of the contentious and complementary relationships between differing groups in our society throughout our history. This is a therapy which is centered in the history and experience of Black people in the United States as well as African diasporic influences that have shaped our culture. Testimony therapy requires the cultural humility and openness of the therapist to recognize the people who come to us for support as experts in their own lives. This is a model for an African-centered, hope-focused mental health practice, consciously intended to decolonize mental health and to contribute to the self-determining cultural ethos that has defined the historical and cultural journey of Black people in American since our arrival on these shores in 1619.

CHAPTER 3

Testimony Therapy: An African-Centered Theory

Testimony therapy is narrative therapy practiced in context of Black culture and history in America. Like the narrative therapy ideas you might be familiar with (White & Epston, 1990; Freedman & Combs, 1996; Madigan, 2019), I believe that people perceive their lives as stories with defining plot lines and meanings. The meanings that people give to or derive from the stories they believe about themselves define and influence their experience of their life. When people see their lives as doom and gloom, they live out a doom-and-gloom existence. However, when people understand their lives as ones defined by significant victorious moments, they experience lives of victory and overcoming.

The primary distinction between the narrative therapy ideas and practices developed by White and Epston (1990) and the testimony ideas and practice that I have developed is in the use of what White calls analogies, which define the central theory about how narrative therapy works. For White, the relationship between the therapist and client is like the relationship between a reader and a writer. The life of the client is like a text to be read.

In his foundational book *Narrative Means to Therapeutic Ends*, coauthored with David Epston, White explains that all modern psychotherapy theories can be understood by analogies (White & Epston, 1990). For example, he argued some modern psychotherapies are grounded in analogies with physical science, and social organization is imagined like a machine's moving parts. For those therapies that imagine human organization to be like biological science, human society is a quasi-organism, and problems are symptomatic of an underlying issue that serves a function in the social structure.

White goes on to explain that analogized as text, narrative therapy then sees human social entities as behavioral, with problems expressed as "performance of [an] oppressive, dominant story of knowledge." It is within this analogy of therapy as text that White and Epston imagine therapeutic conversations as an experience between a therapist reader and a client textual author. The work of therapy then is for the therapist and client to collaborate to help the client "reauthor" their negative problem-filled story to a more ideal story with a plot outcome that is preferred by the client.

While acknowledging that narrative therapists engage in oral dialogue with clients as other therapists might, White makes a strong argument for centering the textual analogy and shifting the therapist's reliance from orality to the use of text documents. He writes, "In a therapy of oral tradition, the re-authoring of lives and relationships is achieved primarily, although not exclusively, through a process of questioning. In a therapy that incorporates the narrative tradition, this is also achieved through recourse to a variety of documents" (White & Epston, 1990, p. 17). These documents primarily take the form of letters, often written by the therapist to the client or to others in the social network of the client (with the client's permission). Sometimes these letters are written by the client to significant people in their network, both real and imagined. Frequently letters are written by friends or family members recruited by the therapist in support of the client.

White and Epston find that this focus on privileging the textual analogy is important because of narrative therapy's conceptualization of the importance of linear time (past, present, future) to how stories are plotted. He writes, "a person requires mechanisms that assist her to plot events in her life within the context of coherent sequences across time—through the past, present and future" (1990, p. 35). He argues that through plotting stories across linear time, we can determine meaning and experience personal agency. Thus White formulates the idea that writing is the most efficient way to document change over time and to generate a sense of meaning in our lives. Thankfully, he acknowledges that this view is based in his own ethnic bias by admitting that non-Western cultural storytelling, such as that of the indigenous Aboriginal people of Australia, can hold knowledge through song, dance, and oral storytelling differently than literary text (p. 35).

Testimony Therapy and Orality

The ideas about the significance of text and literary documents versus the significance of orality and orature (Asante, 1998; Zirimu & Gurr, 1973) is a critical divergence between Western narrative therapy and testimony therapy.* Contrary to White and Epston, I believe that a conscious and intentional focus on orality as culture is critical to decentering colonizing literary culture in therapeutic conversations with Black people in the United States. This is not because I believe that Black people are illiterate or that we do not read. What I do believe is that orality as an Africanism from our West African ancestors is so central to what makes up our culture that even the best of modern Black literary tradition is shaped by orality (Jones, 1991). Following White's analogy of narrative therapy as text, I would say that testimony therapy is like music.

Narrative therapy and testimony therapy agree that people's understanding of themselves and their lived experience is constituted in stories they tell. Testimony therapy raises the critical question: What is the difference when the primary way that people conceive of and tell their stories is centered in the oral tradition rather than in literacy? Walter Ong (1982) argues that "writing structures consciousness":

> *Without writing, the literate mind would not and could not think as it does, not only when engaged in writing but normally even when it is composing its thoughts in oral form. More than any other single invention, writing has transformed human consciousness. (p. 78)*

In other words, there is a difference in the way people understand their world and their experience based on whether a culture is grounded in literacy or in

---

* *Orature* is a term credited to the Ugandan linguist Pio Zirimu as an alternative to the contradictory term *oral literature*. Orature emphasizes that stories, folklore, histories, and remembrances preserved in the spoken word are not inferior to or secondary to literary text but are equally significant to cultural development and maintenance.

orality. The nature of text-based storytelling is linear. The words on the page are permanent and have definite meaning. In literary cultures, "truth" is held in the printed word rather than in the person or the community. To think or conceive of one's world in literary terms shapes relationships. Literary text limits human relationship to the external, easily seen printed word. Printed words isolate humans and limit relationship. On the other hand, Ong writes, "orality fosters personality structures that in certain ways are more communal and externalized, and less introspective than those common among literates. Oral communication unites people in groups" (1982, p. 74).

The centrality of the oral tradition and orature to the culture of Black Americans is conceptualized in Africana studies as *Nommo* (Asante, 1998), a philosophy of the creative power of the spoken word. Nommo posits that the spoken word generates and creates reality and unites the speaker and the hearer as they collectively create and affirm each other's reality. In Black cultural tradition, speaker and audience are not as distinct as in European tradition. This does not mean that Black people don't understand the distinction, but in Black cultural understanding, just as music and dance are a collective activity, speaker and audience are also a collective activity, where speaker/audience is a mutually supportive interplay.

What this all means is that for the testimony therapist, the words exchanged between therapist and client in a counseling session are not just the means of communication. The dialogue between the therapist and client is at the heart of the healing ritual. In Black orature, the testimony therapist pays attention not only to the words coming out of the client's mouth, but also to the rhythm and beat of the conversation between the therapist and the client.

The rhythm of a conversation relates to how the speakers regulate the flow of conversation, using pauses, emphasis, and tones to shift and change ideas behind the words being used. At the same time, the audience in Black conversations defines the communicative boundaries (Asante, 1998) as they respond physically or verbally to what is being said. Through tone, accent, and uses of the body to communicate meaning, a relationship between speaker and audience is created. This is the ritual of Nommo, the creative spoken word.

In addition to paying attention to the rhythm of the therapeutic conversation, the testimony therapist should also be aware of its *beat*. This is evident in the use of gesticulation, body movement, and facial expression, which emphasize and give significance to the words being used. In the rhythm and beat of a therapeutic conversation, ideas, meanings, and concepts may be discovered that mere words cannot express.

As I'm writing this, we are in the middle of the Democratic National Convention in 2024, where the Democratic Party is choosing a representative to run for the office of president of the United States. I just listened to a speech by former president Barack Obama, who is a master of the use of Nommo and Black communication styles to convey ideas and draw audiences into a communitarian sharing of reality. Obama is comparing Donald Trump to the DNC candidate Kamala Harris. Obama, moving into his familiar lyrical style, which is so important to Black people's communication, uses his voice as a musical instrument, all while emphasizing his words with the constant subtle movement of his hands, as if to hold the words and shape them as they pour from his lips. Then at a key point, as he describes the trouble with Trump in between the laughter and goading of the audience, he says of Trump, "Here is a 78-year-old billionaire, who has not stopped whining about his problems since he rode down his golden escalator nine years ago. It has been a constant stream of gripes and grievances; it has been getting worse now that he is afraid to lose to Kamala. There's the childish nicknames"—Obama lifts his right hand into the air as if holding the words to examine them. Then lowering his hand, he turns to the other direction and says, "The crazy conspiracy theories," as he lifts his left hand in a wiping motion, as if he is brushing these crazy theories aside, and then with a small grunt and a pondering look on his face, he continues, "this weird obsession with crowd sizes." As Obama says this, he gesticulates with his two hands in front of him as if measuring the length of something, holding it between his hands. He then gives a sly glance down to see what is between his hands, and with a slight smirk moves his two hands closer together, as if the original thing he holds has shrunk to a thing much smaller. The crowd erupts in laughter and cheering. In just a few seconds, with a few words and gestures, Obama, in the best tradition of Nommo and Black orature, has drawn his audience into a shared experience of ridiculing a pompous and arrogant man who has been thought of by many as invincible, and has spoken truth to power by making the unspoken evident: This man's sense of entitlement and power can all be boiled down to a preoccupation with the size of his own penis.

It's not in the words alone, or the gestures by themselves, but in the styling of words, the tone, the movement of the body, and the verbal interplay. It is the lyrical quality of the conversation and use of voice as an instrument. It is the indirect, circuitous approach to a subject rather than speaking directly about what is meant. All of this combines to give significance to Nommo and orature in the Black storytelling tradition. The testimony therapist values and privileges oral tradition and values over the notion that literacy and reliance on words alone are superior to the storytelling traditions of Black people.

How Do Black Folk Tell Stories?

As mentioned before, I agree with White and Epston that people's lives are constituted narratively in the stories they tell about themselves. The critical question I raise from there is, "How do Black people tell stories? Are our stories told in the linear, externalized, individualizing style of Western literary tradition, or do Black people hold onto the Black traditions of orality and Nommo in our storytelling and expression of meanings?" I am convinced that Black storytelling ways are grounded in oral tradition. To denote this, I use a term that is ubiquitous in descriptions of Black people's storytelling: testimony or testifying, a metaphor from the Black cultural spiritual tradition. In the Black church tradition, testifying is a ritual in which community members are invited to give their testimony or tell the story that they prefer to be known about themselves. Testifying is a ritual of word, rhythm, call, and response. Testifying is a storytelling ritual grounded in the oral tradition of Black people's culture.

Maybe you've witnessed this ritual, or maybe you've seen parodies of it in a movie or television show. In a small church on Wednesday night, an elder begins humming or singing a song, maybe a familiar spiritual or a gospel song. After a few lines have been sung, someone might stand and wait patiently until the singing trails off. The one standing then begins to talk and tell a story. This story likely will begin with a recounting of personal or family problems experienced by the teller. As the person tells the story, they are encouraged at every sentence or so with a response of "amen" or "yes, that's right," or maybe someone will affirm the telling with a knowing "mm-hmmm." The storyteller, who begins haltingly and is uncertain of the direction of the story, seems to gain confidence as the responses become stronger and more frequent. A rhythm begins to build, and the story of doom and gloom begins to transform into a recounting of how, despite the problem, "with the Lord's help," things have gotten better. By this point the witnesses have become full clients in the story, acknowledging their own certainty that the assessment of the good outcome is a correct one. By the end of the story, both the teller and the witnesses have woven their call and response to tell a community story. This community construction of a preferred story is a central idea guiding an understanding of testimony therapy.

While this storytelling ritual based in word and rhythm, call and response is shaped in traditional West African–rooted culture of American-born Black people, it can also readily be seen in hip-hop cypher circles where young Black and Brown people freestyle stories in spontaneous rap battles spurred on by the energetic verbal responses that either encourage or challenge the rappers' creativity in weaving beats and words. You can hear and see testifying rituals as Black women gather to share relationship successes or lament troubles, and the story begins when one musically draws attention to herself by loudly proclaiming, "Giiiirrrrlle, let me tell you!" and the others, turning excitedly toward her, exclaim, "What happened, girl?"

The theme of testifying or having a testimony is endemic in all genres of Black music, from gospel (Rev. Clay Evans, the Winans) to blues and R&B (Johnny Copeland, Stevie Wonder), hip-hop (Common), and jazz (Lou Donaldson, Dianne Reeves). The ritual of testifying as storytelling in community, of sharing the preferred story that we want told about us, is a critical and central part of Black cultural ethos. This ethos is the basis of the sense of us ness and the common cultural meanings among most Black Americans that transcend contexts of class, gender, education, region, or color caste among Black people.

The ritual of testifying in Black people's conversations grounded in the use of Nommo, the creative spoken word, is the method of the social construction of stories in this communitarian culture. Stories are created and given meaning in the play between telling and witnessing of story and in the call and the response.

Social Construction of Ideas

I agree with narrative therapists Freedman and Combs (1996) that all ideas and knowledge are socially constructed. In other words, the beliefs, values, norms, and meanings that people hold are not inherent or natural but are instead created and maintained through social interactions and shared experiences. These ideas are shaped by cultural, historical, and societal contexts and can vary across different groups and time periods. In other words, what we consider to be "real" or "true" in a society is often the result of collective agreement and ongoing social processes, rather than objective facts. For example, concepts like gender roles, race, and even money are socially constructed—they have meanings and significance because people in a society agree on them and perpetuate them through their behavior, language, and institutions.

These knowledges and ideas are socially constructed, and it is important to add that they are culturally mediated. What I mean by this is that ideas are rarely universal and do not apply the same way to all people in all places. This is why in our decolonizing work it is important to challenge the universalizing notions of things like the privileging of text and literacy over orality and orature. The common idea is that people constitute their lives through the stories they tell. The cultural particularity is that story and meanings look different in diverse cultural communities. It is critical, then, that in our healing work we recognize the liberatory importance of creating space where people can tell their stories in ways that allow for their full human selves to be expressed.

The Person in the Community

Gordon (2008) says that a fundamental question engaged in Africana philosophical thought is the question of what it means to be human. What is a person, and who are we as Black people? This is a necessary question, because from 1492 to the present (the modern era), our humanity and our personhood have been challenged by white supremacy and colonization. Even now, as the extreme right exerts itself in movements like MAGA in the United States and other far-right fascist movements in Europe, the idea of Black and Brown intellectual and cultural inferiority is being normalized in daily political discussion, as the right weaponizes ideas like "woke," "DEI," and "critical race theory" to denote something not only inferior but insidious. Decolonization is the struggle to reclaim and assert our personhood, our humanity, in the face of colonizing depersonalization and alienation.

The Eurocentric colonizing concept that makes this Africana philosophical engagement necessary is the Western theory of personhood and identity expressed in the phrase "Cogito, ergo sum" or "I think, therefore I am," formulated by the French philosopher René Descartes. This is the central idea of personhood that guides Western colonizing psychology. It is a basic idea of individualism and individuation as expressed by Jung, Nietzsche, and other Western thinkers. For over a century now, this has been expressed in various ways as the goal of good mental health.

Gordon (2008) highlights an important challenge to Descartes's idea of individualized personhood by Africana philosophers such as Anton Wilhelm Amo, an 18th-century teacher of philosophy born in Awukena in the region of Axim, in what is today Ghana. He was captured and enslaved and gifted to August Wilhelm, the son of a German duke. It was this son who named him Amo, but this enslaved man preferred the name Antonius Guilielmus Amo Afer, a name that emphasized his Blackness to the world. At some point in his life, Amo achieved his freedom and studied to become a professor of philosophy despite intense racial alienation and white resentment toward him. Amo's story is important because in his philosophical work he challenged Cartesian dualism's emphasis on the distinct superiority of the mind.† Amo argued that rather than being distinct entities, the perceptions of feeling and perceptions of the mind are a function of the body. In other words, mind and body are an integrated whole. This idea of wholism and connectedness is an important aspect of the African worldview.‡ Gordon points out that a more recent Gha-

---

† Descartes argued that the mental and the physical are two distinct substances, with the mental able to exist outside the body. This contributed to the biomedical mind/body paradigm. It suggests that personhood and identity exist outside of the physical body and distinct from it.

‡ This philosophy of wholism is beautifully expressed in Dr. Martin Luther King Jr.'s (2018) "Letter From Birmingham Jail," where he writes, "We are caught in an inescapable network of mutuality, tied in a single garment of destiny. Whatever affects one directly affects all indirectly." I would argue that this philosophy of the interrelatedness of all things and beings is a wonderful example of indigenous Black cosmology, evident in everyday Black life.

naian philosopher Kwasi Wiredu (1983) further challenges Descartes from an African perspective. Wiredu argued that from the cultural perspective of Akan people, being located in space and time is essential to the idea of existence. Thought cannot exist independent of spatial relationship and time. From this perspective, then, personhood is defined by relationship.

The idea of the person existing in relationship, as I mentioned previously is found in the South African notion of Ubuntu, which is important to decolonizing ideas and practices of mental health. It challenges colonizing and alienating notions of personhood and individuation with the idea that our personhood exists in the space between human beings. Rather than each person existing alone inside their own thoughts, we exist in relationships. We find meaning in relationships, connection, and community. This implies further that the goal of good mental health lies not in individuation but in balanced communitarian relationship.

This communitarian sense of person and self, again, is reflected in the everyday language of Black people when we hear the use of collective pronouns to express both positive and negative ideas about Black lived experience. It can be heard in such ideas as, "*We* are the only people in America who don't support each other." It can be heard in collective expressions of both pride in the accomplishments or missteps of Black people who are not personally known to us, for example, the collective pride expressed when Black athletes like Muhammad Ali or Florence Joyner conquer in their sports on the world stage, and you may hear someone say, "You give us a fair chance and can't nobody beat us in nothing! We some of the best athletes in the world and they know it!" or when it is revealed that a Black person has committed some unspeakable atrocity and the common response might be, "Oh man, we ain't go'n never be able to live this one down!" In all these expressions there is some sense of collective identity that claims either victory or responsibility for the acts of all Black people. This is expressed as Ujima, which is translated as "collective work and responsibility," one of the Seven Principles of Kawaida, the basis of the Kwanzaa holiday celebration.

Once these concepts of Nommo, the power of the spoken word expressed in Ebonics, the everyday spoken language of the average Black person, and Ubuntu, the communitarian sense of self that is often expressed in our language, is grasped by those of us practicing decolonizing approaches to mental health, we listen differently to healing conversations. We listen to and engage in these conversations as orature rather than literature. We hear the narratives that define the meaning of the lives of people who come to us as testimonies of people seeking victory over colonizing and limiting life situations.

The expression of Ubuntu in the everyday lived culture of Black people explains both the relational pride and the shame expressed in conversations when a widely known event occurs that happens to involve a Black person. I remember the terrifying early days of October 2002. Black and white victims were being shot seemingly at random around the Washington, DC and Maryland area of the country. Many people in Black communities, in the dark humor style of oppressed people, joked that "another crazy white boy is on the loose. 'Cause you know don't nobody be killing folks like that other than white folk." Then on news stations all over the country, TV screens began to reveal the face of a Black man identified as John Allen Muhammad! The first response was disbelief and suspicion. "They must of set the brother up! Ain't no Black man did nothing like that. *We* don't do things like this." Then as the evidence piled up, suspicion turned to collective embarrassment. "Why that brother want to go an do someth'n like that and make us look like this?" Later, this embarrassment turned to community apprehension. "Y'all be careful out there. You know white folks go'n use this as an excuse to stop any brother they see now."

In all this process, Ubuntu guided Black people's understanding and meaning applied to the situation and shaped the stories that people told about "the DC snipers" (Muhammad and Lee Boyd Malvo). This situation also changed the stories that Black people began to reluctantly tell about their collective selves, moving us from "Black people don't do things like this" to "This country is starting to make us as crazy as white folk. Ain't no telling what a brother will do these days." These conversations were usually about the collective *we* and rarely just about the individual John Muhammad.

Ubuntu can be the source of community collective shame but also the root of Black pride, as when we witnessed the brawl on the docks in Montgomery, Alabama, on August 5, 2023. This pride was expressed in social media memes flooding the internet almost immediately and even small folding-chair earrings being sold within days, and chortling expressions that "white folks fucked around and found out!" This conflict between Black ferry boat workers and white recreational boaters on the docks in Montgomery has become the stuff of legend in the Black community and is told and retold with pride as the community remembers the demonstration of racial unity and resistance. The fight is talked about as a *we/us* response to white aggression and arrogance. It is something that *we* did as a final *no* to the centuries of attacks on *us*. This is an example of Ubuntu shaping the way the story is told and the meaning given to the story. I believe it is profoundly important that therapists working with our people understand the profound impact of this relational self and listen for its expression in Nommo as people give their testimony in therapeutic conversations.

Identifying Victorious Moments and Nurturing Hopefulness

Traditional diagnostic psychotherapy emphasizes problem-focused approaches to mental health work. Grounded in the assumptions of Cartesian dualism discussed above, therapists guided by a search for disease in clients' heads seek to identify the problem (diagnose) and then, using their expert healing knowledge, cure the problem. More recent deconstructionist therapies such as narrative and solution-focused therapy encourage therapists to listen for stories that contradict problem-laden storytelling or to seek out solutions to the problems in collaboration with their clients. In this more client-centered tradition, testimony therapy guides therapists in listening for victorious moments in a client's testimony and by focusing on these victorious moments to nurture a sense of hopefulness in the client. By noticing and nurturing these victorious moments, which challenge the doom-and-gloom telling of a testimony, the therapist along with the person seeking help can explore alternative possibilities of the meaning of the person's life.

When people come into the therapy space with a doom-and-gloom testimony, this is what traditional narrative therapists refer to as a *thin telling* of the story. It is important that we listen to these interpretations of our client's story to understand the meanings that they have applied to their life up to that moment. Because of life experiences, teachings by others around them, social conditions that seem to have set limits in their lives, traditions or cultural expectations, and so on, people often are influenced to focus on the negative experiences and life outcomes that contribute to their interpretation of the meaning of their lives. This does not mean objectively that there have been no experiences, events, or actions that contradict the doom-and-gloom narratives they have given to their lives. The work of the testimony therapist is to listen to the doom and gloom but also to listen through the doom and gloom in search of the victories in the client's life that contradict their testimony. As we listen, we focus on these contradictions which represent the victorious moments in the client's life, which they may be too overwhelmed by oppressive conditions to notice. Here is where our ability to be intentionally curious becomes profoundly important. Here is where we slow the dialogue down to review and examine this hidden contradiction in the testimony. Here we ask tentative, exploring questions as we work to draw the client's attention to these moments which have lived with them unnoticed, leaving them focused on only the doom and gloom of their lives.

Noticing Victorious Moments

I Don't Want the Other Inside My Head!
Shabaka is a 50-year-old Black man who occasionally lives with his brother and sister-in-law, when they can convince him to stay, but more often he chooses to live on the streets of the city or in city shelters when it is cold. Shabaka has lived for over 25 years with a diagnosis of PTSD and paranoid schizophrenia since his return from military service and active combat in war. He contacted me through a social service charity after he decided that he wanted to talk to a Black male therapist about his desire to be more proactive in his life and personal development. Over the years he has received services from the Veterans Administration. He has spent time in the VA's psychiatric facilities both voluntarily and involuntarily. Shabaka is both politically and culturally astute, having belonged to several progressive political organizations over the years. Shabaka describes his journey to get help from the VA at a psychiatric hospital, at a time when he was about to give up on himself and his life. He describes this as a time when, out of disgust, he felt hopeless and had lost his will to go on living. He explains to me that he has not worked because of his disgust with working conditions and bad treatment by supervisors.

I look at him deeply and smile slightly, and I say, "So you're saying that disgust starts say'n, 'Shabaka, you don't really want to do this. This is the same old setup!' But there's something else that's say'n, 'No, I got to handle this. I've got to deal with this [working].' . . . *Do* you feel more ready to do that now?" He nods his head slightly and replies, "Yeah."

"Why do you think you feel more ready now than before?" I ask. Shabaka purses his lips in thought and then says, "Before, I got into a thing where the depression became very deep. . . . I had a dream [where] I was going through a park on a bicycle and the bicycle had a flat tire and I wasn't going anywhere. I think that dream was expressing to me where I was at that time in my life, and I became really depressed."

"That was about three years ago?" I ask. "Yeah," he says. I smile again and reflect on what he has told me, and I question him: "So you felt . . . was it disgust again?"

He quickly interjects, "Disgust, despair, hopelessness . . ." We are bantering back and forth now, almost speaking on top of each other and sharing ideas, with each thought building on the next. I point out, "But right now you don't feel that way?" Shabaka looks slightly puzzled and responds, "No, I don't." I recap his push further and, using externalizing language, I pose a question to reweave these new emotions he has introduced into our conversation. "What have you been able to do to defeat disgust, despair, and hopelessness? What have you been able to do to fight it back?" Shabaka lets out a deep sigh and tilts his head thoughtfully. "Well, I left the situation. I went to a hospital down south, to the psychiatric program," he says as I quickly interject a question, "You found it on your own?" He responds just as quickly, "A neighbor told me about it." "He told you about this hospital?" I ask and he responds, "Right . . . right." I slow the pace of our conversation and ask with uncertainty, "And it was helpful for you to go to this hospital?" Shabaka smirks slightly and says, "To a degree." I quickly shift the subject: "How'd you get down there?" He interjects just as quickly, "On the Greyhound." I look surprised at this and emphasize his words: "*You* caught the Greyhound? Who paid for it?" He shot back, "I did." I slow the pace of the conversation again as I reflect to him thoughtfully, "So . . . you had this dream. You say . . . despair, disgust, depression is attacking you, trying to convince you that life is hopeless. And there's somethin' in you that's fighting back against despair, disgust, and depression and say'n 'Look . . . I'm gon'a do something about this . . . ?" He smiles slyly and nods his head, "Umm hmm, yeah!" "*You* got . . . on . . . the . . . bus!" I slow these words down and emphasize each one. Shabaka is following each word as I say it, when suddenly he opens his eyes wide in surprise and exclaims, "Oh yeah, *I* got on the bus. How about that!" and we both laugh hysterically together. "That's kind'a deep!" I exclaim.

Shabaka becomes thoughtful again, "Yeah. But I also had reservations though, about going to the hospital. I don't want people getting inside of my head. I mean this thing now [our conversation] is different. I don't want *the other* [white people] . . . getting inside my head. In essence, they're the ones that scrambled it up in the first place. I don't want to give them a handle on how to keep me in control."

I nod my head in understanding and recap Shabaka's experience once more: "So you have told me that three years ago, despair, disgust, and depression tried to convince you that life was hopeless. Work ain't worth doing. You ain't going nowhere. You need to just give up? Those three . . . *demons* were just trying to speak to you and get you to give up life, but there was somewhere in you that you found to resist. . . . You got on the bus?"

Reflection

Hopefully in your imagination you can hear the rhythms created by the call and response of this conversation. Of course, in print it is very linear. In a conversation like this there is lots of cross talk, give and take, call and response, pauses and empty spaces that all are important to the construction of metaphorical meaning. Though Shabaka begins with a doom-and-gloom understanding of his life, by listening for the victorious moments, I am able to hear and point out his own acts of self-determination and self-reliance in taking responsibility for his own care and mental health. This conversation is filled with metaphors that become places where Shabaka and I can meet for shared understanding of his life experience and its meaning to him. *Getting on the bus* becomes a metaphor for his assertive actions and self-agency in the face of victimization and helplessness. To hear these victorious moments, the therapist must remain curious and expectant that clients bring their own resources and solutions into the therapy room and not just their problems.

Also, in this conversation you may have noticed that I externalized the problems of disgust, despair, and depression that concerned Shabaka. Rather than being something that Shabaka is, or must remain, these problems metaphorically become little *demons*.

Externalizing problems is a common practice in narrative therapy, but I would argue that it does not begin only in this Western therapeutic tradition. Throughout the African diaspora in Black spiritual religious tradition, problem practices and emotional experiences are often externalized as manifestations of evil, or negative spirit forces coming from outside the person. It is common to hear Black folk complain that a person is influenced by "a spirit of greed" or "a spirit of lust." The blame for inappropriate behavior or thoughts or feelings is placed not on the person but on malevolent forces outside the person. The problem is separate from who the person truly is. In this conversation, neither Shabaka nor I understand this as literal, but it is a useful and culturally appropriate metaphor. A recurrent metaphor in conversations between Black people is the expressed resistance to racist domination and manipulation, heard when Shabaka explains that he was hesitant about going to the psychiatric hospital even as he found his way there because he did not want the *other*, that is, white people, to get inside his head. This metaphor describing a stance of defiance and resistance grows out of the healthy paranoia of Black people who have been victimized by centuries of unethical and genocidal experimentation and research on them by the medical and psychiatric establishment.

Paying Attention to the Rhythm and Beat of the Conversation

The conversations of Black people are musical! This is the nature of orality and Nommo. There is a rhythm and a beat to the conversation that conveys meaning and significance. In the example, above you may have noticed that I, as a witness to Shabaka's testimony, responded with lots of repetition and pauses and circling back to previous ideas as well as interjections as Shabaka told his story.

Because the therapeutic conversation with Black clients is grounded in orature, more than in literature, the testimony therapist listens for the meaning of conversation beyond the literal words spoken. The testimony therapist pays attention to tone, cadence, body posture, wordless sound, and silences, which are the context of the conversation.

If you listen with intent to identify the musicality in Black people's conversations, you might hear that some conversations sound like a blues song while others are more gospel or R&B, and still others might feel like hip-hop, spirituals, or jazz. As the therapist, you are witness to the testimony as well as part of the music that is constructing meaning in the story. Are you like a drummer keeping the beat? Are you laid back and just under the conversation, like a bass player in a jazz trio, or maybe a blaring horn emphasizing points of the story and harmonizing with your client who is playing a solo at this moment?

For people in cultures grounded in orality, language is not just in the words spoken but also in the movement and articulation of the body—in gestures and posturing of the arms and head, in rocking and swaying of the hips and in the eyes, looking where maybe there is nothing to be seen. Paying attention to the rhythm and beat of the conversation means being aware of parts of the message and interpreting the meaning in them, knowing that they are significant.

Focus on Emotional Liberation

Black people, the descendants of enslaved Blacks, are emotional in ways that are often deemed inappropriate in Euro-American social settings. We often talk louder, laugh louder, argue with more passion and intensity, gesture, articulate, take up more physical space, and simply bring more energy into social situations than traditional, colonizing, Protestant American culture has traditionally permitted.

We have been shamed for this high-level emotional energy. Many of us have been told from childhood that such big emotion is a sign of unsophistication. It is ghetto or country, and out of place in civilized spaces. The loud, intense emotionality of Black men debating the merits of their favorite basketball team in what seem like angry tones while gesticulating and cursing and calling each other names in a barbershop gathering might be unnerving to some people. The loud cackling laughter of a group of Black women enjoying a girls' trip and wearing intensely colored fashions, seemingly unaware of others around them as they move their bodies and sometimes scream out in mock surprise as one or two share a piece of juicy gossip might move someone not comfortable with their emotional openness to call for their removal from the space because their presence feels so uncomfortable.

Colonization serves to make us hyperaware of our loudness and our taking up space and encourages us to be more civilized and less ghetto in these public spaces. Double consciousness shapes us to be super aware of where and when we are and to tone down our behavior in conscious and unconscious acts of code switching so as not to embarrass the culture. We have been socialized to know that our way of emoting in the world is not acceptable in white spaces, and so we mute ourselves outwardly even though we may rage on the inside.

Testimony is emotional in that it creates space for the expression of grief, anger, and joy that has been historically denied to Black people. This refers to both personal and collective grief, anger, joy, and expressiveness that may often be deemed inappropriate in Eurocentric settings. Testimony therapy is concerned with fostering connections with family and community by utilizing those culturally familiar processes that may help the therapist to elicit testimonies of hope. Kochman (1981), describing Black emotional force, argued that frequently the goal of Black American cultural events is to revitalize energy through emotional and spiritual release. He described this emotional force by discussing three elements that he argued are necessary to achieve spiritual release:

(1) a sufficiently powerful agent-stimulus to activate the emotional (spiritual) forces that the body has imprisoned, (2) a structure like song, dance, or drum that allows for the unrestricted expression of those forces that the agent-stimulus has aroused, and (3) a manner of participation that gives full value to the power of the agent-stimulus and to the individual's ability to receive and manipulate it. (p. 108)

The Black church and other cultural settings have always provided this space of emotional freedom that allows Black people to find their healing by reconnecting with the deepest pain, as well as the deepest joy, that defines the personas and collective Black experience. The goal of the testimony therapist is to create the context for these three elements to be therapeutically helpful. According to Kochman (1981), "the Black cultural pattern of call and response... integrates all three elements of stimulus, structure, and manner of participation (response) into a working relationship with one another" (p. 109). Testimony therapists work to create the space to include a range of emotions in therapy. They do this by being aware of conversational style and call-and-response rhythms in the therapeutic conversation. Testimony therapists and their clients collaborate on constructing a healing testimony.

Because colonizing oppression has often denied us the right to our emotions, sometimes people may come to us for help, and we therapists may notice that they seem to lack the emotional vocabulary to express a range of emotions. Colonization has made it difficult for some Black people to even feel their feelings. Centuries of cultural oppression and perhaps a lifetime of conflict and relationship disconnection may have reduced the person's emotional range to feeling and expressing only anger or satisfaction. All other emotions emerging from relational pain are muted. Fear, sadness, disappointment, frustration, longing, desire, all seem to be reduced to expressions of anger and resentment. In these cases, the testimony therapist learns to empathize and name these other possibilities, even sometimes expressing their own emotional responses and experiences in reaction to the testimony coming from the person coming for help. This empathizing and naming, as well as expressing a range of emotions in the therapy room, creates and lets the person coming for help know that this is a culturally safe emotional space to allow the whole self to be expressed and to explore all the person's lived experience. Here is another example of what this might look like in a therapeutic conversation with a couple.

Afraid to Love

Willie and Charlene are a middle-aged couple who have been married for 15 years. Charlene is a schoolteacher, and Willie works as a truck driver. The couple complains that communication between them is difficult. Willie complains that his wife only speaks to him to complain about things that he has not done. Charlene complains that Willie does not seem to care about her or even himself. Willie has been diagnosed with both diabetes and high blood pressure, and Charlene complains that he is too lazy to even take care of himself. She is tired and frustrated with making demands that he eat better and exercise, and Willie just won't listen. Willie complains that Charlene never has anything good to say and that she is always criticizing him. The couple rarely spend quality time together. There is little intimacy, and neither of them can pinpoint the last time they had enjoyable sex together.

As we sit together in our third session, Charlene recounts all of Willie's shortcomings that justify her lack of positive feelings for him and her lack of desire for intimacy. She sits stiffly with her arms folded and gazes straight ahead, staring into the void. Her voice is low and tense. "He has no drive," she explains, while Willie, sitting in a chair opposite her, looks on sadly. "He's selfish and won't do what he knows he needs to do. It's like he enjoys being unhealthy." As Charlene continues, her breathing becomes shallower, and her face tightens. Willie shifts uncomfortably in his seat. She continues, "He won't even look after his own hygiene the way he should. I just don't understand it. How am I supposed to care about somebody who don't even care about they self? He is just so unmotivated."

As I watch closely, I can see the small tremors that seem to move through her body, and I notice her intense eyes seem to moisten with tears. I move a bit closer to Charlene in my chair and say, "I can see you are really feeling this as you talk about these problems. As you're telling me this, where is it sitting in your body?" Charlene looks at me a little startled, as if I've drawn her attention to something she had not noticed. "Oh," she says, "I . . . guess I feel it in my chest." I nod my head and say, "Yeah, it's looking like you're having to work harder to breathe. Does that happen a lot when you and Willie talk about these problems?" Charlene looks thoughtful, as if trying to remember. "Yes, I guess it does," she says. I lean forward and ask, "Do you think that feeling in your chest that's making it hard to breathe right now is anger, or love? Or is it fear?" Charlene gives a small chuckle and thoughtfully considers this question. "I mean, I do love him. But I'm mad at him most of the time." I smile and reflect to her, "Yeah, I get it. If somebody I loved found it hard to take care of their health, seems like that would be frustrating, and I'd be afraid that I would lose them. I get it. Does it ever feel like that to you?"

In this one sentence, I've attempted to broaden Charlene's sense of emotional choices. I've attempted to reflect back to her the range of possible emotions I am witnessing in her to encourage her to see that her response to Willie might be grounded in feelings that are more positive than anger, and to normalize expressions of care and love to her husband. I'm also interested in Willie, as witness to my conversation with Charlene, hearing that there are more possibilities than anger in his wife's response to him.

Charlene sits back and says, "Yes I'm afraid. I feel like that all the time." "But why?" I ask. "Because he could die, and I love him." "You love him," I repeat as I try to show slight surprise on my face. I say, "I wonder if you would want to say that to Willie right now." I look at Charlene deeply and then turn to her husband. I repeat, "Do you think you could just say those words to your husband?" Charlene takes a small breath in and smiles slightly. She looks directly at her husband and says in a small voice, "I love you Willie."

I turn to Willie, who has been sitting stiffly in his seat with an impassive look on his face, but who now shifts and seems to relax his face as he exhales. "Willie, do you know that Charlene loves you and that she is afraid of losing you?" I ask. He responds timidly, "I guess I don't think about it. It just seems like she's always mad at me." I turn to face Willie completely to shift the conversation to him. I ask, "When you hear your wife describe these problems and her fear of losing you and her love and care for you, what feelings and thoughts come up for you?" Willie takes a deep breath and releases a sigh. "I just keep thinking about how much of a failure I am," he admits. I'm a bit surprised by this response and, moving in closer, I ask, "Can you tell me more about what that means when you say you're a failure?" I glance over at Charlene, who no longer has her arms crossed. She is listening to the conversation. She has often complained that Willie just shuts down when she tries to talk to him, and now he seems to be willing to share his thoughts and feelings. Willie continues, "I don't want to be like this. I want to be healthy. But it don't seem to be no use. I want to do the things that I know I need to do. I want to get up and exercise and make sure I eat the right food. I intend to, I really do, but then..." His voice trails off, and he breathes a sigh of exasperation. I mirror his sigh and say, "Wow, Willie, that sounds so sad to me. Do you feel sad as you're telling us this?" He slowly nods his head. "Sometimes, when people feel that kind of sadness, it feels really hard to get things done.... Even when they really intend to do these things, it just seems like it gets away from them and they can't seem to get going. Does it ever feel like that to you?" Willie looks up directly at me in what seems like a look of recognition. "Yeah, that's how it feels." As I witness this sadness in Willie, I become more curious about other aspects of his life. I ask, "Willie, I've heard you talk about your friends. When was the last time you hung out with your homeboys?" Charlene interjects, "He never goes out with his friends anymore." Willie slowly nods his head in agreement. "Yeah, I got lots of friends, but I can't seem to find the time to see them anymore." I sit up and take notice. "Can you think of anything that's fun for you these days?" I ask. "What really makes you want to get out in the world?" As I've been listening to Willie describe his sadness and feelings of failure, I've noticed that his voice has become more quiet. He seems to be shrinking into his chair. "I haven't been getting out into the world much at all lately I guess." Charlene chimes in, "He is always inside except when he go to work. He never wants to do anything." I keep my gaze on Willie and ask, "Willie, does it feel true that you never want to do anything, or does it feel like something else for you?" He hesitates as he takes a breath. "I really do want to do things, it just seems hard you know.... I can't explain it, but I think about doing things to take care of myself, or calling one of my homeboys to do something, or even asking Charlene to go somewhere with me but . . . then I just . . . I just don't get to it."

As I listen to Willie and hear him describe his experience, what I initially described as sadness seems to be much more than that. I tentatively question him: "Willie, when you think about doing these things, and maybe you get a little excited about doing them, but then . . . that desire just seems to dissolve, does it feel like you're just running out of energy?" "Yeah." He nods his head with some enthusiasm. "Willie," I ask, "Do you think that that sadness you feel that seems to want to keep you at home . . . is it possible that it's not just sadness? Do you think that it might be depression trying to convince you that you are a failure?" He looks puzzled and then says, "I don't know. What's the difference between sadness and depression?"

Here I take the opportunity to share with Willie and Charlene the difference between simple sadness and depression. I use the example of Willie's diabetes, which requires medical attention and care, to help them understand that just like diabetes and other biological illnesses, depression is not something that a person can simply "get over" through willpower. I explain that if Willie has been living with depression for some time, it might explain why he has found it so difficult to do the things that he knows are necessary to take care of his physical health or to be a full partner to Charlene around their home.

Reflection

Charlene, who was sitting as a witness to this dialogue between myself and Willie, began to hear and understand her husband with a more empathetic ear. Her gaze visibly softened as she seemed to begin to realize the emotional weight of depression that may have made it so difficult for her husband to do the things that she demanded of him, and she became more open to the possibility that it was not because he was lazy, or thoughtless, or uncaring that he did not do the things necessary to ensure his health, but he may have been living with depression as an emotional state which was convincing him that he was a failure, because he allowed himself to have diabetes.

My focus during this session with this couple was to create room for emotions beyond anger and resentment and to give them an emotional vocabulary to describe emotions behind their actions. For Charlene, it was important to name and speak about her love for her husband, which moved her to push him to take better care of himself. In later sessions we would focus on discovering loving ways to encourage this better care. For Willie, who often shut down and did not respond at all to Charlene, it was important to be able to share his emotional experience as well as to be able to name his emotional state to himself and share it with his wife. For both members of the couple, it was important to be able to hear and validate emotions without hiding behind basic anger or apparent noncaring.

In the following chapter, I will focus on some of the methods and practices that I have developed to support people in constructing their testimonies and telling their story.

CHAPTER 4

Testimony Therapy in Practice

I began to develop the ideas and practices that inform testimony therapy in the early 1990s as I worked on my doctoral research, which focused on a support and education group for parents who were threatened with the loss of their children to state child protective and foster systems through the legal courts. During this time, I was developing Ujamaa family circles (Akinyela, 1996), the predecessor to testimony therapy. Ujamaa family circles were inspired by the critical pedagogy of the Brazilian educator Paulo Freire.

I first met Paulo Freire in the early 1980s through his books, introduced to me by my mentor and friend Antonia Darder while I was on my path to becoming a family therapist. I had no idea at that time that Freire would be such a powerful and ongoing influence in my life as both a therapist and a teacher in the academy. I was drawn to Freire because of his resonance with anticolonial activist intellectuals like Frantz Fanon (1963), Albert Memmi (1965), Amilcar Cabral (1973), and others who were challenging Western cultural and political domination through their anticolonial practice and writings. During that same time, I became aware that family therapy itself was being challenged and changed by ideas of post-structuralist therapists like Michael White and David Epston (1990), who made a clear shift away from positioning themselves as experts in relation to the lives of those who consult them. While not as overtly "political" as the ideas of the anticolonialists, their narrative ideas were challenging the supremacy of Western knowledge and therapeutic practice from the inside.

Being inspired by the possibility that therapy could, in the spirit of anticolonial work, be done in the interest and on behalf of the oppressed, I imagined that it was possible to link this work to what Paulo Freire (2018) wrote in relation to pedagogy. Freire described how any pedagogical experience can be either an experience of oppression or an experience of freedom. He then went on to explain the principles that underpin a pedagogy of freedom. For instance, with a pedagogy of freedom, Freire emphasizes dialogical learning rather than what he calls "banking education." Dialogue is the core of humanizing education, where knowledge is cocreated through mutual inquiry between the teacher and student. Banking education requires the teacher to be the only expert who "deposits" information into passive students, denying them the power to think critically. Similarly, in relation to therapy, an experience of oppression is one in which the therapist imposes their meaning, their interpretation, their "cure" upon the person who has come for assistance. To assume that somehow as a therapist we can hold the secrets of the meaning of somebody else's life and impose our interpretations on that life can only serve to further colonize the minds and spirits of those seeking our help.

Flowing from this central idea about the importance of ideas of freedom in the therapeutic process, I was also encouraged by Freire's ideas of critical pedagogy and the focus on community building and collective work as a central goal of my therapeutic work, rather than focusing on a therapy of individuation and personal development. For Freire, critical pedagogy is an approach to teaching and learning that helps students question and challenge power, inequality, and injustice in the world around them. Instead of just memorizing facts, students learn to think critically about society, reflect on their own experiences, and take action to create positive change. This is accomplished by engaging students in dialogue with each other and the teacher about their everyday experience as it relates to the world around them. This critical engagement is intended to give students a positive experience of community and supportive relationships. This also fit in with the importance of a therapeutic practice grounded in the culture of the African-descendant community in which I worked and lived.

Freire's pedagogical practice of encouraging community building and interdependence through his dialogical teaching methodology fit well with how I understood the orality-centered culture of Black peoples. Freire (1990) cautioned against "banking" education, or simply pouring imposed knowledge into students' heads. To create the experience of freedom in therapy, it is my responsibility as a therapist to offer a place as free as possible from imposed interpretations, either my own or that of the dominant culture. As described earlier, due to the influence of colonization, all too often Black people live with Eurocentric judgments and values dominating their beliefs and dreams.

One of the key purposes of family therapy is to create a space in which members of the community can make their own meaning of events of their lives, in which they come to define their preferences for their relationships and lives, and where they can have the opportunity to be free of some of the prevalent Eurocentric judgments and values about their lives and themselves. My expertise as a therapist is therefore not in being able to interpret or diagnose the lives of the people who consult me. It lies instead in being cognizant of the ways in which the dominant Eurocentric culture can influence the lives of Black people, and in creating a context in which individuals, couples, or families can come to their own understandings about their lives.

Asking Questions and Testifying

Upon discovering Freire in those early years of my training as a therapist, I had no idea that he would be such a significant actor in my professional and personal development. Perhaps the two greatest things that I learned from his critical pedagogy is the importance of asking questions and encouraging questions from the people with whom I consult. Through the dialogue of asking and answering questions, a communally constructed story can emerge, a story that contradicts and challenges oppressive stories of inevitable domination and taken-for-granted oppression.

Testimony therapy, like critical pedagogy, understands that life and culture are created in the asymmetrical social relationships and intersectional contexts in which humans live. In a society that is defined by stratifications of these contexts and the resultant oppressions which are experienced as "normal," the intentionally subversive conversations and questioning of normality of testimony therapy encourages people to seek their healing in building community, in contradiction to the alienation and isolation that are the life blood of an oppressive society. Freire's critical pedagogical methodology has provided a framework for me to apply therapeutic ideas of cultural resistance and self-determination in everyday practice in ways that are authentic and effective in the real world.

I have developed several practices and styles of questioning that I find useful in helping people who come to me reflect on their testimony stories and begin to shape new meanings out of these reflections. In this chapter, we explore practices such as the four healing questions, as well as using bridging questions to encourage deeper reflection. The testimony therapist invites their client to explore artifacts, which allows them to share significant material articles from everyday life to discover deeper meanings and ideas which may have been hidden to them. I also discuss the practice of creating knotted codes, which are short open-ended stories, and guiding clients with questions to unknot the story and help them discover solutions to problems which have troubled their lives. I explore the use of problematizing questions and victorious moments.

The Therapist's Use of Self

We will come back to all these practices shortly, but first I'd like to discuss the most important tool for the testimony therapist: using the self of the therapist. It is through the self of the therapist that we can engage authentically and build trust with the people who come to us. It is with our selves that we therapists can hear the testimonies of the people who come to us and experience the Nommo of their stories.

The term *using the self of the therapist* is not unique to testimony therapy. Others (Franklin, 2003; Aponte & Kissil, 2004) have also used this concept. What I mean by *use of self* is that you, as the healer, must authentically connect first to who you are. I've read that in ancient Kemet (Egypt), at the temple of Karnak, an admonition was inscribed on the temple walls for those who would enter seeking knowledge. This inscription read, "First know yourself." This is a good reminder for therapists seeking to know the people who come to them for healing. To help develop your sense of self, take some time to sit quietly and explore the following questions:

1. Who am I?
2. What are my values, and where did I learn these values?
3. What are my intersectional social contexts, and how do they shape how I see and experience the world around me?
    a. How do my age and my generational experiences shape my views?
    b. Do I present/perform as a masculine, feminine, or nonbinary person, and how does that impact the way I am seen and the way I see the world around me?
    c. How does my ethnic/cultural experience and expression limit or open my world vision?
    d. Does the color/shade of my skin and the texture of my hair impact the way people approach/see me, and does it impact the way I move in the world? If so, what does that look and feel like?
    e. How do my body presence, my size and shape or my ease of movement, influence my being in the world? How do I see myself, and how do I perceive myself as being seen?
    f. Am I a sexual, asexual, or pansexual person in the world? How does my sexuality affect me internally, and how does it present itself in the world? How does it impact my connections and relationships with the people around me?
    g. How does my financial status and social standing in my community impact the way I initiate, live in, and experience relationships, think about situations, or perceive other people in my community and in the world?

As you reflect on these questions about yourself, what lessons or experiences are linked to each of these for you? Can you remember any stories about personal experiences around these intersectional contexts? Did you learn any life lessons or make any decisions about yourself or about the world from these experiences? How do you think these intersectional aspects of yourself have shaped the way you present as a person in the world?

These intersectional contexts all influence the parts of you that Dr. Naim Akbar (1985) calls the community of self. Even as these intersectional parts affect and shape how we move and experience the world, the alienation from self and others created by colonization and capitalist neoliberal fracturing dissociates us from them, and we are often unaware of how these parts of us play such a huge role in the way we experience and act in the world.

What Does Your Genogram Say About You?

I wrote earlier that an important principle of testimony therapy is the idea of the person in the community. We exist and have our being, for better or worse, in the context of community. I believe that, especially for Black people, community begins with the kin network (extended family) which Robert Hill (1999) said is one of the strengths that helped Black people survive slavery, colonization, and white supremacy. It is in the kin network, that wide-ranging connections of siblings, parents, grandparents, cousins, aunts, uncles, play brothers and sisters, and play cousins (what sociologists call faux kin), that we are grounded and our selves are created. It is from the kin network that we inherit both the trauma and the healing ways of our ancestors. We carry ancestral memories, experiences, attitudes, and values passed on through the kin network. I believe that a valuable tool for rediscovering these and becoming aware of the knowledge we carry from those ancestral kin networks is through genogram work (McGoldrick, Gerson, Petry, 2008; Rigazio-Digilio, Ivey, Kunkler-Peck, Grady, 2005). Both kin network genograms and community cultural genograms can be useful for this work. Just as it is important, as a therapist, for you to experience your own therapy, I believe it is essential for a person seeking to develop their skill in mental health healing to do their own family genogram exploration. This genogram, if possible, should explore your kin network back at least four generations. This work is sometimes difficult for Black colonized people because of our histories of colonial racist violence, enslavement, and family separation, but often through family conversations, stories, documents, or church records we might be able to piece together some of these distant generational stories. As you build your genogram, you might consider these questions:

1. What is your family's history in America, and where did it begin?
2. How was your family development affected by migration patterns and moving about?
3. What traditions, beliefs, values, and resentments have been shared through generations in the family network?
4. Do you notice any cultural patterns such as naming, religion, cooking/eating, or ways of celebrating that have been passed on in the family?
5. Are there any patterns of health/illness that you see or maybe addictions or mental health challenges that repeat in the family?
6. What about relationship patterns of marriage, divorce, childbearing, and parenting? Do you notice anything about these in your genogram?
7. Are there consistencies or inconsistencies of wealth or poverty, social status or class in your kin network, and how are these navigated between family members?
8. Do you notice any values, beliefs, or ideas about the world that may have come through your kin network and are held by you?

Take some time with your family genogram. Explore it and contemplate these questions about your family and your relationship to the family, and ask yourself how this ancestral inheritance might affect the way you show up in the therapy room. Do you ever hear the values, teachings, or beliefs or feel the attitudes of your ancestors when you are having therapeutic conversations with the people who come to you for help? I suggest that even if you have not been aware of these that it has been happening. This practice of ancestral contemplation through reflecting on your genogram can help you become aware of those messages as you receive them.

Emotional Inventory

Finally, as you develop the therapist use of self, I encourage you to do an emotional inventory of yourself. Remember that one of the negative effects of colonization is to alienate us from our own emotions. When we are alienated from our emotions, we are less able to experience our own experience. I believe that a part of the work of decolonizing mental health is to help people who come to us experience their experience in the world rather than to be numbed to it.

Taking an emotional inventory can be incredibly helpful for developing your therapist use of self. Try some of these approaches to challenge emotional alienation and reconnect to your emotional self.

1. **Do a daily check-in:** Set aside a few minutes every day to reflect on your emotional state. Just ask yourself each day, "How am I feeling right now?" or "What emotions did I experience today?" Notice what comes up for you and look for patterns over time. Ask yourself reflecting questions about these emotions like, "Why am I feeling this way?" or "Is there something specific that triggered this emotion?" Reflecting on the *why* behind your feelings can lead to deeper insights and help uncover hidden life issues that may be affecting your emotional states.

2. **Emotional naming:** Begin practicing naming your emotional states as accurately as possible. For example, instead of just feeling "bad," try to distinguish if you're feeling disappointed, angry, or lonely. Look for the distinguishable nuances of your feelings and emotional states. A useful tool to help with this until you get the hang of it might be an emotion wheel, which can help you identify subtle emotions you may not immediately recognize. The emotion wheel is a great tool to help you better understand, identify, and express your emotions. It's shaped like a color wheel and shows how basic emotions like happy, sad, angry, or scared can expand into more specific feelings like joyful, proud, frustrated, or anxious. It can help you name what you're feeling more accurately. These can be found online using a search engine or even bought in poster form from an online store.

3. **Body awareness:** Emotions live in and manifest through the body. They may show up as the tension in your shoulders when you're stressed or the warm feeling in your chest when you are happy. Tuning into physical sensations can be a way to understand your emotions on a deeper level. Take some time and sit alone in a quiet space. Sit as comfortably as you

are able, or lie down comfortably. Maybe close your eyes or look down toward the floor. Notice your breath as you inhale and exhale normally. Begin to notice your body and the feelings and sensations there, scanning from the top of your head down your neck and your back. Notice your shoulders and your arms and hands. Notice your hips and thighs, and notice what feelings or sensations you may have in your legs and feet. What thoughts or feelings do you notice attached to these physical sensations? Is your heart rate slow or rapid? These physical sensations all can be indicators of your emotional states at a deeper level as you become aware of the connections between your body self and your emotional self.

4. **Emotional journaling:** Write freely about your day, what happened, and how you felt about different events. In your journaling, rate your emotions on a scale, say 0 to 10, with 0 being the least intense emotional level and 10 being the most intense emotional level for you. This will help you see which emotions are most present for you and to reflect on what triggers stronger emotional responses. Over time you may notice recurring themes or triggers in your emotions, which can help you understand your emotional self better.

5. **Creative expression:** Allowing yourself to be creative "just because," without the need to share with anyone else, is a great way to explore your emotions. Drawing, painting, splashing colors, dancing, singing, or humming out loud can capture what you are feeling when words are hard to find.

6. **Seek feedback from your community:** Sometimes those close to us can notice emotional patterns in us which, because of alienation, we are unaware of. Ask trusted friends, colleagues, or family how they see your mood or emotional shifts and see if their observations resonate with your own experience of your emotional self.

Over time, as you practice these emotion exercises, these methods can make it easier to recognize your emotions in real time and develop a stronger connection to your sense of self.

An effective testimony therapist strives to adhere to the admonition "First know yourself," as it was inscribed above the temple entrance in ancient Kemet. You should be always reflectively aware of your *physical self* and should ask yourself what role your body plays in the therapeutic relationship. How does where you sit in the room, your posture, or the attitude of your body impact your connection with your client in therapy?

You should be aware of your *mental self* and be aware of your own thoughts as you engage in the therapeutic relationship and listen to your client's story. What is going on with your *internal commentary*? Are you distracted? What has distracted you? What random questions about your client come up for you in the session?

Pay attention to your *emotional self* and be aware of what feelings arise as you are listening to your client's story. Where in your body do you feel these feelings? What emotions arise for you when you are thinking about your client? What is your relationship to fear, joy, anger, happiness, or other emotions as you engage in the therapeutic relationship?

Finally, pay attention to your *spiritual/energetic self*. What does the therapy room "feel like"? This is what Nancy Boyd-Franklin (2003) calls "vibes." How are your spiritual ideas, thoughts, assumptions, and beliefs impacting how you hear your client's story? What are your "gut" or base feelings and assumptions as you sit with your client?

In testimony therapy, I believe that all these awarenesses can be used by the therapist to remain attentive to the place and direction in the therapy in each moment. To be aware of these parts of yourself can be useful to indicate parallel thoughts, emotions, or interpretations that your client is experiencing and can be used to inspire questions or humble tentative thoughts to be shared with your client in the conversation, which may encourage the client to think or reflect on alternative meanings for their testimony.

As you are working to enhance your skills in using the self of the therapist, you should work also to develop six characteristics that will enhance your ability.

First, a testimony therapist is fully engaged in the moment. This requires focus and being fully attentive to and committed to the needs and requirements of your client in that time. It is important to be able to place your own thoughts, day's concerns, and feelings unrelated to the present client work in a safe space until after your session. As a testimony therapist, you should be conveying to your client that your time with them is the most important thing in your shared world for this moment.

Second, a testimony therapist approaches each client with an attitude of having "an open hand," or holding no preconceived ideas, thoughts, attitudes, diagnosis, or interpretations about who your client is or why they bring these problems to you. Your first relationship with your client is as a student to be taught about your client's life. They are the teacher and the expert on their own life, and you are present to learn from them.

Third, being grounded in this "open hand" attitude, the testimony therapist remains teachable throughout the client/therapist relationship, not only in the beginning. Therapeutic humility is extremely important when we consider that colonized people have often encountered social relationships where they are expected to make themselves small in the face of people who may be considered to be authorities because of education, professional status, or social status. This expectation to become "small" serves only to limit the ability of our clients to move toward their own personal and cultural liberation.

Fourth, a testimony therapist expects and respects the unpredictable, although I know that many currently accepted and popular therapies focus on the predictability of outcomes based on evidence. There are good arguments for common factors across therapeutic models, which contradicts the efficacy of so-called evidence-based therapies over others (Wampold & Imel, 2015; Duncan et al., 2010), but beyond that I believe there is support for the importance of expecting and respecting unpredictability in both Black diasporic cultural traditions and even modern physics, from which we can draw metaphorical relationship parallels.

The concept of unpredictability in quantum physics—where particles like electrons don't have definite locations or speeds until measured—can metaphorically resonate with the unpredictability in social relationships and everyday life, which are often characterized by uncertain or unpredictable factors, where people's feelings, responses, or behaviors can't always be precisely anticipated. A testimony therapist is aware that humans are not machines that always function in the same ways. Our interpersonal connections, ambiguity in individual perceptions, and moment-to-moment emotional states serve to shift and change what happens in social and relationship situations regardless of expected outcomes based on what the research predicts. When we expect life to be unpredictable, we learn to flow and move with situations as we encounter them.

Our African ancestors understood this through their myths of tricksters. The trickster is the owner of Nommo, and the guardian of the crossroads (Gates, 2014; Hyde, 1998). Throughout the Black diaspora the trickster is known by many names. The best known is probably Eshu, from the Yoruba of Nigeria. In the United States, the trickster has been known as Br'er Rabbit, the signifying monkey, and High John the Conqueror. In African cultural tradition, when life brings unexpected twists, turns, and surprises, they come from the trickster. This cultural expectation of unpredictability has even been expressed in our folk music. The Black American women's acapella group Sweet Honey in the Rock (1993) sings a poignant song of struggle and mourning which laments, "Can't no one know at sunrise, how this day is going to end." The song goes on to lament that what can be known about the next day is just as unpredictable. This song perfectly captures the Black cultural value of the unpredictability of life and the importance of expecting the unexpected, which the trickster brings into our lives.

This unpredictability in each moment gives us the opportunity for creativity. The great Black Jazz musician Miles Davis is reported to have said, "If you hit the wrong note, it's the next note you play that determines if it's good or bad."* This is the spirit of being open and humble in the presence of the trickster. When a testimony therapist learns to expect and respect the unpredictable, they won't panic when things don't go right in the therapeutic session. They see this as an opportunity to be creative, knowing that the next note they play will make it good or bad.

Fifth, as a testimony therapist you will realize that, particularly early on in your engagement with the people who come to you for help, it is important to nurture hopefulness. Hopefulness, or the idea that change is possible, is a powerful tool for healing when people feel the oppression and alienation of mental

---

* This quote is widely attributed to Davis, though no definitive primary source confirms it. It reflects the improvisational and resilient spirit associated with his musical philosophy.

health problems. A good therapist intentionally practices conveying to the client that they are confident that they will find hope through collaboration with the client and, based on the client's strengths (even if it's just the fact that the client showed up to seek help), the therapist is sure that they and the client can discover a path to emotional liberation for the client.

This does not require making exorbitant and unrealistic promises to your client. The most important thing for you as a testimony therapist, as you engage with your client, is to convey your willingness to journey together as they discover the testimony they want to be told about their life. It is important for your client to know that they will not have to be alone in their search for meaning and significance in life.

Finally, a testimony therapist learns to nurture cultural authenticity. Sometimes we might hear this expressed in Black community environments as "being real" or "not being fake." Or maybe someone will insist that you "keep it real" or "keep it 100." Cultural authenticity does not require you as a therapist to perform Blackness or to "act Black" outside of your own normal way of being in the world. Nurturing cultural authenticity simply means that as a therapist working with people with a shared history of struggle, resistance, and communitarian values, you emphasize the importance of shared historical experiences and cultural practices that have fostered resistance and resilience in supportive ways among Black people. Consider and acknowledge how these elements encourage healthy, supportive relationships, anchored in empathy, mutual respect, and a strong sense of belonging.

Pay attention to the importance of community and collective identity and the significance of strong social networks, even if these are only hoped-for realities at the moment for the people who come to you for help. Healthy relationships involve a balance between individual needs and the well-being of the family, group, or community. Cultural authenticity calls on us to be emotionally open, curious, and engaged in the conversation with our clients. It requires empathetic listening and an attitude of transparency that does not appear to be holding back or hiding a secret agenda, which can appear deceitful to people who may be used to more communitarian ways of being in the world. An inauthentic, disingenuous demeanor in you as a therapist might quickly raise alarms and raise your client's healthy cultural suspicion (Boyd-Franklin, 2003).

As you practice these things we have covered, and as you become more engaged with yourself in the world, you will find that you are able to effectively engage your therapist's use of self as a powerful tool in your therapeutic sessions. As you become more and more aware of all of your selves, you will have learned the secret of the Kemetic admonition "First know yourself," and be able to use this as the doorway to knowing and understanding the testimony of the people who come to you for help.

Helping People Tell Their Story

So once you "know" yourself, how can that knowing help you as you engage your clients in therapeutic, decolonizing testimonies? Building on ancestral knowledge, Africana critical theory, and critical pedagogy, I have developed several approaches you might also find helpful in your decolonizing mental health work. These are ways I use to create safe, inviting cultural spaces that feel culturally familiar and allow the spirit of Nommo to guide my client's in constructing with me the testimony they want told about themselves. Let's focus on four of these methods, which include four healing questions, problem posing, exploring artifacts, and code unraveling.

Dialogue and Creating Healthy Relationships

In his book *Education for Critical Consciousness*, Paulo Freire (2021) discusses the importance of dialogue in creating the experience of democracy (freedom) for oppressed people through a problem-posing educational experience. I think my colleague and mentor Antonia Darder (2024), who is one of the foremost authorities on Freire's ideas, explains this best when she writes,

> *Problem-posing pedagogy entails a horizontal approach that welcomes student participation as free thinkers and actors within their world, with an eye toward the development of critical thought, as such, a problem-posing pedagogy is generated through dialectical engagement of teacher and students, where teaching and learning are understood inseparable to a (subjective-objective) revolutionary praxis within schools and communities that supports conscientização—a communal process of evolving social consciousness. (p. 112)*

Through Freire's critical pedagogy, I understand that the traditional American-Western system of education in which most of us grew up is both a reflection of and the model for the social and cultural relationships that define our lives. It is through our schooling that we learn to accept inequalities of class, race, gender, sexuality, and so on. Freire calls these real life conditions imposed on oppressed people *limit situations*. These are not personal problems, but they are conditions shaped by history, politics, and unequal power that seem to limit or block the ability to have a better life. These limits are often internalized, and people believe "this is just the way life is." This traditional approach to Western education also shapes our understanding and relationships of mental health practices. Our education reproduces and shapes our colonization!

Traditional Western schooling prepares the colonized to accept *limit situations* as normal and discourages us from questioning our conditions and relationships. With this in mind, I believe that just as the "dialectical engagement of teacher and students" is necessary to what Darder calls revolutionary praxis, this same dialectical engagement is necessary between the therapist and client for a decolonizing and liberatory approach to mental health work.

Through dialogue and engaging in critical reflection relying on the storyteller/witness, call-and-response approach of testimony therapy, people who come to us for help are encouraged to unpack and become curious about events, issues, and relationships to everyday life in new and different ways and to apply new meanings to their lived experience.

Dialogue is different from monological conversations where ideas come from only one direction. In these monological relationships, knowledge and truth are assumed to belong to the most powerful, or the most educated or the wealthiest. In a dialogue, there is exchange of knowledge and openness to what might be true for each speaker. One speaker does not assume to always have the expert position but is open to being informed and educated from the experience of the other.

The oppressed and colonized rarely are in situations where they are respected for their knowledge or expertise, even about their own lives. They expect to be diagnosed, analyzed, and judged by superiors whom they come to for help. This assumption keeps the colonized in an inferiorized and subordinate social position. For Freire, this asymmetrical social relationship between people who came for help and their supposed helpers could be brought to a just balance when helpers were critically aware of their own positions and assumed and encouraged the knowledge and expertise of the people they intended to help. Teachers first took the position of students to be taught by the students whom they worked with about their lives. Only after that could they become teachers of their students collaborating in their liberation.

This asymmetrical social relationship is repeated not only in the educational sphere but in all relationships in Western society, including therapeutic relationships. Therapists are assumed to have superior knowledge even about the personal lives of the people who come to them for help. Their expert knowledge is imposed on the colonized client to emphasize the helplessness and lack of agency that the client has in their own life and the necessity of the client's dependence on the expert knowledge of the therapist, sometimes forever. Freire's dialogical, critical pedagogy, privileging and encouraging the knowledge of the student, shapes my own approach to therapeutic conversations and decolonizing mental health work. The following four approaches are my own attempts to invite my clients into dialogical relationship to collaborate with them in creating their own testimony for their lives and to move beyond the limit situations that colonize their lives.

Four Healing Questions

As I began to reflect on what it would mean to intentionally decolonize my therapeutic work over 25 years ago, I was introduced to three healing questions by my colleague Vanessa Jackson. Vanessa is an amazing healer and people's historian who has documented psychiatric oppression of Black people in the so-called "Negro insane asylums" developed soon after the Civil War as an effort to maintain the system of free enslaved Black labor (Jackson, 2002b).

Vanessa described these questions as coming from First Nations (Native American) tradition. I was drawn to this idea, as I believe that despite conflicts between our cultures there is also a long history of collaboration and cultural mixing in resistance to colonization for Black people and First Nations peoples.

These three healing questions are simple and speak directly to the trauma that colonized people encounter both individually and collectively. They focus on our trauma as something that begins outside of us and beyond our control rather than as something that we bring on ourselves. The three healing questions introduced to me by Vanessa Jackson are (1) What happened to you? (2) How does what happened to you affect you today? (3) What do you need to heal?

I later added the fourth question, which becomes the third in order: Despite what happened to you, what gives you the strength to carry on? I was fascinated by these simple questions that invite us to reflect on our situation and to speak to our spirits seeking guidance. Each of these questions is meaningful and impactful in its own right and, when asked by the therapist, has the intention of supporting a liberating testimony. These questions take people's struggles from the abstract to concrete lived experience and encourage them to reflect and search for better outcomes. Let's look at each of these questions in turn.

1. "What Happened to You?"

Often clients will come to therapeutic conversations and find it difficult to say specifically what problems have brought them there. They simply know that "something isn't right." They have vague feelings of unease and discomfort that seem difficult to articulate. This question invites our clients to pause and see themselves and their life experience in a particular space and time; a day, a moment when an event occurred that moved them to seek help.

This question contextualizes experience and encourages clients to reflect on specific events that have contributed to their current life experience. When they understand the *what*, clients begin to develop a context for seeing a way through their life situation.

This question also validates human experience as clients narrate their testimony. Sharing experience to a witness in community helps to acknowledge pain as legitimate and helps people see the impact of events on their lives. As clients recall past events, they are prompted to reflect and give more introspection, and to recognize patterns in their lives and relationships that have evolved from these experiences.

2. "How Does What Happened to You Affect You Today?"

Once a testimony has been situated in space and time, this second question creates space to explore the present-day implications of these past experiences. This question allows people to create a life terrain map and examine their emotional landscapes. Supported by the therapist, a person can trace their emotional journey identifying the important events, feelings, and relationships in their life. They along with the therapist can see where they've struggled (like rocky or steep places) and where they've found strength or joy (like clear paths or beautiful views). This metaphorical mapping can help the person and the therapist understand how past experiences shape the way they feel, think, and act today. As they thicken their testimony, they along with the therapist can examine how life events have impacted their mental health, as well as their relationships and how they move through life. This life terrain map can highlight areas of struggle as well as their victorious moments.

This question helps to highlight how life events and traumas may have affected relationships and help clients identify behaviors and emotional responses that may be impeding positive relationships. Through this question, we can help clients become more attentive to emotional triggers and responses to life situations as we become curious and ask more questions about how our clients have been affected by life events.

3. "What Gives You the Strength to Carry On?"

This question shifts the focus from doom and gloom to the victorious moments. I've found that clients are often oblivious to the fact that they are "carrying on." They have become so invested in the doom and gloom of their testimony that they do not notice that each morning they are waking up, getting up, and getting on with their lives, often in wonderful and exciting ways. They are engaging in uplifting connections with the people in their family or community. They are making positive impacts and achieving great successes. People are expressing care for them and supporting them in small ways. This question allows clients to step outside of the doom and gloom of their lives and witness the victorious moments for themselves. This question highlights a client's resilience and little-noticed strategies which are a source of strength, whether this comes from their personal values or life habits or refusal to give up, or from outside of themselves, from caring and supportive family, friends, or community. The answer to this question could be as simple as, "I know my mother prays for me" or "I read a self-help book that gave me hope." This question helps the therapist to home in on the extra therapeutic factors that are so important to change in therapy (Duncan et al., 2010).

By identifying what keeps them going, clients can nurture a sense of hope, which is also an important factor across therapies for change. This shift in perspective creates a context that allows clients to see beyond the limit situations created by oppressive colonization and allows clients, in collaboration with the therapist, to envision a future beyond their current struggles.

Finally, this question reinforces the idea for clients that they have agency and can make life choices which look different than the doom-and-gloom interpretations they initially brought to the therapeutic relationship. This discovery of personal agency encourages clients to take steps toward healing and change.

4. "What Do You Need to Heal?"

The final question is focused on centering the client as the expert in their own lives. This question prompts clients to both articulate what their goals for healing are and to express their own theory of change. By expressing their needs, clients take ownership of their healing process. This empowerment fosters a sense of responsibility and agency in pursuing their well-being. Finally, this question encourages clients to think about the future and what a healthy state looks like for them, helping to create a vision that can motivate and guide their actions and reconnect them to community.

Four Healing Questions Example

Jerome is a 30-year-old African American man. He is single and reports a history of failed love relationships as well as difficulty maintaining a healthy social circle. He reports that he grew up in a home with his mother, who was 18 years old when he was born. She was unmarried and "liked to party and go to clubs more than she liked being a mother," he said. She was emotionally distant. She married a man when Jerome was 6 years old who was verbally abusive of Jerome and physically abusive to his mother. Jerome wants to be able to forgive his mother and resolve his anger about his life and be able to have more loving and caring relationships with friends, family, and potential lovers.

> **Therapist:** Jerome, thank you for coming in today and for being willing to share your story. In our work together, I want to honor your truth, your voice, and your resilience. I'd like us to begin with four healing questions that I've found powerful in helping people make meaning of their lives. Let's start with the first one. Can you tell me, **what happened to you?**
>
> **Jerome:** I don't know where to start . . . I just know I feel tired. Like, inside tired. My relationships don't work out. I don't feel like I belong anywhere. I've been in therapy before, but I never felt heard. People kept saying I had "abandonment issues" or was "too angry."
>
> **Therapist:** That's a powerful place to begin. Feeling like you've never truly been heard is heavy. Can you tell me about a time or moment in your life that you think might've shaped this feeling?
>
> **Jerome:** Yeah. I guess I'd start with my mom. She had me when she was 18. She wasn't really . . . ready. I remember her always wanting to be out—clubs, parties, boyfriends. I'd be left alone a lot. When she did come home, she wasn't affectionate. Then when I was six, she married this dude who hated me. He yelled all the time. Sometimes he hit her. I would hide in my room. I felt like I didn't matter.
>
> **Therapist:** You've carried a lot, Jerome. You were just a child, and yet you were left to manage fear, rejection, and danger. That's not something a child should have to carry alone. That experience matters, and I want you to know it's valid. Despite what happened to you, can you tell me now: **how does what happened to you affect you today?**
>
> **Jerome:** I don't trust people. I assume they'll leave. I try to keep things casual because getting too close feels dangerous. But then I end up alone and angry. And I keep thinking about my mom. I don't know how to forgive her. I still feel like I'm that little boy waiting for her to love me.

Therapist: That sounds like a deep ache, Jerome. Still waiting to be loved in the way you deserved. You've named how those early experiences affect how you connect with others now. You've learned to protect yourself, but the cost has been high. You don't want to get too close to your mom and you can't forgive her. And I also understand you're often feeling like a little boy wanting your mom to love you. Hearing all of this, I'm curious to hear, **what gives you the strength to carry on?**

Jerome: Huh . . . that's a hard one. I don't think of myself as strong. I mostly feel like I'm surviving.

Therapist: And yet here you are—surviving. Seeking help. Talking about pain others might have buried. That sounds like strength to me. What helps you get through the day?

Jerome: I guess . . . I have this friend, Marcus. He checks in on me. Sends me texts, tells me I'm not alone. Sometimes we go to the gym together. I also journal when I'm feeling overwhelmed. And music helps—especially jazz. Miles Davis. John Coltrane. That stuff calms my spirit.

Therapist: You just named several powerful sources of strength. Friendship. Expression. Ancestral sound. That's resilience, Jerome. Even when things are hard, you reach for life. That's not nothing. That's sacred.

Jerome: I never thought of it that way.

Therapist: Yes, I'm understanding now that you've got some powerful support around you. Understanding that I want you to tell me what happened—despite what happened—and knowing how it's affected you, and seeing the powerful support you have around you, **what do you need to heal?**

Jerome: I think . . . I need to stop carrying this anger. I want to forgive my mom. Not for her, but for me. I want to stop feeling like I'm waiting to be loved and just learn to love myself. I need people I can be real with—people who don't run when I open up. I want to believe I can have love, not just hookups or surface-level stuff.

Therapist: That's a beautiful vision, Jerome. You just spoke your theory of change. Forgiveness, self-love, and authentic connection. What you've named isn't impossible. It's the beginning of your healing map. Let's work together to keep expanding this testimony—lifting up your strengths, unpacking your pain, and moving you toward the life and relationships you want. Does that sound like a path worth walking?

Jerome: Yeah . . . it does. For the first time in a while, I actually believe that maybe healing is possible.

The four healing questions are designed to create a safe space for clients to explore their pain while fostering resilience and agency. By guiding clients through their narratives, these questions facilitate a deeper understanding of their experiences, promote emotional healing, and empower them to take charge of their recovery process. Ultimately, this structured conversation leads to a more hopeful and empowered testimony, allowing clients to envision a future beyond limit situations and doom-and-gloom stories where they can thrive despite their past.

Problematizing Questions

In Black American folklore, the crossroads is place of decision. It is the place where we encounter the trickster and are challenged to make decisions that will have lasting impact on our future. Do we go left or right, or do we go forward, or return to the place we came? The choice is always ours, and we always make a choice. Family and community relationships are crossroad relationships in which we are constantly challenged to make sense of our lives and to create our testimony.

Problematizing questions are meant to intentionally place clients on a crossroad, a place of choices. These questions often encourage clients to deal with contradictions. "Is it this way or the other way?" These questions also may push a client to think more critically and deeply about an idea by asking "but why?" over and over (like a two-year-old) to encourage the client to follow the trail of their logic to its farthest conclusion. Problematizing questions may also offer a bridge to the client who may be stuck in their thinking by simply asking "Because?"

Problematizing questions in testimony therapy serve as a powerful tool for facilitating deeper self-reflection and exploration in clients. By placing individuals at a crossroads of choices, these questions challenge them to confront the complexities of their thoughts and emotions. Here are some expanded ideas around this approach.

1. Crossroads of Choices

Problematizing questions force clients to navigate binary choices—"Is it this way or the other way?"—which can be particularly illuminating. This method acknowledges the often ambiguous nature of human experience, allowing clients to articulate their values and beliefs. By considering seemingly contradictory options, clients may uncover underlying motivations or fears that influence their decision making. For instance, a question like, "Do you prioritize your career over personal relationships, or do you see them as equally important?" invites clients to assess their true priorities and the potential consequences of each choice.

2. Encouraging Deeper Inquiry

The "But why?" technique encourages clients to dig deeper into their reasoning. This iterative questioning mimics a child's natural curiosity and helps peel back layers of thought that may otherwise remain unexamined. Each answer leads to another question, prompting clients to trace their thoughts back to core beliefs or experiences that shape their current situation. For example, if a client states, "I feel overwhelmed at work," asking, "But why do you feel so overwhelmed at work?" can lead to revelations about their work environment, self-expectations, or past experiences that influence their present feelings.

3. Uncovering Assumptions

Asking "Because?" serves as an invitation for clients to elaborate on their statements, prompting them to articulate the reasoning behind their feelings or actions. This question helps bring to the surface assumptions that clients may not have consciously recognized. For instance, a client might say, "I can't change jobs because I need the money." A follow-up question of "Because?"

could reveal deeper fears related to instability, self-worth, or a sense of obligation, providing a clearer understanding of their situation.

4. Breaking Stagnation
When clients feel stuck in their thinking, problematizing questions can act as a bridge to new perspectives. By gently challenging clients to consider alternative viewpoints or implications of their thoughts, therapists can facilitate breakthroughs that lead to personal growth. For example, asking, "What if you approached this situation differently?" opens a space for clients to envision possibilities they hadn't considered before, fostering creativity and resilience.

5. Fostering Autonomy and Agency
Problematizing questions empower clients to take ownership of their thought processes and decisions. By encouraging them to critically analyze their beliefs and choices, clients become more adept at recognizing patterns and taking proactive steps in their lives. Problematizing questions serve as a catalyst for self-discovery, reinforcing the idea that clients have the agency to shape their narratives and outcomes.

6. Navigating Ambiguity
Life is often not about clear-cut choices, and problematizing questions help clients embrace the ambiguity of their situations. By exploring the gray areas between "this way" and "the other way," clients can come to terms with the complexities of their feelings and decisions. This acknowledgment can reduce anxiety and lead to a more nuanced understanding of their circumstances.

Problematizing Questions Example

Tamu is an African American woman married to her husband George for five years. The couple has a five-year-old and a two-year-old. Tamu reports ongoing tension and conflict with George and feeling that he does not appreciate her or respect her. Tamu acknowledges feeling overwhelmed by care of two small children and working as a teacher. Tamu reports feeling judged and criticized by George during daily conversations. Tamu said she has expectations of her husband, and said "I want him to lead," but she has difficulty explaining what this means and what George should be doing. Tamu seems to become confused when attempting to explain her desires and expectations for the marriage and her relationship with her husband. She becomes tearful as she struggles to explain her needs and finally says, "I'm just blah!" She continues. "I don't feel anything."

> **Therapist:** Tamu, you mentioned feeling overwhelmed and exhausted. You've been juggling so many responsibilities at home and at work, and that's been affecting how you feel about your marriage and yourself. I can sense there's a lot you're carrying right now. Let's take a moment to step back and look at your story from a different perspective. Can we do that?

Encouraging Deeper Inquiry. This question invites Tamu to explore her story from a new, reflective angle, encouraging deeper inquiry into her emotions and situation.

> **Tamu:** (tearfully) I'm not sure . . . It just feels like nothing's going right. I don't know if I can even see anything good in my life right now.
>
> **Therapist:** I hear you. It sounds like things feel really heavy for you. When you say "nothing's going right," I wonder, can you think of a time, maybe even just a small moment, where you felt like you did something well—where you felt proud of yourself? Something that helped you get through the tough times?

Encouraging Deeper Inquiry. The therapist uses this question to encourage Tamu to dig deeper into her experiences, allowing her to reflect on positive moments that she may have overlooked.

> **Tamu:** (slowly) Well . . . I guess . . . I mean, there was this one time last year when I had to handle a really tough situation at work. A student was struggling, and I felt like I was losing control over everything. But . . . I stayed after school for extra help, worked with him

one-on-one, and by the end of the semester, he passed his exams. I was proud of that.

Breaking Stagnation. This response represents a breakthrough for Tamu, where she moves from feeling "nothing's going right" to recalling a victorious moment, breaking the stagnation in her thinking.

> **Therapist:** That's powerful. You took time out of your already busy day to support that student, and it paid off. That's an example of your leadership and care. So, you had a choice then, right? You could have just gone home the way you were feeling, but you chose to stay. What made you push through when it might have been easier to just give in to exhaustion?

Crossroads of Choices. The therapist highlights the moment of decision—Tamu had a choice to stay or leave. This moment frames Tamu's action as a crossroads where she made a choice to push through.

> **Tamu:** I guess . . . I wanted to do right by him. He didn't have a lot of support at home. I wanted to be the one person who would help him get through.
>
> **Therapist:** That's beautiful, Tamu. You stepped into that moment with intention, even though it wasn't easy. I wonder, could this experience tell us something about you as a person? What does it say about your strength and your ability to rise up even when you're feeling like everything is too much?

Uncovering Assumptions. The therapist invites Tamu to uncover deeper assumptions about herself—her strength and ability to rise up even in difficult circumstances. It challenges her to reflect on her internal resources.

> **Tamu:** (surprised) I guess it says I care a lot. Maybe even more than I realize. I don't always see it, but . . . I do care.

Fostering Autonomy and Agency. Tamu begins to recognize her own care and strength, which is a key moment where she acknowledges her autonomy and agency. She realizes that even in exhaustion, she has the ability to make choices that align with her values.

> **Therapist:** Exactly. You care deeply, and even when you're tired, that care shows up. Now, let's go a bit deeper. When you're feeling "blah," overwhelmed, and disconnected from your husband, could it be that what you really need isn't just for him to lead, but for you to lead in a way that's true to who you are—someone who gives and cares but also needs to be supported?

Crossroads of Choices. Here, the therapist asks Tamu to consider a different choice in her relationship with her husband—one where she also takes the lead in articulating her needs. This moment of reflection presents her with a new crossroads in her marriage.

> **Tamu:** Yeah, I've never thought about it that way. I guess I'm waiting for him to step up, but maybe I need to be clearer about how I can step up for myself too.

Breaking Stagnation. Tamu's realization that she can take leadership in her marriage breaks through her previous stagnation—she no longer sees herself as helpless in her relationship but as someone who can initiate change.

> **Therapist:** Hmm . . . that's a really important insight. You're recognizing that leadership doesn't only come from him; it can come from you too. What would it look like for you to lead in your marriage, to set the tone for what you need, while still feeling supported and appreciated?

Encouraging Deeper Inquiry. This question invites Tamu to explore what leadership in her marriage might look like, encouraging her to go deeper into her own desires and actions.

> **Tamu:** I think it would look like being honest with him about how I'm feeling and not just waiting for him to figure it out. Maybe I need to ask for help, not just hope he sees it.
>
> **Therapist:** That's an empowering shift. By taking the lead in that way, you're also modeling what it means to care for yourself. In that

moment, you're creating a new possibility for how your relationship can function, one where both of you feel supported. Now, if we shift this focus from "doom and gloom" moments to victories, would you say that this moment in your marriage—where you decide to be more open and direct about your needs—could be one of those victories?

Navigating Ambiguity. The therapist invites Tamu to see the ambiguity in her situation—not everything is black and white. While her relationship has its challenges, there is potential for a new, victorious direction that honors both her needs and the relationship.

Tamu: (softly smiling) Yeah, I guess it could be. It feels like a big thing... but it also feels like I'm stepping into something bigger. Like, I'm not just a victim of all the stress anymore.

Fostering Autonomy and Agency. Tamu recognizes her agency in stepping into a new possibility. She is moving from a victim mindset to one of empowerment and self-leadership.

Therapist: Yes, exactly. It's a victory. It's not about pretending everything is perfect, but about choosing moments where you can stand tall and lead—whether in your marriage, in your career, or in how you care for yourself. You've had those moments before. Like the time you helped that student. Your capacity for growth and strength is already in you, even if it's hard to see sometimes.

Fostering Autonomy and Agency. The therapist reinforces Tamu's autonomy and agency, highlighting her past moments of strength as a foundation for her continued growth.

Tamu: Yeah... I guess I have had those moments, haven't I?

Therapist: Absolutely. You have. And every time you make a choice to show up, even when it's tough, that's a victorious moment. How do you think this new way of seeing yourself—one that recognizes your victories, even in small moments—can help you with the challenges you're facing now?

Navigating Ambiguity. This question invites Tamu to navigate the ambiguity of her current situation, recognizing that the victories she's experienced don't erase the challenges, but offer a new way to approach them with a sense of agency and empowerment.

> **Tamu:** I think it'll help me not feel so stuck. If I can see the victories, even if they're small, then maybe I won't feel so defeated all the time. Maybe I can start making choices that lead to more of those victories, even in my marriage.

Fostering Autonomy and Agency. Tamu acknowledges her ability to make choices that lead to further victories, demonstrating her growing sense of agency and self-efficacy.

> **Therapist:** I love that. You're beginning to see the power you have in your choices and actions, Tamu. By acknowledging your victories, you're rewriting the story of who you are, and that makes all the difference in how you approach the future.

Fostering Autonomy and Agency. The therapist reinforces Tamu's agency, framing her recognition of victories as a powerful shift in how she will move forward in her life.

In summary, problematizing questions in testimony therapy serve as a vital mechanism for fostering critical thinking, self-exploration, and empowerment. By encouraging clients to confront contradictions, delve deeper into their reasoning, and navigate ambiguity, therapists can facilitate meaningful change and personal growth.

Exploring Artifacts

The plotlines of the stories that we humans tell about ourselves to give meaning to our lives are linked together by situations, people, locations, and artifacts. When we explore life artifacts, clients are invited to bring a personal item to the session that represents some important aspect, idea, connection, success, or problem experience in their life.

This can serve as a powerful approach for fostering self-reflection and meaning making by having the client explore their relationship with an object that holds personal significance. The process involves selecting a meaningful item, such as a legal certificate, photograph, or any other object tied to the client's identity, experiences, or social world. This object becomes a symbolic entry point into the client's personal narrative, as the therapist uses curiosity and open-ended, problematizing questions to encourage a deeper exploration.

The therapist's role is to remain in a state of "not knowing," creating a safe space for the client to unfold the significance of the item in their own terms. The emphasis on the client's own interpretation encourages a critical reflection on their life story and how it is shaped by social, emotional, and historical contexts. By problematizing aspects of the client's narrative, the therapist helps the individual to interrogate assumptions, question the impact of external forces (such as societal norms or family interactions), and uncover unacknowledged influences in their life.

This reflective process not only deepens the client's self-awareness but also helps them make connections between past experiences, their present condition, and future possibilities. It opens the door to reframing difficult or limiting narratives, such as how a legal document (e.g., a birth certificate or divorce decree) might represent not just a legal status but also layers of identity, relationship dynamics, or social position.

By anchoring therapy in the materiality of a personal object, exploring artifacts moves beyond abstract conversation and grounds therapy in the tangible. This allows clients to externalize problems or successes, making them easier to address and reframe within the therapeutic setting. The process enables clients to reshape their self-understanding and foster empowerment by gaining new insights into how they perceive their place in the world.

Exploring Artifacts Example

Let's say that Tamu has returned for another therapy session. This time the therapist will help Tamu explore artifacts in her life to uncover her hidden testimony.

Therapist: Tamu, I'm really glad you're here today. I'd like to invite you to bring an artifact—a personal item, an object, or a photograph—that represents something meaningful to you. This could be anything tied to your identity, a past experience, or something you connect with deeply. Do you have something in mind?

Tamu: I do. I have a photograph of me and my grandmother when I was young. It's one of those black-and-white pictures where I'm sitting on her lap in her garden. She always made me feel safe and loved, especially when I was feeling upset.

Therapist: That sounds like a powerful image. Tell me more about that photograph. What do you notice when you look at it now? How do you feel about it?

Tamu: When I look at it now, I feel a mix of warmth and sadness. It's comforting to remember her care, but I also feel like I've lost that sense of peace in my life now. I can almost hear her voice telling me to "stay rooted like the trees." She always said that when life felt overwhelming, I should find my center and hold onto it, just like those trees in her garden.

Therapist: That's such a meaningful image and advice from her. It seems like "staying rooted" was something she wanted to pass on to you. In the context of your life now, how do you interpret that advice? What does it mean to you today, and how might it relate to the challenges you're facing?

Tamu: I think it means staying grounded in the face of all the stress, especially with my kids, work, and marriage. But sometimes I feel like I've lost that grounding. The pressure of everything can be overwhelming, and I don't always know how to "stay rooted." It's like I've forgotten how to do it, or maybe I've let the "wind" of life blow me around too much.

Therapist: You're describing a lot of internal tension between what your grandmother taught you and what you're experiencing now. The wind seems to represent the overwhelming pressures you're facing. Can you think of a time recently when you felt this "wind" most strongly, when you felt ungrounded or pulled in many directions?

Tamu: I feel it all the time, honestly. Especially with my husband—there's a lot of tension between us. I feel like he doesn't respect me or appreciate what I do. It's like there's this constant storm of criticism and expectations, and I'm just trying to keep up with everything. It feels like there's no space for me to just be.

Therapist: That sounds exhausting, and it seems like these external pressures are making it hard to find your center. How do you think your grandmother would want you to respond to these pressures? How could her wisdom help you now, in the middle of all this tension?

Tamu: I think she'd want me to remember that peace doesn't have to come from everything being perfect or easy. She'd probably remind me to take a moment to breathe, to pause, and reconnect with myself—no matter what's happening around me.

Therapist: It sounds like you're saying that grounding could be a choice, even in the midst of everything swirling around you. What if, instead of waiting for things to calm down, you allowed yourself moments of peace during the chaos? What might it look like to "stay rooted" amid the storm?

Tamu: Maybe it's about being mindful of the small moments. I could pause and breathe for a second, or focus on the bracelet my grandmother gave me. I used to wear it every day. It was a reminder of her strength and wisdom, but I've stopped wearing it lately.

Therapist: That bracelet seems to hold a lot of significance. It's not just an object; it sounds like it's a tangible link to your grandmother's strength and the peace she encouraged you to find. What do you think it would mean to bring that bracelet back into your life—how might it support you in grounding yourself again?

Tamu: I think wearing it again would remind me of her love, and of her belief that I can be strong and centered, even when everything feels chaotic. It would be like carrying a piece of her strength with me, a reminder that I'm not alone.

Therapist: It sounds like the bracelet could serve as an anchor, not just to your grandmother's memory, but also to your own inner strength. If you allowed it to be that anchor, how might it shift your experience when life feels overwhelming? How could it help you reshape the way you respond to those moments?

Tamu: I think it would help me reclaim my power in the moment. It's not about everything being perfect, but rather about remembering that I have the ability to stay centered, even if it's just for a brief moment. Maybe I can start wearing it again and using it as a tool to pause and refocus, even when things are tough.

Therapist: I love that idea. It seems like the bracelet isn't just a piece of jewelry; it's a symbol of your resilience and your connection to a deeper sense of self. As you wear it again, what other practices or actions could help you stay rooted in the midst of life's storms?

Tamu: Maybe I could also start thinking about how I set boundaries, especially with my husband. I've been so caught up in trying to meet his expectations, but I think I've lost sight of my own needs. I could use the bracelet as a reminder to advocate for myself and take care of my own well-being.

Therapist: That's a powerful realization, Tamu. By reconnecting with the bracelet and what it represents, you're also reclaiming your right to take up space, to assert your needs, and to prioritize your peace. It's amazing that you're already thinking about how this artifact can be a tool for both grounding and setting boundaries.

Tamu: Yes, I think I can start by wearing the bracelet again and using it as a symbol of strength. I want to be more intentional about grounding myself, both in moments of tension and in moments of peace.

Creating Codes

One of the most exciting practices of critical pedagogy is Freire's use of what he calls codes. In teaching literacy in poor and oppressed communities, teachers would first learn about the daily lives of their students by becoming curious about every aspect of their lives, asking questions and showing interest in what they did and what this meant to them. After some time of curiously observing and learning about their clients and encouraging them to be experts in their own lives, the teachers would take what they learned and create representations of elements of the daily lives of the clients using pictures. These representations were called *codes* because they created puzzles for the students to collectively decipher. In presenting these codes to their clients, the teachers would pose problematizing questions about how the students understood and interpreted the picture. What did they see? What was the situation? What issues were being solved in this situation, and why did this solve the issue?

By (re)presenting familiar life situations and experiences to their clients through codes and encouraging critical reflection about their meaning, the teachers helped clients to experience their own lives as significant and meaningful. Through the dialogue and problematizing questions, clients were encouraged to look beyond their limit assumptions about life situations and to think creatively about possible solutions and changes to their lives beyond what has always been. By doing this in conversation with others, the power of relationship was encouraged and reinforced, connecting clients to empowering community.

In the decolonized therapy room, dialogical coding and decoding can be a useful resource for the therapist to collaborate with their client to give new and empowering meaning to their lives and to create their preferred testimony. This means that the most important first steps of the testimony therapist are to assume a position of humble curiosity and not knowing. You may be an expert in your field, but you are not the expert in the life of your client. Now is the time to be open and reflective. Now is the time to focus not just on what is wrong with your client but on what is going well. How do they live day to day? What are the important relationships in their lives? What is enjoyable for them and why? From these dialogues, if you listen closely, you are likely to hear themes arising in the stories that clients tell about their lives. You are challenged to bring these themes to your client in such a way as to make them valuable to the client. Many of these themes raise deep emotions and may appear to have no solution. For example, how simple is it for a parent to resolve the dilemma of trying to parent a child who is aware that the parent is under court order not to use corporal punishment? The child may threaten to call the police or social services each time a conflict arises with the parent. The parent may now simply back off any attempt to discipline the child for fear of more court or police involvement. This does not help the parent, the child, or their relationship.

The task in problem posing is to provide a structure for positive, solution-directed dialogue that encourages communitarian values. Testimony approaches avoid allowing these conversations to degenerate into opportunities to voice powerless complaints. By using codes as objects for discussion and by involving testimony principles of speaker/witness dialogue in an inductive process of questioning, the discussions may be kept focused on personal experiences. At the same time, a client's personal experience may be fit into the broader cultural context, and solutions may be worked out in the conversation between client and therapist.

A code is a concrete physical representation of a particularly critical issue that has come up in the stories that clients tell about their lives. Codes should be a representation of problems and situations which are familiar and would be immediately recognized by clients. Codes should not be one dimensional but should represent a problem with many sides and more than one solution. The code should be ambiguous to avoid sending the message that there is a good or bad point of view. There should be no implicit solutions in the code. Keep it open and simple and only deal with one issue at a time. They should require only small steps for making change.

Remember, a code is a representation of a theme which has been heard in your dialogue with your client. For example, a couple may tell a story about an incident of situational (as opposed to characterological) intimate partner violence. Though this violence has occurred only once in the relationship, it still is causing emotional pain and distrust between the partners. As a therapist you might present the couple with a scene from a novel which you read to them, or a movie scene which you watch together, that portrays a similar example of situational intimate partner violence. Here you can be creative. The code could even be a verse from a song or a photograph depicting the familiar situation, a drawing, or anything that represents the themes heard in the client's story. It's important to remember that the code should reflect the cultural and social reality of your clients.

Presenting codes in this way allows the people who have come to you for help to gain some emotional distance for what could be an embarrassing or overwhelming subject. It also allows issues to be examined in a supportive therapeutic relationship rather than in the limiting place of individual isolation and alienation.

The Decoding Questioning Cycle

Problem-posing therapy utilizing the developed codes follows a sevenfold process which carries clients from the familiar, individual, and concrete to the abstract, collective, and analytical. In reflective dialogue with the therapist, clients experience knowledge being gained in relationship. They also learn that their own problems are not peculiar to themselves, nor are they insurmountable. In the process, clients are asked to observe or listen to a code and:

1. **Describe what they see or hear:** This means simply reporting what is observable without giving input as to the meaning of what is seen or heard. They are to act as reporters of data, not interpreters.
2. **Define the problems with what is observed:** Now clients are asked to interpret and problematize the code. Even if the code appears benign and insignificant, they should be encouraged to look for contradictions and problems. Who is helped and who is hurt? Are there any power inequalities? Is there injustice in the situation? Is this limited to only the people directly involved, or is this a social problem? Why? Does racism, sexism, or child abuse/neglect play any part?
3. **Share similar experiences:** Here the therapist encourages the clients to normalize the situation. Group members may feel that the problem represented only has significance to them. By sharing similar experiences or knowledge of similar situations, the group becomes aware of the social nature of the situation and can collectively break through the feeling of isolation and alienation.
4. **Question why there is a problem:** It is not enough to see problems. If they exist in this situation, why are they problems? What is at the root

of the problem? Is it only personal, or are there social conditions which influence or enhance the problem? Is it only a problem now, or is there historical precedent in the family or the society?

5. **What can be done to resolve the problem:** This is a chance for clients to create visionary solutions. If problems have been identified by the clients and the source of the problems and their implications explored, the solutions can be found in this question.
6. **Define the benefits in the resolutions:** Now we are asking the client to create a new telling of the story which redefines the situation and reconstructs their environment. They are not only seeking solutions, they are examining the implications of the solutions they raise.
7. **Describe how the new situation might look:** The therapist is inviting the client to name and define their own reality. As they describe the new imagined situation, they are daring to visualize what a different world would look like. They are taking responsibility for their own lives and forging new directions for them.

Each part of this cycle should involve discussion and ongoing questioning of answers given. The therapist should encourage clients to question and even challenge their own thoughts and each other's ideas. In this process, clients will have the experience of intentionally looking at a problem in the context of relationship and together weaving a collectively decided-upon shared story and understanding of the world. They will have worked together to solve a familiar problem from their daily lived experience. They also will have been empowered to take responsibility to define their own lives and to communicate with the therapist their own perceptions of the world. We call this approach problem posing rather than problem solving because there is no one solution to any code raised. It recognizes the need for ongoing action, investigation, and challenge in the lives of clients.

The therapist is active throughout this process and has not been an "objective" outside observer but an active critical participant who collaborates with the client and accompanies them as they find solutions and create their own testimony. The therapist has been open and ready to say simply, "I don't know, I'll have to investigate that," if in fact a question is raised which cannot be answered.

The therapist has not been infallible, but has been knowledgeable and willing to share their knowledge as well as to hear and affirm the knowledge of the clients.

Decoding Questions Example

Willie and Cheryl are a married couple with three children who are 17, 15, and 10 years old. They are having severe discipline problems with their 17-year-old son, Robert, who has been skipping classes in school, getting into conflicts with teachers, and smoking marijuana almost daily. Robert has left home and stayed away all night at least twice in the past year. Both parents are exasperated, and Willie has even threatened to kick Robert out of the house. This has caused conflict between him and Cheryl. Tensions are running high in the home. The therapist shows the couple a short music video telling the story of a mother who wants to protect her son from street danger. In the video she argues with him and tries to force him to stay home, but he leaves in an angry huff, running to meet friends who are planning to rob a corner store. The video ends without resolution.

> **Therapist:** Welcome, Willie and Cheryl. I'm glad we're here today to work through some of the issues you're facing with Robert. To start, I'd like to show you a short video. It's about a mother who argues with her son, trying to protect him, but he gets angry and leaves, heading toward danger. Let's watch and reflect together. *(The therapist plays the video.)*

1. Describe What You See or Hear

> **Therapist:** After watching the video, let's begin with simple observation. What did you both notice about the mother and son in this video? What are some key moments or actions that stood out to you?
>
> **Willie:** The mother looks really worried and is trying to keep her son home, but he's not listening. He just gets angrier and leaves.
>
> **Cheryl:** Yes, the mother seems really frustrated, and the son—he just

doesn't care about what she's saying. He walks away and gets even more upset. It feels like a power struggle between them.

2. Define the Problems With What is Observed

Therapist: Now, let's think about the problems that are happening in the video. What do you think the mother is struggling with, and what problems do you see in the son's behavior?

Willie: The mother seems like she's trying to protect him, but he's rejecting her. She's controlling, and it's pushing him away.

Cheryl: The son is clearly defiant. He doesn't seem to appreciate her concern. Instead of listening, he's running off into danger. It's almost like neither of them can see the other's side of things.

3. Share Similar Experiences

Therapist: This situation feels familiar, right? Think about it from a broader lens. Have you seen or heard of situations like this before? What does this remind you of, either from your own life or from things you've observed?

Willie: It reminds me of stories I've heard about teenagers pushing back against their parents, especially when they don't want to be controlled. They just want independence.

Cheryl: It's also similar to how some people get angry when they feel trapped or like they can't make their own choices. It's a common thing in families, I think, where a parent wants to protect, but the child just wants to break free.

4. Question Why There is a Problem

Therapist: Now that we've identified the problems, let's dig a little deeper. Why do you think these issues exist in the video? Why is the son rejecting his mother's protection, and why is the mother using control to try to keep him safe?

Willie: The son probably feels like his mother doesn't trust him. He might see her attempts to control him as a lack of respect for his ability to make his own decisions.

Cheryl: The mother's reaction might come from fear—fear that something bad will happen to him. She's probably scared, and that's making her more controlling. But it's not helping him trust her.

5. What Can Be Done to Resolve the Problem(s)

Therapist: So, knowing what we now understand about the problems, what do you think could be done to improve the situation between the mother and son in the video? What other options could the mother try to get through to her son without pushing him away?

Willie: Maybe instead of trying to force him to stay home, she could sit down and ask him about what's going on in his life, why he feels like he has to leave. She could listen to him and show him that she understands his need for freedom.

Cheryl: Yes! I think the mother could try to have an open conversation where she expresses her concerns, but also gives him space to explain himself. She could ask questions like "Why are you so determined to leave?" without just assuming he's wrong.

6. Describe How the New Situation Might Look

Therapist: Now, imagine if the mother tried something different. If she listened more and showed she understands his feelings, how might the situation look in a better, more connected way? How would things feel different between them?

Willie: If the mother took that approach, it might lower the tension. She might start to build trust with her son, where he feels like she actually sees him as an equal in the conversation.

Cheryl: It would definitely feel less stressful. If she stopped trying to control him so much, maybe he'd feel less pressure and more willing to listen to her concerns. They might even be able to find a middle ground.

Therapist: That vision of open communication and mutual understanding sounds like a healthier dynamic. It's important to think about the future, where both the mother and son are respecting each other's feelings and needs. This is the kind of relationship we're trying to create in our families—one where understanding, not control, leads the way.

These four approaches are not mandates. They are useful methods which I have found help me to bear witness to the testimonies of my clients and collaborate with them in respectful dialogue as I help them experience a healthy decolonized relationship, which invites them to see beyond colonizing life limits. You may have other ideas and approaches which you find helpful in your own work, grounded in your own cultural experience and knowledge. I encourage you to explore these approaches along with your clients and community.

CHAPTER 5

Supervision and Testimony Therapy

When I entered the field of mental health and was being trained as a marriage and family therapist several decades ago, Black people certainly tended to avoid seeking mental health support specifically because of the alienating and colonizing experience of walking into white spaces with Black people's problems. In those days it was difficult finding mentors and teachers of mental health practice who understood the problematic and oppressive contexts of traditional Western mental health practice, or who understood the cultural and social issues that I as a young therapist encountered on a regular basis when I worked with Black people who would risk coming to see a therapist. Even beyond teachers and mentors, it often felt lonely and alienating even to find other therapists who were of African, Asian, Latinx, or indigenous (AALI) descent.

Though there are more AALI therapists working across all mental health fields, the reality is that only 4 percent of all licensed mental health workers in the United States are of African descent, while 8 percent are Hispanic, 11 percent are Asian, and 3 percent are made up of other ethnic groups (Norris, 2025). The fact that only about 25 percent of trained and licensed mental health professionals come from and are available to provide healing services for communities that have experienced colonization and racist oppression for years is appalling in itself! This clearly highlights the underrepresentation of healers for these communities, which have faced ongoing social, cultural, and racial trauma which affects their mental health. No data are being kept on how many of these licensed AALI therapists are trained to mentor and provide clinical supervision for new therapists of color who may be trained in the future, but a 2021–2022 demographic report from Auburn University's Marriage and Family Therapy program indicates that out of eight American Association for Marriage and Family Therapy (AAMFT)–approved supervisors, seven were white non-Hispanic and one was Latinx, with no Black American representation. This is likely a good indicator of the lack of Black American mentorship available to supervise new Black therapists coming into the mental health field and to train them in decolonizing mental health practices.

I decided to become an AAMFT approved supervisor in 2010 after conferring with a group of other AALI family therapists at a national AAMFT conference. We had spent several years discussing our frustration with the marginalization and dismissal we all felt in the profession and recounting our own experiences in being supported to develop in the field. By the end of that discussion, several of us committed to becoming approved supervisors to provide for younger therapists being trained what we often did not get, which was the opportunity to be mentored by a professional who looked like us and, more importantly, who shared and understood the experience of marginalization and resistance to coloniality in America.

In a white paper published online by Motivo Health (2025), we learned that 57 percent of students who complete mental health training programs to become therapists never attain licensure to practice. There are a range of reasons for this, with one of them being listed as "barriers specific to clinicians of color," so we can see that even with the increase of Black people needing and seeking mental health services, there is an abysmal lack of trained mental health workers available for these communities. When we add to this the lack of a focus on the need to decolonize mental health practice and the absence of people who have experience and desire to teach new therapists decolonizing practices, we can see that the future of decolonizing mental health can be discouraging.

We are living in an unnerving and uncertain time. I am writing this in the first few weeks of the second presidency of Donald Trump, and between news reports, social media confusion, attacks on immigrants, and the dismantling of anything related to social justice safety nets for Black and other communities. More than ever, we should be concerned for the mental health of our community. More than ever, we are in need of healers, therapists, and mental health workers who will be more than gatekeepers for the status quo gaslighting people into accepting the system and fitting in. This will require teaching new generations of therapists to decolonize mental health and to create space for the emerging testimonies of resistance and resilience that will be necessary to survive and get through this next period.

This will also require building on the Black educational tradition of what Jarvis R. Givens (2021) calls *fugitive pedagogy*: The tradition of Black people teaching about and for Black people's interest and survival despite the efforts of white racists to deny us education or to shove us into traditions of miseducation (Woodson, 2017).

Often when therapists from Black communities begin learning about testimony therapy and decolonizing mental health, it is unsettling for them. The possibility that healing work can be done while decentering Western assumptions is both surprising and in some ways frightening for many. For most of our lives, we have been taught that the Eurocentric assumptions about psychology, identity, and relationships are what is normal, and our lived experience of the fact of Blackness is at best diverse, or at worst a symptom of pathology. This means, for Black and other people experiencing coloniality, we learned to put our authentic selves in a box while we practiced mental health work, and we even tried to fit our colonized kin into that same box.

Now the reality is that while they may not have heard of testimony therapy or even about decolonizing mental health, some of these therapists have listened to the voices of their ancestors and have instinctively learned to code switch in the therapy room. They have relied on ways of talking to and connecting with their Black clients which feel more authentic and significant, even though they may be filled with self-doubt that somehow they are "doing it wrong" by not sticking to the methodology and theories that they learned in school. To learn that the ways of engaging people and thinking about and performing relationship that they may have grown up with, and the beliefs, spiritual concepts, and idioms that come from their culture, can be codified and used clinically to help their people heal, without fear of "being wrong," is a liberating revelation.

Because of the medicalization of mental health work by the health insurance industry, I find that young therapists coming into the field have been trained to approach their work as technicians, viewing the people who come to them as "broken" objects with little agency over their own lives, who need to be diagnosed to find the most broken parts inside their heads and then saved through the "expert knowledge" of the therapist, based on methods which have been shown through research to be the only valid approaches to deal with that particular brokenness. This "expert knowledge" orientation makes it difficult for these new therapists to engage with the humanity of the people who come to them through unhindered and authentic relationship. These therapists come into the field with several challenges that make it difficult to work in the interest of decolonization.

First, I have found that even those new therapists trained in professions like family therapy, which traditionally distinguished itself from other mental health work with its focus on family systems more than individual brokenness, find it difficult to see beyond individual, internal state psychology as they search for problems to fix. Second, these new therapists have difficulty trusting that clients can be experts in their own lives. Their assumed expertise makes it difficult for them to allow themselves to be taught by the people who come to them for help. Third, new therapists often fail to join and engage with clients. The objectifying distance they often maintain makes them appear inauthentic to their clients. Fourth, I find that an excessive dependence on protocols and techniques, which were most important to demonstrate research repeatability, only serves to discourage and even extinguish the curiosity of new therapists. Their positivist orientation and trust in manipulative techniques diminishes the therapist's relationship to themselves and their own intuitive connection to the humanity of the people they are working with. This positivist approach often leads to self-censure and fear of asking questions of the clients for fear of being too intrusive in their lives.

Teaching new therapists to take a decolonizing stance in their practice of therapy should reflect the Africana critical theory and liberatory teaching attitudes related to testimony therapy. With the heavy emphasis on the medical model and so-called evidence-based practice geared toward satisfying the economic bottom-line needs of insurance companies rather than the real emotional, cultural, and social needs of people, this is a difficult task to accomplish and requires patience and commitment on the part of both teachers and their students.

Because of medical model training, new therapists must be encouraged to unlearn the attitude of coming into a therapeutic situation as an all-knowing professional focused first on diagnosing the people who come to them. As the therapist is invited into the relationship network, their first task is to join with the family as a student, allowing themselves to be taught by the clients about their lives and what they might like to see differently. The therapist also invites the client to experience a sense of hopefulness by noticing and focusing on strengths that may be helpful in challenging the pain caused by the presented situation. This hopefulness is encouraged using analogy, metaphor, and testimony between therapist and client. The therapist is working along with the client to divine the situation.

A testimony therapist introduces the *unpredictability* factor that opposes the doom-and-gloom familiarity of the client's lived experience. This is done through humor, paradox, signification, hyperbolic language, and other approaches. When clients tell their life story only through doom, gloom, and suffering, this can reflect *narrative determinism*, or the belief that "life has always been this way and will always be this way." Unpredictability interrupts this rigid, limit-focused narrative. When something unexpected is introduced, such as a humorous reframe, or a hyperbolic response that makes no immediate sense, it creates a brief pause in the client's thinking. In this pause, clients are invited to reflect on their testimony from a different perspective. Using humor through a light reframe might bring a smile. The therapist might say, "You telling me you've been holding up the whole world since birth? Even Atlas only carried the sky—you out here holding it all! That's heavy!" Using paradox the therapist might offer a counterintuitive observation to disrupt linear thinking by saying, "You say you're invisible, but I see someone who's hard to disappear—that takes power to pull off." A hyperbolic response might exaggerate aspects of the client's story to reveal their constructed nature. For instance the therapist might say, "So you're telling me, if you don't fix everyone's problem, the earth will crack open and swallow the whole block? That's a lot of responsibility for one person." Signification is word play in Black oral tradition.

A therapist might affirm a client's decision by drawing on a familiar cultural idiom: "Ain't nobody mad but the devil. Even doom and gloom has to take a break sometime."

In testimony therapy supervision, just as in therapy itself, the supervisor's role is not simply to teach techniques or correct mistakes. Rather, it is to cultivate a witnessing presence that refuses to collude with silence, invisibility, or the marginalization of emotions, experiences, and cultural truths. Often supervisees speak about their cases in technical language, diagnostic codes, or neutral summaries that obscure the emotional, cultural, or political realities present in the room. The testimony supervisor notices and names these subtle layers—whether it is the supervisee's own fear, racialized dynamics, power issues, client despair, or unspoken hope hiding these issues in plain sight.

By following their own curiosity and bringing unspoken issues into the therapeutic circle, the therapist participates with clients in creating a safe place for stuck power struggles to be played out in the direction of transformation. In a parallel process, when training new therapists, we should become curious about their intentions and actions with clients and raise questions to encourage them to reflect on the work they are doing in the therapy room. These ways and attitudes of working with people can be admittedly difficult if a new therapist has spent several years being trained simply to help people "fit in" to society rather than to collaborate with people to discover and cocreate chosen testimonies with them that feel more liberating.

My approach to teaching new therapists is like my approach to providing testimony therapy to people who come to me for help. For example, just as in therapy, I assume that both my supervisee and I are shaped and influenced by grand public stories about ourselves related to ethnicity, class, gender, sexuality, color/caste, and other socially constructed narratives. As a therapist, I focus on my client's personal and cultural strengths and invite them to take notice of these strengths. I take a similar approach to my work with supervisees, in that I focus on their strengths and invite them to notice and use more of those strengths in their work. In my work with clients, I focus on the present or the *now* moment as a liberating space. In a similar way, I work with new therapists to trust the process rather than focusing on a wrong step or worrying about what technique to use in the next 20 minutes.

Therapy is a ritual performance providing space for a client's hidden testimonies (unspoken personal and cultural stories) to take shape. In supervision, I likewise strive to work with new therapists to discover how their own testimonies shape the work done with their clients. In much of the supervision literature there is discussion about the stance of the supervisor, that is, whether he or she acts collaboratively, as a coach, or as a teacher with the supervisee. I assume that different moments and different situations in the supervision relationship require that I take on differing stances to be effective as a supervisor. With new supervisees, relying on principles of critical pedagogy, I initially work as a student to learn from the person I am supervising about themselves. With the knowledge I gain from that relationship, I am better able then to be a teacher, completing my knowledge of them through dialogical conversations.

With supervisees who have some experience, I often work as a coach, and with experienced colleagues, I focus on collaborative work. I am also aware that I may need to work from any of these stances at any time. It is important that I be open and aware of the situation demanded in the supervision relationship. I am also aware that I am always in a sense working collaboratively with my supervisee, as we share testimony, metaphor, and analogy to name a particular situation and give it meaning for the supervisee.

One method that I use for this and which I also focus on in therapy is the problematizing question. I tend to ask tentative and curious questions about the supervisee's work. This encourages the supervisee to consider what they are doing, and to deconstruct and critically think about their work. This is important, I believe, because it gives space and encourages the supervisee to be the expert on their own casework, rather than me projecting myself as having the expert answers. At the same time, I remain aware of my responsibility as a supervisor to provide information and knowledge that I may have beyond the experience or training of the supervisee. As a therapist, I strive to remain comfortable with ambiguity and to allow the stories of clients and their meanings to reveal themselves. This requires humility and honesty and no defensiveness on my own part. As a supervisor, I strive to model this stance with my supervisees, not by demanding answers but by being patient and asking questions that allow the process of supervision to provide answers to issues raised about the supervisee's work in therapy. Just as in therapy, I believe that in supervision dialogue and learning to question rather than having the answer is our most powerful tool.

My approach to supervision parallels my approach to therapy and is guided by the same philosophical outlook. Supervisees need encouragement around their strengths, support, and feedback as well as critical reflection on their work to help them develop into fully competent therapists. From our first meeting throughout our supervision experience, I discuss the significance of context with the supervisee (Hardy, 1990; Leitch, 1992; Libow, 1985; Storm, 1991). I require focus on context in case presentation and consideration of context throughout the therapeutic process. I include discussion about how contextual issues may be affecting the supervisor/supervisee relationship, with ongoing opportunities for the supervisee to give critical feedback about their experience. Prior to meeting for the first time with a supervisee, I give her an agreement form, as well as a values and goal questionnaire to be completed before our first meeting. The agreement form allows us to clarify exactly what the supervisee will need from me as a supervisor. It also allows us to clarify my responsibility to her as well as our mutual responsibilities as they relate to issues of ethics. The questionnaire asks the supervisee to think about her own theoretical orientation, her strengths and weaknesses as a therapist, her goals as a therapist, and other such questions. These items provide a framework for the supervisee to critically think about what she would like to work on and achieve in our relationship and gives us clear areas of discussion as we learn about each other in the first meeting. Prior to arriving for the second meeting, I ask the supervisee to prepare a genogram of her family to include at least three generations, including herself. This genogram is helpful, particularly for new therapists or for those who are unfamiliar with relational/systemic conceptualizations (Braverman, 1997). The genogram also helps the supervisee to situate herself and her own experiences in the context of therapy (Liddle, 1988; McGoldrick, 2016). From the very beginning of our relationship as supervisor and supervisee, I am aware of and strive to model my understanding of the various contexts through which the supervisee and I interact, such as class, gender, color/caste, and ethnicity. I constantly question my own positioning as it relates to power relationships with the supervisee and periodically ask for reflections by the supervisee on these issues.

First Do No Harm

I believe it is imperative that we take advantage of technology as new therapists are being trained. Our first responsibility with new therapists we supervise is to make sure that they first *do no harm*. It is our responsibility to make sure that new therapists are working ethically and being attentive to the safety of the people who come to them for help. This means it is important for those of us who supervise to witness the work of the new therapist, either by reviewing video or audio recordings of their sessions, or by viewing them live through closed-circuit video, two-way mirror, or even on occasion sitting in with them as a nonintrusive cotherapist. This is because I believe that learning is social, and that more effective learning occurs when supervisees can share experiences and knowledge with colearners. Recorded therapy sessions provide the opportunity to see or hear directly what the supervisee did and said in the therapy session, while at the same time providing the cognitive distance and abstraction to allow critical reflection on the therapy as a teaching/learning experience.

New therapists sometimes become stuck with clients as they are pulled into the vortex of client's subordination/domination power dances, and they find themselves in contention with the client. The relationship between the client and therapist then reflects the relationship, in the case of family therapy, between members of the client's family (Liddle & Saba, 1983). As a supervisor, my most frequent means of intervening in this isomorphic situation is to first learn from the supervisee how they are experiencing this relationship. This is a place where the therapist's use of self becomes an important skill to develop.

While being caught up and focused on technique and doing proper therapy, new therapists may lose sight of their own experience of the relationship with the client and not be able to experience their own emotional, somatic, and intellectual responses to this relationship. They, like their clients, are not able to feel their feelings and are simply moving through the encounter without awareness. This can also be a good opportunity to encourage the new therapist to practice the self-knowledge exercises discussed in Chapter 4 to help them appreciate what we mean by the therapist's use of self.

When I notice this, as we observe the recording of the session, I may ask the therapist, "What were you feeling as you asked your client that question?

Did you notice any sensations in your body, or did you have any intrusive thoughts as the client responded to your question?" By shifting attention from proper technique to the therapist's thoughts, emotions, and bodily sensations, I am reminding the therapist to use their whole self as an instrument of therapeutic intervention.

I also work here to help new therapists develop other testimony-focused skills. Of course, as a decolonizing therapy grounded in oral tradition, it is important that the new therapist is cognizant of the rhythm and the beat of the conversation with their client and the call and response as they collaborate with the client to construct a testimony. It is important that the therapist remain aware of their own physicality and the messages and meaning carried in facial expressions, posture, distance between themselves and the people they are helping, and even subtle hand movements.

I'll suggest that new therapists listen to various genres of Black music such as jazz, gospel, blues, hip-hop, and R&B or, even better, watch videos with these types of music performances and to imagine themselves as one of the musicians. I ask them to imagine the music as conversation and to name emotions they may hear in the music. I ask them to develop stories about the musical interaction they hear. What is the problem the music is trying to solve? Which instrument or voice is centering the conversation? Which is maintaining the rhythm and intensity of the conversation? How do the various parts collaborate, and how do they contend with each other?

From this exercise, I then ask the new therapist to imagine that they and their clients in conversation are all taking musical parts. What part are they taking in the conversation? Are they maintaining the rhythm and flow of the conversation or, like a drummer, providing a steady beat supporting someone who seems to be carrying the melody of the testimony? With this exercise I strive to invite the therapist to hear and find meaning beyond the words spoken in the therapeutic conversation.

I want to know how they see the client, what they have done with them so far, what they expected to happen, what they believe has happened, and why they believe they are stuck. I work with the new therapist to revision and reconstruct their relationship to the clients by using humor, paradox, signification, analogy, and shared testimony of my own experiences, particularly those in which I have felt equally stuck. This last part is important because I believe it challenges the myth of the perfect and infallible therapist. I ask reflective questions such as, "What problems do you see here?" "What's the problem with the problem?" "You chose to go in this particular direction because . . . ?"

I model for the new therapist the stance of collaboration in the process and coconstruction of theory and practice with their clients by raising tentative and curious "I wonder (why, what if) . . . " questions rather than emphasizing directives or rushing to give my opinions. Most of our conversation in supervision is guided by my own curious questions about what the therapist was doing, thinking, or feeling in a particular moment. At the same time, I am mindful of my own responsibility to make use of my wealth of knowledge in the field in giving support and guidance to the new therapist (Anderson, 2000). When I teach testimony approaches, I strive to maintain an atmosphere of collegiality and collaboration while not abdicating my responsibility to provide for the new therapist what they expect as it relates to sharing my own experience and knowledge as a therapist.

Supervision With Imani

The following is an example of working with a new therapist and encouraging testimony approaches to the work. Using experiences and circumstances from several sessions with new therapists, who collectively I'll call Imani, lets us explore teaching a decolonizing approach to therapy.

Imani is a 29-year-old Black woman who is a master's-level therapist working toward licensure in a family support agency. Our supervision is held biweekly at the main office of the agency in a large family therapy room. This is also the space in which most of Imani's sessions with the families are held. The room is well furnished with comfortable chairs and a sofa as well as with child-sized furniture and a cabinet for toys, games, and books. There is also a two-way mirror looking into the room that allows live supervision from behind the mirror. Imani presents at our supervision sessions with video of her sessions with families. With the permission of the families, we also sometimes conduct live supervision using the two-way mirror.

In my first meeting with Imani, we discuss the significance of context, including both the context of our supervision and of the therapeutic relationships with her families. We discuss how contextual issues such as age and gender differences between us might affect our supervisor/supervisee relationship. We discuss the fact that we are both African American marriage and family therapists working in a city with very few of us in the entire state. This is important in terms of issues of cultural and professional isolation that might be felt by a new therapist in the area. We continue down this line to discuss Imani's experiences in school as a Black woman, and I ask what she had noticed about this experience. I ask her how her own cultural and social experience was included or excluded from her learning.

I also open discussion about what impact racism and economic and political marginalization have on the people we see as therapists as well as on ourselves living in this society. As I approach these subjects, I introduce the idea of decolonizing therapy with a focus on helping the people we work with see beyond the cultural and social limit situations that coloniality creates in our lives. Imani is curious about these ideas and excited. She says these are things she has personally thought about, but have never been discussed with her in the context of therapeutic relationships. She is excited to see how these ideas might show up in the therapy room.

Prior to our first meeting I gave Imani a written agreement to read and sign. At our first meeting, the agreement allows us to clarify exactly what Imani needs from me as a supervisor. It also allows us to clarify my responsibility to her as well as our mutual responsibilities as they relate to issues of ethics. Along with the agreement, I ask Imani to respond to a questionnaire which asks five questions. She is asked to reflect on why she decided to become a therapist. I also ask about her goals as a therapist. I ask her to tell me about her strengths and weaknesses as a therapist, and to name and describe her theoretical orientation in therapy.

With this last question I often discover that new therapists have not seriously thought about the theory that guides their work since leaving the classroom behind. They may have vague memories of theories and may timidly respond that they prefer narrative or solution-focused or, more often than not because of the emphasis on so-called evidence-based approaches, they will declare themselves to be cognitive behavioral therapists. Beyond remembering the names of therapy theories, however, I often find that new therapists have not thought or practiced these beyond the classroom. When this is the case, I'll focus our conversation on the importance of theory, not so much because any one theory is superior to another (Duncan et al., 2010), but because a theory gives us as a therapist a sense of direction for the work we do. It provides us with a proverbial flashlight through the woods and helps us to know where we are and where we are going at any moment in the therapeutic relationship. Once I explain this, I describe my own work and the ideas of testimony therapy to the new therapist. I explain that I will be working with them guided by these ideas and practices, and that I will insist that they be able to tell me how their own theory of practice influences their work in the therapy room, whether they rely on testimony ideas, traditional narrative, or any other theory which they choose to work from.

For our second meeting, Imani prepares a genogram of her family. We are able to discuss issues of systemic relationships and how her own experiences situate Imani in the context of therapy with the families she consults with. Through her genogram, Imani and I are able to discuss how issues of race, gender, class, and color/caste have affected her development as a therapist and how these issues shape her way of living in relationships. This issue of color/caste is important and may be overlooked by someone who has not experienced or is not cognizant of the fact of Blackness. Colorism, or the bias between Black people of different skin tones, is a tragic result of the legacy of slavery and colonization of Black people by white America. It has meant that lighter-skinned Black people both carry a skin privilege, with more benefits and opportunities because they are closer to whiteness, but also may experience alienation and resentment among Black people. Colorism has a terrible legacy of limiting dark-skinned Black people's material life chances, choice of romantic partners, or inclusion in spaces of privilege because of their epidermal badge of shame, which is a reminder of their descent from Africa in the Western mind. This antagonism and conflict based on skin tone becomes even more problematic when you consider the wide range of skin tones, from the darkest brown to the nearly indistinguishable from European white, which is possible even in one family kin group. This is a legacy of racist coloniality and is part of the fact of Blackness.

Conversations like these on the internal cultural secrets of Black people may seem difficult to introduce into a therapeutic learning situation. These are the secrets that colonized people rarely discuss openly even among ourselves, and these conversations can provoke feelings of shame when others witness them. They are necessary for decolonization, however, because these remnants of coloniality are the elements of Du Bois's double consciousness and Fanon's zone of nonbeing that keep Black people alienated from ourselves and from other Black people. A new therapist who has not been liberated to confront this will not be able to do the work of decolonizing mental health in the everyday lives of the Black people they work with.

As a dark-skinned Black woman, Imani has experienced this. She is surprised that I have introduced it into our conversation about therapy, as she has never been invited to discuss her thoughts and experiences of colorism in a clinical setting before. "I've thought about it," she says, "but I didn't think it was appropriate to bring up in therapy since that's just my individual and personal problem." I asked Imani to tell me of times when she has had thoughts about a client's feelings about her darkness, or times when she has noticed the skin tone of the people who have come to her. I ask her to reflect on her own ideas about colorism and relationships and where she had learned them.

I notice that Imani seems to lack confidence in her own skills and development as a therapist, which seems to influence her to take rigid stances both with the people who come to her for help and in our sessions together. She is often overly formal and unsmiling and seems guarded about her own presence in the therapy room. She seems physically uncomfortable in the session, often sitting bolt upright. I mention this to her and ask if she has noticed any discomfort for herself during our sessions. "No," she says. "This is just the way I am. I think it's important to set an example of order and correctness in the session." I smile and ask Imani if, while she is in her sessions with clients, she notices her own thoughts and emotions or the sensations in her body. She chuckles and says, "I'm too busy focusing on the next step in the session. I don't have time for that."

I take this as a good time to discuss the therapist's use of self and the importance of being connected to the various aspects of ourselves as an instrument in the therapy session. I discuss with Imani the importance of being aware and curious about our physical reactions to clients' stories as well as to our seemingly random and fleeting thoughts and even our own emotional reactions to what people may bring to the therapy room. All of this can be used as a therapeutic tool by the self-aware therapist. Imani admitted that giving herself too much freedom to feel her own feelings in a therapy session seemed risky and unprofessional. "After all, the session is not about me," she challenged. I agreed. "No, the therapy is not about you," I say. "But nevertheless, you are there in the therapy session, and your presence and responses to the people who you sit with impacts them and the relationship whether you want it to or not." I notice Imani looking thoughtful as she slowly nods her head in understanding. I continue, "By mastering the therapist's use of self and connecting to your own responses, you can use these as guides for helpful directions in your work with your clients."

As Imani shares the story of her family through the genogram, she becomes tearful as she talks about the divorce of her parents. When I ask what about her family story brought the tears, she looks confused and says, "I don't know. We're not discussing anything that I don't already know."

In later supervision sessions, I notice that Imani seems even more stoic and quiet than usual. I am somewhat confused and concerned about what seems like a thick wall between us. I speak to this directly with Imani, and she becomes tearful once again. She then explains to me that since our discussion of her genogram, she has tried to understand the tears that came. She also admits that she had been very embarrassed by the tears and felt the need to be very much "in control" around me. She says that she believes that this is because I reminded her of her father, who was very important in her life, and the idea of being tearful in that situation may have felt too intimate. We focus on how this kind of relational countertransference might come into play in her work as a therapist, and reflect again on the importance of knowing one's own story and how all of our relational experiences enter into the therapeutic session with us. When the therapist has a knowledge of self, they are better able to use this knowledge by being curious and asking questions of themselves and of the people who come to them for help.

I take this moment and opportunity to revisit the tears from our previous session. I gently nudge Imani to reflect more deeply on her tears from that session. "If you did know what the tears were about, what do you think you'd say?" I ask. To ask the question in this way is an attempt to get Imani to allow another part of herself to come to the fore and be curious about her own emotions, rather than the staid, professional woman she always presents to the public. She sits back thoughtfully and finally says, "I might say, I felt sorry for myself and what I had to go through. And then I might say, these were horrible situations and experiences my family had. But they are so like a lot of Black families I knew." I ask Imani if she ever has these thoughts or emotional responses as she listens to the stories of the families she works with. When she acknowledges that she has had similar thoughts and feelings, I talk to her about ways that she can use this information to open up emotional spaces for her clients by simply being curious and inviting her clients to reflect on the meaning of these emotions and experiences.

By engaging new therapists in conversations about their own family and life experience, we help them to become comfortable exploring the life experience and meanings that their clients bring into therapy. By demonstrating openness and freedom to discuss even the internal cultural secrets that we colonized people hold and to normalize this discussion, new therapists are helped to develop skills in decolonizing mental health with their clients through the therapist's use of self.

Feedback and Assessment

Ongoing feedback and evaluation are important to help new therapists have a sense of their own skill development. With Imani, I did an ongoing evaluation of her work and our work together using the reflection paper and contract agreement as references to track her development. Imani and I, in addition to our biweekly supervision sessions, met once a month for evaluation of her work. I asked her to talk at these evaluation sessions about how she was experiencing her work with the families she consulted in the month prior. What good experiences did she have, and why did she see them as such? What difficulties was she aware of and why? I asked her to identify any ethical issues that may have arisen in cases reviewed during this time. I also asked Imani to identify and differentiate specific issues of process and content. Because she was working for an agency, I also discussed and gave feedback to Imani on her work and competence as it related to agency policy, note taking, and case management. Though you might question how these issues relate to decolonizing work, it is particularly important that therapists from colonially impacted communities become proficient at these skills, as our experience is often that we are more closely monitored and criticized in these areas and labeled as inefficient and unprofessional in work evaluations.

I gave a reflection on my own observations of Imani's work, pointing out sessions and situations that I had observed either in live supervision or recorded. I focused on strengths in her development. I then wrapped up these evaluation meetings with a briefer discussion on any difficulties I observed in live or recorded sessions. These observations were expressed in problematizing questions. For example, in an evaluation session with Imani concerning a couple who was significantly older than Imani with a 14-year-old foster son, I noticed what seemed to be a "tit-for-tat" power struggle between Imani and the foster father. The couple was concerned that their foster son was avoiding talking to them and seemed to be hanging with kids who had a negative influence on his behavior. The father, a man in his 50s with a conservative, crisp military demeanor, was expressing his frustrations and said, "Sometimes it just feels like sh..." Imani smiled and said tersely, "It's OK, you can say '*shit*' in here." The father sat up straight and returned, "Well, I prefer not to," in a matter-of-fact tight-lipped fashion. Just as tight-lipped, Imani shot back, "Then I'll say it for you... SHIT!" After she recounted this part of the session, I asked her, "I wonder what kind of power issues are in play here. I mean, an older conservative Black man, a young Black woman, and you're both committed to fighting over... shit!" Imani and I both laughed. She then began to reflect on the issue that my rude attempt at humor highlighted. My concern in this question was to highlight the issues of gender and age that may have been inviting Imani and her client into a power struggle. By raising these issues of context as significant to the interaction, Imani and I were able to evaluate her own awareness of these issues in her therapy work and plan for future sessions in that context.

Finally, in our evaluation time together we discussed the original reflection paper and supervision goals set in our work agreement. We reviewed the theoretical stance initially identified by Imani and discussed what in her work best reflected that theoretical orientation. We also discussed whether this orientation still felt like a good fit for her as a therapist. If there had been any question about this, we may have discussed other theoretical approaches and how these might be helpful in work with identified cases to be presented in our next supervision session. Throughout the monthly assessments, I encouraged Imani to think about her work in a theoretical context. I also encouraged a willingness to "let go" of theory that did not fit, as well as a willingness to experiment with new approaches and to remain cognizant of new ideas in the field.

From the beginning of supervision, I invited Imani to be in collaboration with me about what was going on. At the end of our supervision, I provided her with a narrative assessment of her work over the entire time that we had worked together. In this narrative I recounted our initial agreement about how we would work, as well as the goals that we agreed on for our work. I then asked her to evaluate how well we have worked on these goals. I asked her to tell me what in our work has been most useful and helpful for her own development. I also asked Imani to discuss with me what in our work, and especially in my own method, has been least helpful in her development. I explained that her responses to these questions were intended to help me to do better work as a supervisor.

From this I reflected on my own experience of how successful Imani had been in attaining goals for therapy, using specific instances and cases to illustrate my thinking. Just as I did in our monthly evaluations, because I supervise therapists working for an agency, I discussed and gave feedback on Imani's work and competence as it related to paperwork, case management, and agency policy. I then reviewed her responses in the original reflection paper about theoretical orientation, professional strengths, weaknesses, and goals as a therapist. Next, I reflected on my own assessment of where Imani was at the end of our time together as it related to this initial reflection paper. I finished my reflection by summing up how I experienced Imani in her work and then by suggesting possible goals for development in the future. I read this assessment out loud, and then I invited Imani to reflect to me her own understanding of what I read, as well as her understanding of the supervision experience.

Training new therapists who understand the importance of decolonized mental health practice is more necessary at this time than it has ever been. Bringing new therapists into the field from communities impacted by historical colonial oppression has been an ongoing failure in the mental health profession. We have seen that even when young Black people are trained in the mental health profession, they often do not complete the requirements for licensure because of "barriers specific to clinicians of color." From this we see that even the work of training new therapists is decolonizing work. It requires that we create brush harbors; the proverbial safe spaces in which new therapists feel at home and can be taught in ways that resonate with their life experience while providing them with the confidence to build a professional sense of self that is authentic to their own culture and is resilient to outside cultural forces that might attempt to make them feel that their own approaches to mental health work are inferior to colonizing Eurocentric approaches to therapy.

My effort in this chapter has been to suggest testimony practices that can help create those safe spaces, while sharpening the skills of new therapists and making them even more impactful as helping agents in their own communities. We can do this by practicing comradely collaboration, walking alongside the new therapist and sharpening their own awareness of the therapist's use of self, using problematizing questions that help them move beyond the stuckness of limit situations that confront them, and freeing them to become curious and creative in doing therapeutic work rather than being chained to the demoralizing and dehumanizing medical model of the insurance industrial complex. I believe we can accomplish all of these things while being attentive to the best practices of ethical and clinically sound decolonizing mental health work.

CHAPTER 6

Repaying and Repairing Our Souls

Soon after the second inauguration of Donald Trump as president of the United States, Congresswoman Ayana Pressley reintroduced HR 40, the so-called reparations bill to establish a federal commission to examine the legacy of slavery and to develop reparations proposals for the descendants of enslaved people.

This bill was first introduced by Congressman John Conyers in 1989 and has floated in and out of public notice over the years to little effect, yet the demand for reparations and repair for the damage done to enslaved Black people and the continuing harms of enslavement experienced by their descendants was established and fought for since the end of the American Civil War. The "40" in the bill's title refers to the rescinded promise of 40 acres of land to every formerly enslaved Black family. The promise of land and a farm animal to cultivate the land was made by General William T. Sherman, the commander of Union forces in the defeat of the Confederate States in his Field Orders, No. 15. The field order was rescinded by President Johnson, who came to office after the assassination of Abraham Lincoln. Johnson, who was a Southerner, made several reversals which impeded freedom for formerly enslaved Black people. This land along the southern seacoast and inland of the southeastern United States would have provided formerly enslaved people with the resources and stability to build self-reliant and self-determining lives. But, like the many treaties made between the United States and Native American people, Field Order 15 was a broken promise to Black freed people.

As the reparations movement grows among Black people, it is important that spaces for bearing witness and telling our stories of oppression and resistance be intentionally provided. These intentional healing spaces will help us begin to make sense and give meaning to our journey and will help to clarify for our collective selves the four healing questions. This chapter reflects my own concern for externalizing and making public discussions about the mental and emotional health of Black people and the relationship of mental health to ongoing fights for social justice in the face of structural racial oppression.

Since that time, as Jim Crow racism after the end of the Southern Reconstruction period hardened the racist domination and enslavement of Black people, the demand for reparations has been largely thought of as financial repayment for the centuries of unpaid labor extorted from Black people during enslavement. But this raises the question, what is the cost of a human soul? How does one place financial value on the collective spirit of a people once that spirit has been damaged, and what would it take to heal the spirit? These are some of the more profound questions that challenge us as we ponder the issue of reparations and the struggle for justice and human rights for the descendants of enslaved Blacks in America.

As a result of the legal enslavement of Blacks in North America from 1619 until 1865, and then the continued state-sanctioned Jim Crow apartheid for a century longer until 1964, and continuing structural racist oppression, state-sanctioned police violence, and economic superexploitation via racial capitalism, Black people continue to be impacted by ongoing psychological trauma and harm. Because of this ongoing harm, there is a need for a decolonized mental health practice in support of Black families. Beyond working with families and individuals in the therapy room, this is a vision of the possibilities of testimony therapy as a decolonizing, culturally liberating mental health practice focused on social justice and community healing.

The issue of reparations involves not only repayment for the material loss and damage done to African descendants but also should be focused on documenting and telling the story of the impact of historical racist oppression from the standpoint of the descendants of enslaved Blacks. The fight against racist oppression and the struggle for reparations can be a healing process if we intentionally go about creating sacred and safe spaces where our testimonies can be spoken and witnessed.

Some people, on hearing Congresswoman Pressley's news conference, might assume again that this was just a stunt to counter the unsettling shock and awe assault of the second Trump administration against DEI programs and other efforts for economic and social justice in both the private and government sectors of the United States, but it is important to emphasize that demands for and efforts aimed at getting the U.S. government to take responsibility for the ongoing impact of enslavement and centuries of social, economic, and cultural oppression did not just "pop up" as a reaction to Donald Trump.

Even after the initial failed promise of 40 acres and a mule to each Black family, the National Ex-Slave Mutual Relief Bounty and Pension Association, led by Black women, organized over 30,000 members to call for repayment for their uncompensated slave labor (Barry, 2005). Also, in the same period, the African Methodist Episcopal church, the oldest organized Black church denomination in America, made a demand for reparations led by Bishop Henry McNeal Turner to allow Black people to return to Africa.

Audley "Queen Mother" Moore, who was the foremost organizer for reparations from the 1950s, influenced Malcolm X and Elijah Muhammad to include the demand for reparations in the program of the Nation of Islam, a Black religious movement representing thousands of Black people throughout the 20th century.

The National Coalition of Blacks for Reparations in America (N'COBRA), founded in 1987, has been the major leading organized effort seeking reparations for enslavement and oppression. Representative Conyers supported HR 40 from 1989 until his tenure ended in 2017. This bill has never made it to the floor of Congress but is being kept alive by Black political figures like Congresswoman Pressley. But, beyond even this national effort, cities like Detroit, Los Angeles, and Evanston, Illinois have established commissions to support reparations for Black people living in those cities who have been marginalized by discriminatory practices such as redlining and police abuse.

So, we can see from this brief history that reparations are not new. Most of these efforts have emphasized needed financial and land-based compensation not just for enslavement but for the ongoing injustices that have been faced by Black people living day to day since the slavery era. As I have tried to make clear throughout this book, the effects of oppression, especially racial colonial oppression, are not just economic but psychological, impacting the oppressed people's ability to function in healthy ways or to maintain supportive relationships with others. This is why a decolonizing approach to mental health and testimony practices centered on community reconnection becomes so important.

When damage has been done to a people, when there has been exploitation and one group has benefited from it, then a key aspect of repairing the relationship between these groups is processes of reparation. Processes of reparation enable the damage that has been done to be mended and relationships to be healed. This is true in therapeutic contexts. Where abuse has occurred, it is of great importance, for healing to take place, that the effects of the abuse be fully acknowledged and that the perpetrator of the abuse engage in acts of redress and reparation. In my experience, where this occurs there is a much greater likelihood of relationships being restored. This also seems true in wider social contexts.

There is abundant evidence of the profound abuse of Blacks sanctioned by local and national, private and public European organizations in the history of the United States of America. There is also abundant evidence of the genocide attempted against those who were indigenous to this land. The history of the ways in which Black people have been treated in this country continues to profoundly affect the lives of Black people. This history also affects the relationship between Blacks and whites in this land. For healing to take place, processes of reparation need to take place. This will require many things, one of which is an engagement with history and an unashamed telling and retelling of our testimony.

At every step along the way, Black people have argued that it is crucial to come to terms with the history of the enslavement of our people to heal its legacies. The United Nations World Conference Against Racism, held in Durban, South Africa in 2001, passed a resolution stating that the slave trade in African people conducted by European countries and states was a crime against humanity and therefore carries no statute of limitations. By the standards of international law, reparations are owed to the descendants of the victims of this trade. Furthermore, it can be argued that reparations are also due in relation to the ongoing effects of the hundred years of Jim Crow segregation that followed slavery—the ways in which Black people were excluded by law from education, property rights, and social and human rights.

These are issues that have directly affected the lives of Black people living today, not just those who suffered in the distant past. My father lived under Jim Crow. He could not go to school and could not amass or pass on wealth because of those laws. I was born in a state and at a time under Jim Crow law and can clearly remember seeing "white only" signs and trying to make sense of their meaning. The effects of these laws flow through our lifetime. These laws have affected the life chances and possibilities of Black people in the United States. This history is directly linked to current health and mental health conditions of Black people.

One reason to create space for testimony in the reparations movement in relation to these histories and their ongoing effects is because these testimonies can overturn the myth that Black people are somehow to blame for the conditions of oppression they face. It has often been charged that Black people are the source of the profound economic, cultural, political, emotional, and psychological damage that has been done to Blacks. Rather than acknowledging the real effects of the policies and acts of oppression perpetrated by racist American cultural, social, and political institutions, we have been held responsible for our own victimization. Black people are poor not because of economic exploitation of our labor, land, and resources, but because we are lazy. Sadly, many Black people have been recruited into believing this racist dominant story about us, so that once again the story is telling us.

A key aspect of any process of reparation is acknowledgment of the wrong done and the ongoing effects of the injustice. Such an acknowledgment has never happened in this country in relation to slavery or segregation. There's never been a formal acknowledgment or any kind of an apology for what happened in this land to Black people. And so, many Black people believe that the reason so many of us live in poverty, or under the regime of the police and prisons, is not due to history or ongoing injustice but because we are somehow not good enough. At the same time, many white people believe that they don't have to take any remedial action in relation to the events of the past and its ongoing effects.

If there is ever to be reconciliation between Black people and Euro-Americans in this country, both these things must change. Creating spaces for testifying and storytelling about what has happened to us would enable us as Black people to be released from the sense of internalized racist guilt for our lack of development. Truth telling and testifying might also release white people from the sense of superiority that many have in this country, a sense of superiority that is only possible when the history of privilege and its basis in oppression goes unacknowledged. Acknowledging the true effects of the past is a crucial first step in any process of reparation.

A History of Psychological Oppression

Of course, any conversation about reparations, mental health, and Black people in the United States must first confront the reality that the mental health profession, in particular psychiatry, has been a primary offender in the oppression of Black people (Jackson, 2002; Breggin & Breggin, 1998; Tomas & Sillen, 1979). This goes a long way to explain the general reluctance of Black people to engage in any sort of mental health or therapeutic projects. There has always been a strong link between the American mental health profession and racist oppression. Louisiana physician Dr. Samuel Cartwright diagnosed diseases in Blacks to explain why they might run away from slavery and be oppositional toward their enslavers (Thomas & Sillen, 1979). Cartwright, a well-known physician in the antebellum South, diagnosed a serious malady among enslaved Blacks that drove them to run away. The malady, which I mentioned only briefly in Chapter 2, was called drapetomania, or flight-from-home madness. He also diagnosed dysaesthesia aethiopica, a malady that resulted in what the overseers called *rascality*. This terrible disease of the mind made enslaved Blacks talk back to white overseers, break and steal white people's property, and slight their work. G. Stanley Hall, the founder of the *American Journal of Psychology* and the first president of the American Psychological Association, argued that Blacks, along with Indians and Chinese, were members of "adolescent races" and in a stage of incomplete growth and must be treated gently and understandingly by more developed (i.e., white) peoples.

These and countless more testimonies by influential members of the

American mental health profession can be found that justify and promote policies in both the private and public sector that have resulted in human rights abuses and genocide practices against Black people in America. For example, throughout the 1950s, Black prisoners in New Orleans were forced to submit to psychosurgery experiments involving electrodes being placed in the brain (CCHR, 1995). In addition to this atrocity, Dr. Robert Heath of Tulane University conducted ongoing LSD experiments on Black inmates in the Louisiana state prison for the CIA to test whether the drug could cause "loss of speech, loss of sensitivity to pain, loss of memory, loss of will power, and an increase in toxicity in persons with a weak type of central nervous system." These types of experiments were also conducted in Kentucky (CCHR, 1995). These efforts to pathologize Black people's responses to everyday racism are not relics of the past. Atkinson et al. (1996) published research in which they found that Black clients were more likely to be given a poorer prognosis and more serious diagnosis (e.g., borderline personality disorder) by white psychologists than Black psychologists. They argued, "until it can be shown empirically that harm is not being done to Black clients by pairing them with European American psychologists, every effort should be made to assign [Black] clients to an ethnically similar help provider." Breggin and Breggin (1998) make a strong case for their contention that the medical industry, in collusion with government agencies and the psychiatric profession, has targeted inner-city Black and Brown children. They argue that the proposed federal violence initiative aims at identifying inner-city children with alleged biogenetic predispositions that supposedly make them violent when they reach adulthood. Under the auspices of vestiges of this so-called violence initiative, drug companies searched for a violence gene and sought to find so-called biochemical imbalances that supposedly caused Black and other children to have a greater potential for violence. Of course, the hoped-for outcome of this research was to produce drugs that would "cure" this propensity for violence. As a result, psychotropic drugs such as Ritalin and other medications have become the intervention of choice by which to control Black children in the care of public schools and government agencies. We also can't forget the "colored insane asylums" from the 19th until the late 20th centuries researched by Vanessa Jackson (2002b) and more recently by Antonia A. Hylton (2024).

All of these and the many more extant examples of the complicity of the mental health profession make it clear why Black people in the United States may be distrustful of psychotherapy and psychotherapists. The master narrative in America about mental health as it relates to Black people has been a story of oppression and genocide. It has been a story of Europeans and their representatives attempting to "get into our heads" to better control us and force us to fit into a more servile place within the status quo.

The reality of the collusion of the mental health profession in the colonization and oppression of Black people is irrefutable. However, there is still the reality that slavery, Jim Crow segregation, and decades of racial violence, neglect, and marginalization have had a profound negative impact on the mental health of Black people. There is a need for a decolonized and decolonizing healing processes. The lived experience of Blackness includes living with day-to-day emotional and mental pain expressed in stressful relationships, alienation, and experiences of depression, anxiety, rage, and feelings of hopelessness. For many of our people, these emotional experiences provide the dominant meanings that define the stories of our lives. These emotional experiences make it difficult to bear witness to the experiences of goodness and hopefulness that we may also have, but that seem trivial and insignificant in the wake of our racially impacted past. It is as if the initial trauma and terror faced by our ancestors in the Middle Passage between Africa and the Americas has been given to us to live out in millions of daily interactions, conflicts, and dilemmas in our relationships with each other and with outsiders. The task of the testimony-informed therapist, when it comes to seeking reparations, can be to help the people discover alternatives to the doom-and-gloom story of oppression and victimization.

As stated in previous chapters, I am using the notion of testimony in the way that our ancestors came to understand the term. In the hidden religious community of the brush harbors and in the country churches and urban storefront churches of poor and working-class Blacks, sacred space was created before worship when the people were able to sing and pray together in a loving community circle. At some moment when the spirit seemed right, a voice would often ring out and exclaim, "Somebody oughta' testify!" In other words, someone needs to tell a story of overcoming defeat and surviving adversity. Someone needs to tell a story about how they got over despite the hardships and the hard times. And in that sacred space, as someone stood to testify and tell their story, the story was thickened and given deeper meaning by the call-and-response action of the community who could bear witness, cajole, encourage, express surprise and awe, and give praise for what they had heard. In that process of testifyin' and bearing witness, call and response, the story of struggle took shape, and a collective meaning was gained from one person's story. That story became the collective story of triumph and thanks for survival, victory, and overcoming.

This kind of therapeutic space, intentionally created as a program of the reparation movement, would go a long way in strengthening our people for the struggle to come. As we tell our story and reconstruct our past, we at the same time challenge and undermine the dominant story constructed by our enslavers about us. This dominant story is one that continues to influence and shape our interactions with each other, with our oppressors, and with the rest of the world. The construction of counterhegemonic, African-centered narratives will help define liberating meanings about our experience through our enslavement and into the future. These stories can in fact be collective action to redeem the names and lives of our Black ancestors who have struggled and died under the new Jim Crow and the racial colonialism that Black people in America currently experience with the rise of anti-Black MAGA extremism. This is a cultural and political conversation about our day-to-day pain and its source, as well as about individual and collective healing, and how we can accomplish it.

Testimony approaches to this healing process give recognition to the tradition of orality in the culture of Black people in America. Testimony reparations groups will help Black people to bring meaning to the world in the power of Nommo.

A therapeutic process grounded in narrative ideas recognizes the importance of testifyin' and telling our story. Stories are retellings of experiences of events. These events are connected in a particular sequence across time, and then a meaning or interpretation is applied to the connected events. It is a combination of the events we choose to highlight, the order in which we link them, and the meaning we give to these connected events that make a plot to the story and interpreted meaning. Human beings are always telling and retelling stories to each other and themselves to make meaning in the world. The story of Black history has been dominated by the racist disempowering interpretations of our colonizers seeking to influence and control our lives. We then find ourselves hearing about and thinking about our lives not out of our own center and in our own interest, but in the interest of our colonizers. The story according to someone else is telling us.

In the Eurocentric version of our history told about us, we lack agency and are dependent on the goodwill of benevolent white people, or we are reduced to passively accepting the imposed dominance of others so that we are perpetual victims, only knowing the doom-and-gloom interpretation of our testimony.

On the other hand, stories that recognize the sources of our pain as well as identifying those victorious moments in which we have resisted and overcome pain, and those stories that ask challenging questions about how we can become pain-free by our own agency, are thick and complex stories that add agency and power to our memories of our history. These are interesting and empowering stories. As Black people build a reparations movement, mental health workers can take on the task of organizing community circles and rituals of remembrance focused on repairing our fractured sense of history and cultural integrity, and helping communities gain meaningful interpretations of what happened to us.

I realize that this is a different and new way of thinking about mental health work. This moves the work of mental health out of the therapy room working with individuals, couples, or families and imagines the power of testimony approaches to mental health as community work. The work of the therapist as organizer is to now be a witness to the empowering testimonies of national Black communities as these communities recall what happened to us, how what happened to us affects us today, where we find the strength to overcome, and what it will take for us to heal.

Much of the history told and remembered about the Black experience in America has blamed us for our own troubles. Daniel Moynihan blamed Black mothers for being too dominant. The Clintons blamed Black youth for being superpredators. The political right consistently blames Black people's problems on a lack of moral character and values, and liberals argue that Black people simply have not had the opportunity to prove themselves worthy. As we employ testimony and the power of Nommo for reparations, we challenge the practice of victim blaming. As community stories are gathered and collective memories are recalled, as we bear witness to our own story told by us, we can depathologize our experience and focus on the collective Black power that has helped us survive despite continuous racist oppression and exploitation.

Community testimony circles aimed at decolonizing the mental health of our people will focus on externalizing the problem. Rather than reinforcing the idea that the pain we experience is genetic to either individual Black people or to our culture, the stance of the healer/witness is that "our people are not the problem, the problem is the problem" (White & Epston, 1990). We can identify the problem as coloniality and its accompanying racism, economic exploitation, dehumanizing conditions of life, genocidal health conditions, and racist miseducation aimed at reinforcing the superiority of European culture, knowledge, and aesthetics.

All these problems and more are the contexts in which Black people experience the emotional and psychological pains that can make life difficult. When the problem is externalized, our conversations reflect this. Our people no longer hold problems inside themselves as parts of their being. Communities are no longer described as unmotivated. We have conversations about how "limiting situations may sometimes influence a community's progress" (i.e., conditions from outside the community). This is important because this stance makes it possible to also discuss those times when communities have become energized and in fact powerful changes have influenced the life of the problem! We can identify those victorious moments when the community has found the power to push back against the problem identified as a limit situation and, in pushing back, has changed the influence of the problem in the community for the better.

In similar ways, we may identify and externalize such problems as sexism, poverty, or white supremacy rather than pathologizing the behaviors in Black people that these problems often influence. In such a case, we would be interested in the tricks that the problem uses to influence our people toward destructive or painful behavior; the intentions of the problem in its efforts to influence, coerce, or trick people into unhealthy actions; the problem's purposes for existing in the lives of our people; their problem's tricks and lies; the problem's allies enemies; and more.

Restoring Harmony and Balance

To determine an appropriate process of reparation, there are two significant, different but related, concepts: repaying and repairing. Racism and the oppression of Blacks have not simply been about irrational white hatred of Blacks. Racism in the ideology of white supremacy has material benefits for both active and passive participants. This means that ultimately all people who identify themselves as white have benefited from the oppression and exploitation of Blacks in America. In the United States, settlers colonized the land, ravaged the indigenous peoples, and exploited the labor of enslaved Blacks to claim the land and extract the wealth from it. Only through a process of giving back or repaying what was taken can some balance be brought back into the relationship between Blacks and Native peoples and European exploiters.

Alongside the realms of repayment (an economic realm) and repairing (a healing realm), there is also the matter of spirituality. Justice has a spiritual component that is about restoring balance and harmony to relationships. The Kemetic (Egyptian) notion of Maat encapsulates this spiritual realm. Maat is about ensuring and maintaining reciprocity, balance, and harmony in all relationships. Within much of Black spirituality, maintaining the balance and harmony in relationships between humans is of fundamental importance. This is true in relation to the living but also with our ancestors.

In many Black churches, spiritual communities, and homes there is a tradition of pouring libations and calling the names of remembered ancestors to honor them and acknowledge the link between the living and the dead. This is a tradition we have retained from our African ancestral cultures. At the beginning of important events or celebrations such as Kwanzaa gatherings, births, funerals, or religious services, water or wine or another drink is poured as first a libation statement is given, and then the participants are invited to name their personal as well as Black community ancestors and historical figures. Even informally, young men and women in the community sharing beer, wine, or other drinks together will often pour the first bit of liquid onto the ground "for the brothers and sisters who ain't here," to honor and remember dead and departed loved ones.

This ritual is about restoring balance and harmony in ancestral relationships. Pouring a libation is a ritual of acknowledging the debt that we owe to our ancestors. It is offering an acknowledgment that the presences of our ancestors give us support, strength, and guidance. Fundamentally, undergoing this ritual is about maintaining the reciprocity of relationships between the living and the no longer living.

When Black communities are at their best, this attention to reciprocity occurs regularly. Younger people give honor and respect to their elders, while elders give honor and respect to their ancestors and at the same time are the caretakers of small babies. This whole system of reciprocity is perhaps best described in the symbol of the circle, which is the dominant metaphor of much Black spirituality (Raboteau, 2004). In a healthy world and in healthy relationships, there's a circle of respect—of offering and receiving. The idea of this kind of reciprocity is captured through the Nguzo Saba in the principle of Ujima—collective work and responsibility. The question of reparations can also be understood in this broader spiritual context. Creating a relationship of reciprocity between Black people and dominant U.S. culture requires that the balance of the relationship be restored. In this light, honoring and acknowledging the experience, history, and stories of Black people and our ancestors, and making genuine efforts to repay and repair the harm that has been done, can be understood as spiritual action for freedom.

There are several ways that we can pay attention to this in the reparations movement as an act of soul healing along with our efforts to be repaid materially for the damage that has been done. We mental health workers can begin to pay attention to themes of pain that seem to be embedded in stories of racist injustice. We can consciously ask questions about racism and experiences of injustice, thus inviting those persons and families who consult with us to feel free to openly talk about these issues. Second, we can organize ourselves and make ourselves collectively available to be knowledgeable witnesses and guides to help communities testify to their stories of pain and resistance, and identify those things that will be needed for their reparation.

This type of national healing and repair of ethnic, social, and class ruptures between people condoned or perpetuated by state governments has been done before, most famously in the South African Truth and Reconciliation process at the end of the war to end apartheid. This process, led by Bishop Desmond Tutu, attempted to avoid further violence and bloodshed and to heal the spirit of the South African nation by inviting both white and African ethnic groups to tell their stories and uncover the truth about past injustices, promote national healing, and foster reconciliation between different ethnic and political groups in South Africa. The focus of the commission was to implement restorative justice rather than retribution by allowing victims to share their experiences and to hear from perpetrators the pain they had caused, which had been unacknowledged for so long. A significant point to consider is that the South African government, which is now an African government rather than a racist apartheid government, is committed to paying reparations to those people who were harmed by the racist policies and practices of the former apartheid government.

Many other countries have also attempted to apply truth and reconciliation restorative justice practices in the wake of political atrocities and human rights violations, including Argentina after the end of the 1976–1983 dictatorship, Chile after the end of the Pinochet dictatorship, Rwanda after the end of the 1994 genocide of Tutsi people, Canada to address the kidnapping of indigenous children into residential schools between the 1870s and 1996, Sierra Leone to examine the causes of the 1991–2002 civil war, and many more.

Healing processes and efforts to unveil the truth and give voice to the testimony of people harmed by political and cultural violence is not a new or unusual demand. These are efforts to repair not only the material deprivation and economic exploitation that people have experienced, but also the mental, emotional, and spiritual harm of state-sanctioned or condoned violence such as the violence experienced by Black people in America through enslavement, Jim Crow, and in the years following.

An Example From Down Under

A small example of taking restorative justice and repair seriously was told to me by my friends from the Dulwich Centre (Aboriginal Health Council of South

Australia, 1995), founded by Michael White in Adelaide, Australia, working with Aboriginal people who have suffered harm at the hands of the Australian government. Here the Aboriginal Health Council of South Australia implemented a healing retreat for the families of Aboriginal men who had died while in police custody in Australian jails. This retreat allowed family members to come together to find healing for themselves. According to a report on the camp, the purpose was to provide context for:

a. Aboriginal people to express and address their grief in relation to the loss of their loved ones.
b. Appropriate healing ceremonies to take place.
c. The honoring and re-empowering of special knowledges and skills related to healing that were available to these families as part of their culture and their traditions.
d. The provision of forums for the sharing of these knowledges and skills.
e. The exploration of how such knowledges and skills might be taken up in service provision.
f. The further clarification of recommendations for future service provision.
g. Some determination of how such services might play a significant role in the prevention of further deaths of Aboriginal people in custody, and in the prevention of "mental health" problems within the Aboriginal community.

This retreat used the cultural power, traditions, and spirituality of the Aboriginal people to both seek healing and discover remedies for the problems. This was done by facilitating storytelling space and defining uniquely Aboriginal interpretations of their story.

I am hoping that in a similar way, as the movement for Black reparations in America builds, that mental health workers, therapists, and counselors committed to human rights and decolonizing mental health will organize sacred spaces throughout the United States that will invite people to tell their testimonies and hear the testimonies of others, and gather the histories and memories of our ancestors as told by them so that we can purposely make meaning of our collective experience and recall what happened to us, reflect on how what happened to us affects us today, share our stories and resources about how we have survived and carried on despite what happened to us, and decide collectively what we will need to heal. Stories guided by the healing questions will not only provide the context and opportunity for personal and family healing but will also provide documentation for the reparations movement to demand justice and repayment for the damage done to our families and communities. This process can be repeated in communities throughout the United States. The possibility for healing testimony to be gathered is endless, and the opportunity for documenting evidence while doing healing is full of hope for the success of the reparations movement.

Honoring Ancestry

In many ways, seeking reparations is about honoring our ancestry. It is about honoring our fathers and mothers, and their fathers and mothers, and so on. Black culture at its best privileges honoring of elders. Therefore, when white supremacy refuses to acknowledge in meaningful ways the realities of our ancestors' lives, it creates a context in which many of our people experience shame and guilt about our Blackness. For Black people, negating history is dishonoring to our ancestry, which is to dishonor everything about us. What's more, when the injustices of our ancestors' lives remain unacknowledged, and when their stories of resistance remain unspoken, many Black folks can be recruited into feeling ashamed of their ancestors. There can be no more painful experience than this. And so, we continue to seek justice for those who have come before us. We do so for many reasons. It is our duty. It is what we owe those who lived in the past. We also know that honoring ancestry is profoundly healing for us in the present and the future. And so, we do this not only for our ancestors and ourselves, but also for our children and grandchildren. What white supremacy refuses to acknowledge, we ourselves reclaim. There is considerable work now being done to reconstruct stories and write biographies of our people who were enslaved. There are also those who are working to find gravesites of enslaved people and to recognize these as sacred places. People are performing rituals at these sites and are reclaiming histories that are sources of pride. Today and every day, we acknowledge our ancestors and their sacrifices for us. We will continue to seek reparations in relation to all they suffered. We will continue to reclaim history until their lives are properly acknowledged.

CHAPTER 7

A Hundred Flowers Blooming: The Future of Decolonization

We are living in hot, critical, and unnerving times. As the calendar progresses quickly through the first quarter of the 21st century, this is particularly true for Black, Asian, Latinx, and indigenous people in the United States. As I write these finishing chapters, we are several weeks into the second presidency of Donald Trump. He and his MAGA Republican Party cohorts are steamrolling over what remains of American liberal democracy and dismantling all semblances of security and civil rights, with a particular focus on those rights which MAGA has identified as supporting and enabling DEI policies aimed at providing a relatively equal playing field for all people regardless of their ethnicity, gender, sexuality, or physical ability. These policies are being labeled as discriminatory against white people, though the aim has been to correct historical social imbalances within society that have kept oppressed ethnic groups, LGBTQ people, the disabled, and working-class women at a social disadvantage since the founding of the United States.

With its goal of deporting thousands of undocumented immigrants and even the children of immigrants, whether they were born in the United States or not, layoffs of millions of federal workers (which particularly impacts the Black community), and the normalizing and protection of white supremacist militia groups like the Proud Boys, Black communities across the country are understandably on edge.

For months prior to the elections during the presidential campaign, there was a noticeable tension in people's conversations, even when it was expressed as joking. In the therapy room, it is rare to get far into a conversation without some acknowledgment of the day's craziness or the terrifying new development coming from Washington, DC, through the news or on social media. Now more than ever, a decolonizing therapy is necessary to validate people's concerns and fears and to acknowledge that these are indeed difficult times that will require a strengthening of community over individual interests. These conversations have seemed to make it easier to refer to our ancestors' struggles and the strengths and cultural ties that helped them survive. As a therapist, I'm learning the importance of remaining authentic and open with the people who come to see me. I'm learning that in crisis, there seems to be a natural urge among the oppressed to come together and to look for connections with the community.

Beyond the presidential elections, since October 7th, 2023 people in the United States and around the world have been reminded that occupation and resistance are the central forces shaping the identities of the peoples of the world today, as we have seen daily news reports of Israel's war in Palestinian Gaza after over 1,000 Israelis were killed and 251 were taken hostage by the Palestinian group Hamas, leading to the deaths by incessant bombing of thousands of Palestinian women, children, and men in Israeli missile attacks and troop incursions.

Watching this tragedy unfold has been particularly sad to me as I remember that in May 2016 I was honored to be a guest of the Palestinian people in the West Bank city of Ramallah, traveling there with other international therapists to learn about the decolonizing mental health work performed by Palestinian therapists for Palestinians traumatized by the Israeli occupation of their lands. During my short visit, I was able to learn from the Palestinian people about their amazing history of resistance to the Israeli occupation and their determination to create a unique Palestinian identity. I experienced the vibrancy of Palestinian daily life and tasted their amazing foods infused with millennia of creativity and care. I witnessed young people dancing the folk dances of their ancestors and heard songs of faith and love for God and for the land which God has provided. In just a few days I witnessed the suffering of the Palestinian people under state terror which so closely reflects the terror experienced by Black people in the United States. This familiarity of experience is what has generated the rising support and solidarity and sympathy for Palestinian freedom in Black communities in the United States and around the Black diaspora.

Today in Gaza, the people seem to be left with nothing. They have suffered the loss of their homes and the lives of their loved ones. They have suffered, yet they resist by returning to the rubble of their homes, caring for their elderly and children, and even finding and caring for lost pets. They resist by not allowing war and terror to destroy their relationships to loved people and places. In Black cultural tradition, we believe that suffering and resistance to it is the source of our creativity and our ability to survive. We believe that the times when we have been left with what the oppressor believes is nothing is the time when we are at our most creative! This is the source of what is called "soul power" in Black cultural tradition. It is out of this crisis of emptiness and nowhere to turn that we become our creative best, and are able to develop the resources necessary for our own healing. This place of deep despair, which we call "the blues," forces us to sit in contemplation and reflection and draw on the memories of our ancestors to know what must be done.

With the ongoing tragedy in Gaza and the Palestinian West Bank, the emerging cultural and political crisis for Black and Brown people in the United States, and similar recolonizing efforts becoming clear around the world, I would ask my friends from other oppressed communities to consider if perhaps there is some indigenous tradition which allows you to reflect on and trust the memories of healing of your ancestors. If there is such possibility, could indigenous therapists who know the significance of storytelling study those memories and gather the meanings, metaphors, symbols, and other things which would be familiar to your cultural community and codify them so that the therapeutic healing practices learned from them can be taught to others committed to healing people and decolonizing their lives? In taking these steps, you would be re-presenting healing practices which may seem new, but at the same time they will be culturally familiar. Additionally, in relying on indigenous resources there will be a strengthening of the oppressed people's will for self-determination and cultural self-reliance. You will be placing your own history, culture, knowledge, and metaphors at the center of your narrative project and ending the psychological occupation of our cultures.

As I have thought about, developed, and practiced testimony therapy over the years, I have learned from and been inspired by therapists from oppressed communities who have also drawn on their own indigenous practices and traditions to decolonize mental health for their people. During this time of emerging crisis with efforts to reassert Eurocentric white supremacist cultural and political dominance in our lives, these efforts are more important than ever. New therapeutic voices are rising, and those which have been here all along but unnoticed are stepping forward to fight for justice and cultural democracy, where the voices of the oppressed must be heard.

In this chapter, I invite you to speculate with me about what a liberated future could look like. Here I want to create for you a vision for a society which honors the cultures of all its people and is committed to a cultural democracy. This work is already being done in communities all around the world, where indigenous therapists are creating spaces for their people to testify and tell their stories in their own ways. Imagine what mental health practice can be like if the various cultural communities which make up our society are free to mine their own histories and cultural resources to discover healing practices and storytelling traditions which speak to their unique communities. I want to introduce you to some of the brilliant practitioners and thinkers I have met over the years who involve themselves in challenging the effects of inferiorization, alienation, and fractured relationships imposed by coloniality on the lives of their communities.

Tileah M. Drahm

Tileah M. Drahm is an Aboriginal woman from inland Queensland, Australia, in Gimuy. She proudly traces her Aboriginal ancestry and her connection to the Kulilli and Yidinji people of the land. These are people who have been on the land and have lived in harmony with the land, she said, for over 9,500 years. She acknowledges that like many colonized people she also shares ancestry with the Irish settlers who came to Australia in the last two centuries.

Before Europeans arrived on the continent in 1788, there were hundreds of Aboriginal societies with their own languages, customs, and traditions. Over thousands of years, they learned to live with the land, which they experienced as a living being to which they belonged. They had rich oral traditions that included stories, songs, and dances that held the knowledge and cultural values which were shared with each generation.

When white settlers arrived on the continent in the 18th century, they immediately began to fence in the land and dominate the Aboriginal people, separating them from their lands and their ways of life. Thousands died as new diseases from Europe were introduced to the continent and in skirmishes with settlers.

Beginning in the 19th century and continuing to the 1970s, Australian settler governments began a policy of removing Aboriginal and Torres Strait Islander children from their families and communities with the idea of "civilizing" them and making them less Aboriginal, in a massive effort at forced assimilation into white society. This was an act of genocide similar to the Indian school programs in the United States and Canada. In the United States, the objective of the program was to "kill the Indian, save the man." In Canada the objective was stated as "killing the Indian in the child."

In Australia this program had devastating impacts on the culture of the Aboriginal people as thousands of children of "the stolen generation" lost their languages, connection to families, and cultural memories, alienating them from themselves, their people, and their lands.

Tileah was trained as a social worker, and she is an instructor in the University of Melbourne and Dulwich Centre Master of Narrative Therapy program in Australia.

I was excited to invite Tileah to speak with me about her work as a narrative therapist and the ways that she and other Aboriginal people have shaped narrative therapy as a decolonized therapy for the people who come to her for help.

> **Makungu:** Are you able to say a little bit about your home and its history? What do you know about the life of the people before you were colonized by European settlers?
>
> **Tileah:** In our Yidinji cultures, we have stories that go back to when we lived off the land of the Great Barrier Reef about 9,500 years ago, which isn't that long in the history of our connection here on this land. Those stories have persisted. It's rainforest country here, and

when I go into the rainforest now, I'm just in awe of my ancestors and what they must have known about living in harmony with the planet! It's a harsh environment. Sometimes it rains for 6 months at a time. I can just imagine. We think about the knowledge and skill that it would have taken to change your way of life from having all that country over that period, and we adapted. We changed, and we continued to live in harmony. It wasn't as though we conquered it and built, you know. That wasn't about being primitive. I believe it was about knowing the effects that humans can have on nature and deciding to live in harmony with nature. And when you think about it, we have only been colonized for 200 years, and in some areas only about 150 years. I mean, when you think about it, it's not been that long ago that the generations of Aboriginal people who experienced massacres have passed away.

Tileah pauses for a moment and reflects on the history of colonization for her people and the impactful change it has brought into their lives in Australia, and the similarities between this experience and the experiences of indigenous and colonized people's in other settler colonial societies like the United States and Canada.

Tileah: I don't know. It blows my mind a little bit when I talk to folks in the U.S. and in Canada and hear about the tactics of colonization and invasion that happened there. They are so similar to what happened here. There was so much cruelty, and there is so much of that legacy that is still here today. It was just this last year that a big five-story statue of Captain James Cook [the first European on the continent] with its arm stretched out in, like, a Nazi-type salute was taken down in Cairns. That was only last year, and it was this big, ugly statue. We Aboriginal people hated that statue. We'd have a physical response of revulsion when we drove past it. Even today there are still places around here named after massacres of Aboriginal people. The beautiful land we used to live in harmony with, 99 percent of it has been cleared for cattle now. There are only pockets of the rich rainforests left. It's so sad when you think about how much destruction has happened and how we have been driven from the lands we belonged to.

Makungu: *When you think about emotional and mental well-being, how has this history affected Aboriginal people? What are the effects of coloniality and colonization on your people?*

Tileah: There is not a place that you can go that doesn't center that problem story about our people. In primary schools, you know, children are taught that problem story. On the news, there's the problem story. Just everywhere—the health statistics, you know. I mean, I work at a hospital, and what we promote in the community is, you know, this tiny little improvement in maybe diabetes care, or something. But the story comes back to, oh, you know all the poor Black people and their huge problem with diabetes, because they have this terrible diet. So, we're always swimming in this problem story.

I'm thinking of an example of a particular community in Cape York: Here there is a huge problem with alcohol, and so they have alcohol restrictions. You can see big signs around the community about this. Well, not that long ago, in my lifetime—this was in the '80s and kind of early '90s—for all public services and social services, the funding model was changed by a genocidal maniac named Joe Bijelke Peterson, who was the premier of Queensland. He was a white South African. He changed that. All services were now going to be funded through the sale of alcohol. In that community things just deteriorated after that. Now about three generations after that time, we're still living with the effects of that. We're blaming young people and imprisoning them for these problems. In Queensland they've just created a policy, "adult crime, adult time," where they are imprisoning 10-year-olds! There has been a lot of pushback on this from groups like Amnesty International, who say it's not OK to lock up children.

Makungu: *Can you talk a little bit about yourself and how you personally became interested in doing this work?*

Tileah: I was politicized very young, you know. My mum and dad were laborers, and they organized for the rights of workers. There were always conversations about social justice at the kitchen table. I don't know why I did social work. I don't know how that bit really came about. I would have dropped it about six months in except one day I showed a photo of my great-grandmom to the only other Aboriginal woman in the class, and she burst into tears, and then we realized how closely related we were. And then she kind of took me under her wing and got me through those studies. She would just translate everything we studied and ask the question, "What does this mean to us?" Working with her like that, focused on our culture and our people, got me that diploma by making social work meaningful for Aboriginal culture for me.

Makungu: *And what drew you specifically to narrative practices?*

Tileah: Well, my dad learned about narrative practices first. He did a one-week training with Michael White in Cairns. I was newly graduated and really green about working in these areas. I asked my dad what the training was like, and Dad said, "It was good. . . . It's what we already do, but you should do the training." I did do the training, and later I learned from the first indigenous narrative therapist, Auntie Barb, that what my dad said was true. Auntie Barb would tell us, "This is our Aboriginal way. Narrative practice belongs to us." One of the things we have been doing over the years is [to] find the wording that both respects and honors what Michael White and David Epston did in collaboration with many others, but also, we want to name those parts of narrative practice that are really in line with our Aboriginal tradition.

Makungu: *So you recognize indigenous ways in the narrative practices that we learn about through Michael White and David Epston?*

Tileah: Yes, that's right. I think in their quest to divine this therapy that is nonpathologizing, nonblaming, they searched far and wide. They explored bodies of knowledge in many different places. I think through that really broad search they came across something that fits us . . . something that we had already invented. We were already doing it in many ways. Our ways are much more intricate, but the sum of all of that broad knowledge is something closer to a whitefella's perspective.

Makungu: *Are you able to identify some of the specific indigenous Aboriginal aspects of your approach to narrative practice?*

Tileah: Well, first our mob doesn't really take to the whole language about "therapy." If I say to someone, I want to interview you, or let's have a counseling session, they might look at me sort of strange, you know? But if I say, "Let's just have a yarn," then they say, "Yeah, let's yarn." It's like I've heard you say, narrative therapy comes through the metaphor of literature and stories told in literature, but when I think about how we just like to yarn and how our stories are told in our oral culture, it's circular, and it goes everywhere. Our stories are fluid, and who knows where we're going to go, you know? So when we're having yarns with family, it can go anywhere, and different stories come up, but in narrative practice when people are talking to us about problems, what I value about Michael White's description is that there is that theme, but our yarn still follows that theme. It's a similar way but also different. I think one of the things that is so profound about our way of doing this and what we offer to the field is how we stretch time. We live in our ancestors, into the past, and we live in our descendants into the future. If somebody is having trouble talking about a story, we don't need them to talk about the problem. They can talk about their ancestors or their future generations. We can always find a healing story for their situation. If someone is struggling in the family or in the community, then we all are there for that person. So in the yarn, we get to think about the collective understanding, so it's not just an individual problem.

Makungu: *So how does this community thinking affect your practice?*

Tileah: Well, in narrative practice we talk about therapeutic posture, but then on top of that for us there's the kinship structure, which means it matters who you are related to. We're all related, but in our practice we can find out how we are related in just a

30-second exchange using our Aboriginal tradition. We do this mapping when we first meet. We see that first meeting and our practice time as ceremony. We all say where we are from, the land we belong to and the mob we come from and who our family is. Our age relationships matter and in the ceremony, we honor that. If there is an older woman, I'm really aware of questions that I can ask, or if it's an older man the relationship between us may change. If it's a younger person, I become "auntie" and so I can be more centered or influential. I can correct a bit more or guide a bit more. If they are the same age as me, it may be different. We're always adjusting depending on how we are in relationship with them or where you sit in the generational map. But if we're related, we can fast forward. You know whitefellas talk about building rapport. Well, we do that in this 30-second ceremony, because we find that connection. Once we've found that connection, now we can talk.

Makungu: *So this generational mapping ceremony which builds connection between the practitioner and the people who come for help is a distinctive Aboriginal practice for you?*

Tileah: Yes, we start there. Even when I work with whitefellas I do the same thing. I start with doing the generational mapping. For us this is all ceremony. Not metaphorically, as it's sometimes used in narrative theory, but for us this is truly ceremonial work that links us to our traditions.

Chaste Uwihoreye

Dr. Chaste Uwihoreye is a psychotherapist in the central African country of Rwanda and an honorary lecturer at the University of Rwanda in Kigali, the capital of the country. While Rwanda is now considered one of the most stable and peaceful countries on the African continent, this is only after a devastating 100-day genocide of people of the Tutsi community of Rwanda, perpetrated by some political leaders of the Hutu community in the spring of 1994. It is estimated that over 800,000 people were killed in the brutal massacre of Tutsi people. The traumatic impact of this devastating atrocity was the context in which Chaste came into adulthood. I am honored to be able to speak with him and learn about his work and the story of his land.

> **Makungu:** *Can you say a little bit about your homeland and its history before colonization?*
>
> **Chaste:** Rwanda is a beautiful country known as the "Land of a Thousand Hills." It is a nation where all people share the same language (Kinyarwanda), the same culture, and deep-rooted traditions in agriculture and tourism. Rwanda is home to mountain gorillas, among other unique attractions.

Before colonization, Rwanda had a harmonious and well-structured sociopolitical system led by a monarchy. Society functioned through traditional mechanisms of governance, justice, and conflict resolution. However, colonization disrupted this unity. The German and later Belgian colonizers introduced a system of ethnic division, classifying people into Hutu, Tutsi, and Twa, which later led to deep divisions and, ultimately, the genocide against the Tutsi in 1994.

Despite this painful history, Rwanda has emerged as a resilient nation, pioneering reconciliation efforts through the Gacaca courts, a traditional justice system that helped restore unity and heal wounds. Today, Rwanda is a model for postconflict recovery and development.

> **Makungu:** *What impact did colonization have on your homeland?*
>
> **Chaste:** The biggest impact of colonization was the division of Rwandans into artificial ethnic groups, which fueled tensions and ultimately led to the genocide against the Tutsi. Colonization also disrupted traditional belief systems by suppressing indigenous rituals, religious practices, and local methods of conflict resolution.
>
> **Makungu:** *Once the colonizers left, what were the aftereffects? How did the people live?*
>
> **Chaste:** After colonization, many Rwandans adopted the cultures, religions, and ideologies of the colonial powers, often at the expense

of traditional Rwandan identity. The artificial ethnic divisions created during colonization led to waves of violence, including periodic massacres and the 1994 genocide against the Tutsi. Additionally, colonial borders divided families, leaving some as Rwandans, while others became Ugandan, Congolese, or Burundian, leading to cross-border conflicts that persist to this day.

Makungu: *Have there been any mental health problems directly related to the history of colonization?*

Chaste: Yes, colonization and its aftermath have contributed significantly to mental health challenges in Rwanda. The forced ethnic identities imposed by colonizers led to decades of violence, exile, and genocide, resulting in collective trauma. This trauma has been passed down across generations, manifesting in PTSD, depression, and anxiety disorders. The loss of traditional coping mechanisms due to colonization also made it difficult for communities to process and heal from these wounds.

Makungu: *Can you tell me how you personally became interested in being a mental health healer? What got you started?*

Chaste: My journey in mental health began after the genocide against the Tutsi, when I was a secondary school student. I witnessed the deep collective trauma among my classmates and community, many of whom were orphaned or had lost loved ones. This experience motivated me to pursue a career in clinical psychology. I began working with children and adolescent survivors of the genocide, who were struggling with trauma and other mental health challenges. This experience deepened my commitment to mental health healing.

Makungu: *How did your attention begin to move toward thinking about and including cultural practices from your own culture in the mental health work you do?*

Chaste: When I started practicing as a mental health professional, I realized that Western psychological approaches which I had studied in French and English were often not accessible or meaningful to many Rwandans. The language and concepts did not reflect

Rwandan reality, making therapy difficult to implement. I began to explore how mental health issues were named and understood in Kinyarwanda. I incorporated Rwandan proverbs, rituals, songs, and communal storytelling into my therapy sessions. I also introduced family-based approaches, such as *igitaramo cy'umuryango* (family gathering for storytelling and healing), which helped bridge the gap between Western psychology and Rwandan cultural practices.

Makungu: *Why do you believe this is necessary? Why not simply stick to what we have learned in our training programs?*

Chaste: Western mental health models are not always directly applicable to non-Western contexts. For example, there are language barriers. Many Western psychological terms do not have direct translations into Kinyarwanda. We Rwandans often have different cultural understanding of emotions and healing. We often express emotions metaphorically, so that direct translations of Western therapeutic techniques can feel foreign and ineffective. Traditional Rwandan approaches such as community storytelling, music, speaking in proverbs, and group healing rituals are often more effective than individual talk therapy in some cases. By integrating Rwandan cultural practices into therapy, I found that people connected more easily to the healing process, making mental health care more accessible and meaningful.

Makungu: *Tell me a bit about your own practices of healing and how your cultural perspective informs your thinking.*

Chaste: My healing approach is based on individual, collective, and family therapy. My process includes naming mental health issues in Kinyarwanda and encouraging people to describe their emotions using traditional metaphors and proverbs. For example, "Ijoro ribara uwariraye" (Only the person who spent the night awake knows its darkness), meaning only those who experience pain can truly understand it. Another example of the use of metaphors and proverbs is "Ibuye ryagaragaye ntiriba rikishe isuka" (A stone that is seen does not break the hoe), meaning recognizing a problem is the first step toward solving it. I also use a lot of arts therapy in my work, such as drawing, painting, storytelling, and traditional songs to express emotions. We also focus on social healing through community engagement, organizing group discussions, traditional dances, and rituals to promote collective healing. We create *mingos*, which are special friendship groups for emotional support of those who may have lost family connections because of the genocide. Finally, when it is time to end therapy with the people I'm working with, we always end with ceremony. We provide some symbolic gestures such as giving flowers or singing songs or hold some other sort of closing ritual. By grounding my practice in Rwandan culture, I ensure that mental health care is not just about treatment, but about restoring social harmony and resilience after our people have suffered so much trauma due to the genocide and the aftereffects of colonial oppression.

Marcela Polanco

Marcela Polanco is a professor of marriage and family therapy living in San Diego, California, and teaching at San Diego State University. Dr. Polanco is a Colombian woman who situates herself in the complicated meanings of race, gender, and ethnicity of her native land. She would quickly be visually identified in the United States as an Afro-Latinx woman, but explains that in her South American, Colombian context she would be considered a white person by indigenous communities. Marcela is a thoughtful scholar, activist, and therapist who has made amazing contributions to decolonizing mental health for the oppressed.

The land that is now known as Colombia in South America was invaded and colonized by the Spanish beginning in 1525, when the first Spanish settlement was established there. Before colonization, the territory was inhabited by several indigenous peoples such as the Muisca, the Tairona, and others who were agriculturalists, workers of gold and beautiful pottery, stone masons, and architects building sophisticated urban and agricultural societies. Like many other indigenous cultures, these diverse peoples had a deep spiritual connection to the land and nature, with belief systems centered on ancestor veneration and honoring the forces of nature. Marcela is very conscious of this history and the impact of colonization on the indigenous peoples, the forced importation of enslaved Africans with the following centuries of enslavement and oppression, and the resulting culture that is a mix of indigenous, African, and European. I was privileged to speak to Marcela while she was on sabbatical from the university and spending time in Colombia to continue her research.

> **Makungu:** *Marcela, can you talk about the impact of colonization on the cultures and the people of Colombia?*
>
> **Marcela:** Yeah, so it is still very prevalent. Even though, interestingly enough, I think many academics from very different perspectives situate the constitution of Colombia as one of the most progressive constitutions in Latin America. One of those ways is in the way in which indigenous Black and campesinos are situated politically. The population of the indigenous people of Colombia is very small compared to other countries because of the genocide against indigenous people. It came about through the eradication of language and worldview of the people. It is also connected to the contemporary violence of the drug cartels. The cartels have been like the contemporary colonizers that are stealing the land to cultivate cocaine. In the 18th century a law was made imposing Spanish as the official language, similar to what Trump is doing now in the United States with English. In Colombia, Spanish was made the official language, and it was forbidden to speak any of the indigenous languages. Also there was the imposition of the Catholic religion on the indigenous people, forcing a totally different view of the cosmos.
>
> **Makungu:** *In your work, do you see a direct relationship between this history of colonization and oppression and mental health and emotional problems amongst the people in Colombia?*
>
> **Marcela:** Yes, but thinking about this has helped me rethink mental health itself. In conversations I'm having here with folks, the conceptualization of individualized psychology is out of place, this conceptualization that people possess mental health problems

individually, or that people have individual psychological problems. Everywhere people find that assumption ridiculous and out of context. So everyone thinks systemically, like family therapists here, because it's very clear that it's not an individual problem, but in reality, colonization and coloniality has fucked us up communally by stealing the land, the traditions, the community relations, and the fracturing of relationships! Currently I'm doing work around suicide, and in Colombia, they don't consider suicide to be a personal problem, but it is a family and a community problem in which the community is about the relationship with the land. The people's relationship with the land is where they intervene. There is a relationship between ecology and psychology. So yes, colonialism has affected the mental health of the people, but not in the way that the West conceptualizes mental health.

Makungu: *How did you come to be interested in mental health and therapy work?*

Marcela: I don't think I have ever been interested in mental health per se. I was raised by people who were very conscious about the social political context, so I've always been interested in the socio-political aspects of suffering, even though I am a psychologist here in Colombia, but psychology wasn't taught like that, in the individualistic way. So, I have to attribute that to the way in which I was raised and by the circumstances of violence in Colombia that were very intense and in your face when I was raised here, though it's very different here now. So I would say history and location drew me to this work.

Marcela explains that she came to the United States to complete her schooling, and it is here that she was attracted to and began her studies in psychology with a focus on family therapy.

Makungu: *Marcela, can you remember when and how, as you studied to become a therapist, you became focused on your own historical and cultural experience in the work? When did you start thinking* about the importance of decolonizing the theories of mental health that you were taught?

Marcela: As a student I was very obedient, because I am an immigrant, so I was very—because of what America was offering me in being able to live in the U.S., so I think I lost sight of the legacy of my parents. I think that narrative therapy helped me reconnect to it. I think learning about narrative therapy, that was very helpful to locate my social and cultural concepts about therapy and mental health outside of the colonial structures. It helped me be more critical of what I was experiencing. Then I think it was as I began to teach, which gave me the monetary possibility to sit down and think, it became clear to me how therapy is conceptualized as individualistic but understanding the social politics of the practice.

Makungu: *As you studied psychology and began to focus on family therapy as a profession, it seems you somehow also began to consider the role of culture in this work and what it would mean to center your Colombian experience to guide what you do. Can you tell me more about that?*

Marcela: Well, narrative therapy helped me think about these things in ways that resonated with my experience of being a woman of color in this Western environment. I also began to pay attention and to become curious about the worldview of my community. Our people have a way of looking at the world which is not just material. History is not lineal in this worldview. This requires that I translate even my understanding of narrative therapy into my own Colombian version of narrative. I call this a therapy of solidarity. This is a solidarity constructed by a therapist who refuses to draw a sharp distinction between their life and the lives of others, but refuses to marginalize those persons who seek help. I started to remember and pay attention to the ways in which men and women that identify culturally as Latin American arrange their stories and use language and bring metaphors and analogies and make reference to their religious accounts and even their superstitious accounts of life.

I also began to think about the importance of the literature of magical realism in our culture. I began to turn to the work of magical realist novels, the work of Isabel Allende as well as Gabriel García Márquez. I enjoyed reading these stories and experienced this sense of being completely recruited into a reality that is so fantastic, but yet it felt really real. So I looked for ways in which I could translate magical realism into my practice. How can I help people tell stories in magical realist ways which shape our worldview?

Makungu: *In your work on decolonizing, you focus strongly on the politics of mental health for colonized people. Can you say something about this now?*

Marcela: Telling stories is not just [an] activity of unveiling new events that are significant for the person, but within the general context of Colombian culture, the term I found to better depict the importance of giving one's account was the term of *testimonios* or testimonies. This has been a significant term within social and feminist movements in Latin America in general. *Testimonios* provide a political consciousness to the performance of one's stories. It unveils the importance for us as Latin American people to tell our stories, to raise our voices about our struggles, about our successes, about our experiences in general in that sense. The word *testimony*, having found the word and bringing it into my practice, it was very clear to me that I was starting to conceptualize my therapeutic encounters with the people that come to consult me as a space for the performance of social activism. When I speak about the importance of keeping at the forefront the histories of colonization, that immediately invites me to understand my practice as social activism. It is a reclamation of people's wisdoms, which comes with the reclamation of their word and their memories and histories and their imaginations and relationships.

Ncazelo Ncube-Mlilo

Ncazelo (Nah-zelo) Ncube-Mlilo is a psychologist and narrative therapist living in South Africa for over 20 years. She was born in neighboring Zimbabwe. Much of her work has centered on working with women and children dealing with the HIV/AIDS crisis in South Africa as well as working with men dealing with issues of domestic intimate partner violence. She began her work in response to the rise of violence and trauma among young people in the country.

Both the peoples of her birth country and her adopted country have long histories in southern Africa. Zimbabwe is a beautiful, lush land inhabited by several ethnic and national groups such as the San, Ndebele, and Shona peoples. With the arrival of Bantu-speaking people over 2,000 years ago, several significant kingdoms formed in the area, including the kingdoms of Mapungubwe, and later Great Zimbabwe, two trading empires. The Khoisan people, who largely populated the Western Cape area, were the earliest inhabitants of what is now South Africa. The Bantu migrations also played a significant role in South Africa, with Bantu-speaking groups gradually settling in the eastern and southern parts of the region. They introduced farming, ironworking, and complex social structures. Over millennia, ethnic and national groups such as the Zulu, Xhosa, and Sotho-Tswana people migrated to the area, with the Zulu eventually dominating with the founding of the Zulu kingdom just prior to the arrival of Europeans and the imposition of colonization. I was able to catch up with Ncazelo from her office in Johannesburg to discuss her work in decolonizing mental health for her communities.

> **Makungu:** *As you think about it, as a psychologist, would you say that there have been any mental health problems directly related to the history of colonization and the aftermath of colonization on the people?*
>
> **Ncazelo:** I think one of the things that I've grown up with, which has been a challenge, I think, has been sort of the tribalism in our country, particularly between the Shona and the Ndebele people. We grew up knowing that there was a lot of animosity, and this

was one of the outcomes of apartheid, the divide-and-rule type of thing. And this unfortunately has persisted until now. I'm from an Ndebele community, and we've always felt that Zimbabwe is not our home. The Shona people have more opportunities. They are more progressive, and there is just dwindling influence, you know, of the Ndebele people in terms of national issues. And then there's the whole Gukurahundi story about the massacre of the Ndebele people.* And up to today, there's never been anyone who's taken account, who's been accountable for what's happened. And that has remained in our psychology as a people, that so many people died and were hated simply because of their tribe and their ethnicity. And so, yeah, it always comes up, and I don't think it's ever been tackled and dealt with. It's just those divides that have continued to impact on our relationships, on the economy, on the politics, and yeah, and have really very long-term sort of consequences in terms of the psychological well-being of the people.

Makungu: *You have lived in South Africa for several years. As you think about your work in South Africa, would you say that the problems that people bring to you are related to South Africa's history of colonization in any way? In your work, do these things show up in the therapy sessions? I know you do a lot of group work. Do these problems show up in some kind of way? And if so, could you talk about it?*

Ncazelo: Definitely. And they are such a huge challenge. We're talking about how South Africa is the leading country in terms of inequalities and the differences between the rich and the poor. This is why we focus on community mental health. We go into communities, and we run group therapy interventions with women, with men, and particularly in our work with men, you know, I've developed a methodology called Outraged, which is an 11-step structured group

---

* Gukurahundi is a Shona term which translates loosely to "the rain which washes away the chaff before the spring rains." It is a term connected to the genocide of Ndebele by Shona people in Zimbabwe from 1983 to 1987, when a Unity Accord was established in the country.

therapy intervention, which is about the prevention of gender-based violence and trying to work with men and boys as champions of this issue, because men are largely seen as perpetrators. We want to support men using a very nonblaming, nonjudgmental approach to talk about these issues of inequality. We want them to explore other ways of being and to understand what recruits them into all this violence that we hear about on a day-to-day basis. And the men will talk about how a lot of their anger is about the inequalities that exist. And they will talk about how they feel after apartheid. They had many dreams about having jobs and being able to look after themselves and be independent. But this has not happened. Unemployment is currently at over 40%. There is a sense of disappointment, disgruntlement around what is going on. There is no access to land, because I think 90% of the resources that matter in this country are still in the hands of white people.

And so you [have] Black people being poor, unemployed, and they are still begging to find a job and be given employment because the economic power has stayed with the white people. The men talk about how this anger often leads to rage, and sometimes they take it out on their children and their partners. And that's why there's just so much violence in this country, because the inequalities are just too much. There is a sense of disappointment that the government of the day has not really moved to try and foster equality and come up with progressive policies that will have Black people included in the economy in a significant way. This is how problems show up in therapy session[s]. When we run a group with communities, the first thing they'll tell you, we are hungry. Yes, we want mental health services, but we also want food. And we've been in positions where we've had to buy food for people because it just doesn't make sense to invite people into a space to talk about their mental health when some of their immediate sort of physical needs are not being taken care of. . . . Mental health for me is about social justice. We cannot separate the two.

Makungu: *Can you talk about how you personally became interested in* *being a mental health healer? What got you started in this field of mental health?*

Ncazelo: I always loved people. I've always had, I don't know if this is a proper word . . . an inclination toward those who are disadvantaged and marginalized. And I remember my earlier days in high school, and my dad would be driving with me through the markets, and I'll be seeing women selling things. And I would always say, get down and buy something from each and every one, because I was somebody who noticed people who were vulnerable, people who struggled. And so I can identify as early as that time that I started to care about issues of inequality and people who were disadvantaged. And I suppose it's something that continued to grow on me until I decided to study psychology in university.

My first job was in a special education department where I was working with people who had intellectual challenges. I used to do a lot of assessments and placing them in special schools. And then I moved from that to working with children affected by AIDS. And I suppose it just continued to grow. I never looked back. That's how I sort of started working with young people. But I think my experience of responding to HIV/AIDS and the dilemmas that young people were experiencing, I think was a very significant part of the journey that brought about an awakening of the importance of culturally appropriate mental health intervention. I witnessed the children and heard their stories when they expressed the dilemmas they were going through in their lives, losing multiple caregivers, moving from one community to another, feeling totally disconnected from land and country. I heard these sad stories about their diminished sense of who they were as persons. They talked about rituals and cleansing ceremonies to get rid of bad luck because they'd lost so many people in their lives. These were things that we did not talk about, in my psychology textbook from school. This is what the children understand about what's going on in their lives. I knew that I would need to meet them somewhere. And if I was not culturally competent, it was not going to happen.

I realized how important it was to work closely with families and communities who are the custodians of the different traditions and cultures and rituals that the children were talking about. I then realized the limitations of psychology in addressing some of these things. So I think that became a huge, huge turning point in my life and the decision to become a mental health practitioner who's aware of issues of culture and the need for approaches and practices that meet people where they are at in terms of their own values and their own beliefs. Otherwise, what we do just becomes meaningless and does not touch them.

Makungu: *You have developed an approach in your practice called the tree of life. As you began to become aware of the role of culture in the work you were doing, can you describe how you actually began to include cultural ideas and practices into the mental health work you do? How did the tree of life approach come about?*

Ncazelo: It was probably in the early 2000s. I was a team leader in a life skills camp program for children affected by AIDS and talking to them and hearing them talk about how they'd not been involved in funeral and burial processes because it's taboo in their communities, in their cultures, for children to witness death at that level. And kids talking [about] how they felt sad. They never had closure. They told me that they didn't remember what their parents looked like. They'd been totally excluded from conversations linked to the death and the burial and whatever rituals that came with burying their parents. And so it was really very distressing for a lot of the children. Some of them coming to our 10-day camps and not even knowing that their parents had passed away because they'd simply not been told. And so a lot of the challenges and the stresses that young people had were linked to issues of culture, traditions, belief systems, and so on. And so when you talk about counseling, I remember one particular girl who said, "You know what, I don't need counseling. I just need these rituals done. I need somebody to go and do this because that is what's going to fix my life."

A lot of what children spoke to us about is what inspired the development of the tree of life. Because if you think about how we talk about the roots of the tree and what they're about, it was honoring children's desires to be connected to country, to their heritage, their culture, and their people. And so we wanted those aspects of their lives that they felt were being threatened by HIV and AIDS to be the very things that the tree focuses on. And so we then created a tree of life or a methodology that would speak to those things. Children struggling to go back home because there are so many challenges [in the] village and the community. How do we help children to be less alienated from their families? What could we do to bring families closer to children to understand what they are suffering or going through? Because they probably did not know even what the children were going through because these were just things not to talk about with young people. And so we had to start a lot of initiatives and projects that involved having, you know, "Let's talk about HIV. How does it affect children? Do children mourn? Do children grieve? What is it that you can do as communities to involve children in these rituals?"

It was groundbreaking work that we began to do in the region as we became aware that the taboos against talking to children about death was based on a lot of fears. This is such a difficult, emotive topic. People are thinking, "If we can't deal with it ourselves, let's protect our children." We realized that these taboos were really coming from a perspective of "We want to protect the children. We want to keep them safe." And then we had to say to them, "The children don't feel protected. They don't feel safe because the lack of involvement leaves them with a lot of pain and a sense of not having had closure." This conversation changed a lot. It shifted a lot of things and started having families and communities involved alongside the children in ways that were more helpful and understanding, but we could not leave them behind. We couldn't have this one-on-one counseling, you know, sessions with children. We had to involve the village, the community, and we had to talk about culture and rituals and think about how we could move together to support children. So I think for me this experience with children affected by AIDS was just an awakening of sorts.

Makungu: *You have a beautiful metaphor from southern African culture that you use to name your therapeutic practices. You call what you do imbeleko practice. Can you tell me about that?*

Ncazelo: I was once asked the question, if you look at your tree of life, and all these other methodologies that you've created, you know, what is this work about? What do you call it? What came to me was *imbeleko*. And I say this work is about *imbeleko*. And so I suppose that is at the core of what I do or what I have learned to do, which is very meaningful. *Imbeleko* is a practice that women use in most African cultures. It's just this act of carrying children on women's backs wrapped tightly in a blanket. So in thinking about what my work is about and what I'm seeking to accomplish with this therapy, I thought a lot about this tradition and what it might mean symbolically for mental health work. *Imbeleko* symbolizes a way in which we keep people feeling a sense of safety, warmth, and a deep connection to the community. It taps into our own indigenous ideas of what it means to be safe. It's not the methodology itself or alone, but it's also how we make people feel in the spaces, how we hold them. We wrap them and create that warmth, that safety, reassurance, that connectedness, that humanity that people want to experience when they are alongside others. It really does contribute to the positive outcomes that we see in our community mental health.

Makungu: *Your innovation of the tree of life approach to help people tell their stories has been taught to therapists from several different countries around the world. What is the tree of life?*

Ncazelo: We first began using the tree of life method working with children affected by AIDS. It was an effort to move away from problem-saturated stories and to create hopeful ways of working with children. With the tree of life, we invite people to draw their own personal tree. Each part of the tree metaphor represents something specific in your life. Your roots talk about where you come from, your heritage, your culture, things that make you feel strong and rooted, things that make you feel proud about your identity, your heritage. And so that's what the roots are about. And then the ground represents where you live, what you like to do, who you spend your time with, favorite songs, favorite places, and so on. And then the trunk talks about your skills and what you're good at. And then we inquire about where you got the skills from, who passed the skills. And then the leaves represent important people that have supported you, cared for you, and then your branches are your hopes and dreams, your fruits, and the gifts that you've been given in life. When people draw their trees, they are then given an opportunity to present their tree in front of a group and to be interviewed by a tree of life practitioner who's been trained how to help thicken the preferred stories of people's lives, sort of creating islands of safety for people.

That is Part 1 of the method. Part 2 is about the forest. Here we talk about what it means to be standing with other trees in the forest of life. And we invite people to think about who's in the forest with them and what people can do to keep their forests beautiful and strong. What can they do to nourish their forests? And so you can use the forest of life to strengthen a sense of connectedness, belonging, collective identity, community, and helping people to think about how to be alongside others in caring, kind, and respectful ways. In that way, it really supports community building and helping people to look at their relationships and the things that matter in those kinds of connections. The forest of life is great for community work, for teams, for example, working with families to help them. It helps individuals to feel more connected to each other. And so that's what is powerful about the forest. So you move from the tree, Part 1, where you're looking at your individual tree, and then with the forest of life, you now start to look at yourself in the context of relationships and your communities and what that means for your life and so on.

And then we have Part 3, which is the storms of life. Here we talk about what are some of the challenges that these beautiful trees can experience in their lives? Finding ways to look at the storms and where they come from, how they affect us, but also how can we tackle storms? What are the skills and knowledges that we can use to tackle different storms of life? This is sort of a double telling approach where you are acknowledging storms, but you're also acknowledging the skills and the knowledges that people can use to tackle storms and looking at some of the initiatives that they're already carrying out in their lives to tackle storms of life. And then it ends with Part 4, which is awarding people a tree of life certificate. It is important that we document and celebrate what this experience has been about for people. We celebrate what their hopes are, their dreams and their skills. We do this with a ceremony at the end of it all, where you invite people to be present, to witness the participants tell their stories about what this journey has meant for them, where it's taken them to the steps they want to be taking in their lives, what has shifted. This celebration is a rites-of-passage metaphor that acknowledges you are no longer at the same place where you were when we began this journey. You're now in a different place, and we ought to celebrate. This whole process can be done in communities in one day over several hours, or over several weeks.

This Is What Democracy Looks Like

In this chapter I've shared with you only a very small sample of the thinking and practice in decolonizing mental health that colonized and formerly colonized therapists are developing all around the world. These ideas move us beyond diversity and inclusion and beyond multiculturalism and cultural competence toward cultural democracy. These decolonizing practices dare to imagine a world in which people impacted by coloniality and the domination of Eurocentric ideas can create their own indigenous self-determined practices of mental wellness grounded in their own traditions, metaphors, spiritualities, and life meanings. Cultural democracy, rather than requesting that these cultures be permitted at the table of Eurocentric domination, demands that people have their own culturally centered tables which give meaning to their existence while maintaining relationships and connections to all the other cultures and peoples of the world in Dr. King's inescapable network of mutuality (King, 1964).

Ngũgĩ wa' Thiong'o (1993), the great Kenyan novelist and playwright, in his book *Moving the Centre*, offers the metaphor of "a hundred flowers blooming" in a chapter on creating a democratic world literature, resulting in a plurality of cultural centers in which each people has a right to create literatures in their own indigenous languages, cultural perspectives, and creative meanings free of domination and oppression. This vision of cultural democracy is also important to the way we tell our stories in the therapy rooms and healing circles within our communities. Through building on the vision of cultural democracy, as more mental health workers seek to decolonize mental health practices for their people, the oppressed peoples of the world will have the opportunity to shed centuries of alienation from self, nature, and others and emerge from the zone of nonbeing and double consciousness to be their authentically human selves.

Conclusion

Decolonization Is More Urgent Than Ever

As I said in a previous book, *Culture, Politics, Spirituality, and Practice* (Akinyela, 2025), these are disturbing times. Even as I was writing this book, the world changed around me to make the situation for Black, Brown, LGBTQ, non–English speaking, and working-class people even more precarious. With the election of Donald Trump to the presidency of the United States, the social, political, and cultural conditions that enforce coloniality have been made obvious with the spoken-out-loud white supremacist domination of the MAGA movement.

A ubiquitous quote of dubious source is very meaningful at this time: "When fascism comes to America, it will be wrapped in the flag and carrying a cross." This is the MAGA movement—an authentically American fascist movement that, with the help of evangelical fundamentalist white Christians and the financial support of billionaires, has captured all three branches of government and is working feverishly to dismantle even the meager constitutional protections that Black people have fought for and gained over the past 160 years, beginning with the First, Thirteenth, and Fourteenth Amendments and even threatening the 1964 Civil Rights Act with anti-DEI policies.

Since January 20, 2025, in a flash of shock and awe seemingly intended to make resistance impossible, Donald Trump has, by executive order, rescinded the Equal Employment Opportunity rule, eliminated DEI programs, and threatened to defund any institutions that receive federal support that insist on retaining cultural, gender, or ability-focused supports for people other than specifically those focused on Euro-American culture. The Trump administration has redefined gender policies by restricting the recognition of gender to strictly male and female categories, though years of scientific and social research have shown that gender is more complicated than male and female. To date there is an ongoing effort to eliminate the Department of Education, which plays an important role in enforcing educational civil rights and administering federal education funding.

There has been a massive purge of federal workers led by billionaire Elon Musk's DOGE (Department of Government Efficiency), leading to great tension among the millions of workers in federal government positions. This is important to the issue of Black people's mental health when we understand that the federal government is the largest single employer of Black workers in the United States (U.S. Office of Personnel Management, 2023). This means we are looking at massive unemployment in Black communities across the United States, with the potential to raise tensions resulting in anxiety, depression, and anger among Black people and disrupting relationships.

As MAGA extremists are emboldened in their fascist racism, and in some states have even been encouraged with potential rewards for reporting on their neighbors under the slogan "if you see something, say something"—which encourages citizens to report evidence of DEI practices in businesses and schools or the possible undocumented immigrant status of their neighbors.

Over the past 10 years, with the rise of the MAGA movement, there have been verbal and physical attacks on people in public spaces speaking Spanish, or Krio, or Arabic, and now with an executive order making English the "official" language of the United States, there is even a rising fear among Black, Brown, and other people of speaking in their own native tongues for fear of being attacked by racists in the streets.

In a concerted attack on the fight for justice related to the abuses of police force against Black and Brown people highlighted in the first Trump administration by massive demonstrations and actions led by groups like Black Lives Matter, the Trump administration (Cauchi, 2025) has dismantled a federal database that tracked misconduct by police, known as the National Law

Enforcement Accountability Database (NLEAD), which had been established under Executive Order 15074, signed by President Biden in 2022. The intention of this executive order was to promote police accountability and prevent police officers with histories of misconduct from transferring between agencies without being questioned about their previous conduct. With Trump's reversal, this program has been shut down, sending a clear message that MAGA wants no accountability for racist police, and raising the fear among Black people that police violence will go largely unchallenged in Black communities under MAGA fascism. This, along with the hundreds of violent felons convicted for the January 6 terrorist attack on the U.S. Capitol in 2020, raises a fear that MAGA is encouraging fascist violence against oppressed people, similar to the violence of Hitler's Brown Shirt Nazi movement prior to World War II.

Perhaps if you are not Black, or an immigrant, or speak a language other than English, or if you present as a biological male or female, you're thinking right now that I'm being hysterical and that things "can't be that bad" or that "MAGA is a little harsh, but we have protections and things will get back to normal soon." However, for Black people and other people who have been colonized and oppressed, this whirlwind of shock and awe has made it evident that our equality and acceptance as citizens in this country have been no more significant than the paper documents they are written on. We are seeing all of the civil and human rights that our ancestors fought to gain since 1619 being wiped away with the stroke of a racist pen in a matter of weeks. This is unsettling. We have been thrown even more deeply into Fanon's zone of nonbeing as we are faced even more blatantly with the Fact of our Blackness.

It seems we have difficult times ahead, which will require us to call on the strength, experience, and support of our ancestors who have gone through similar times. Our ancestors' testimonies will remind us that we have seen this face of America before, and we resisted and we survived. Our ancestors and elders have left us some powerful messages to get us through times like these. The ancestor Derrick Bell (1992), one of the architects of the legal theory called critical race theory, reminds us that

> *Black people will never gain full equality in this country. Even those herculean efforts we hail as successful will produce no more than temporary "peaks of prog-*

> *ress," short-lived victories that slide into irrelevance as racial patterns adapt in ways that maintain white dominance. This is a hard-to-accept fact that all history verifies. We must acknowledge it, not as a sign of submission, but as an act of ultimate defiance. (p. 12)*

As we think about this assessment, many in the Black community, particularly Black women who have worked so hard to fight against the rising tide of injustice and racism, resonate with the testimony of ancestor Fannie Lou Hamer (1964) when she declared, "I've been tired all my life, and I'm sick and tired of being sick and tired!" On the other hand, the testimony of our ancestor Frederick Douglass (1857) reminds us that despite the reality of the permanence of racism and our ongoing exhaustion,

> *If there is no struggle, there is no progress. Those who profess to favor freedom and yet deprecate agitation, are men who want crops without plowing up the ground; they want rain without thunder and lightning. They want the ocean without the awful roar of its many waters. This struggle may be a moral one; or it may be a physical one; or it may be both moral and physical; but it must be a struggle. Power concedes nothing without a demand. It never did and it never will.*

We can be inspired by the reassurance of our ancestor Dr. Martin Luther King Jr. (1986), who wrote in his book *Testament of Hope*, "They fail however to perceive the sense of affirmation generated by the challenge of embracing struggle and surmounting obstacles" (p. 314). And finally, we are inspired by our ancestor in resistance and struggle, Assata Shakur (1987), who lived in exile outside of the United States for over 50 years, "It is our duty to fight for freedom. It is our duty to win. We must love each other and support each other. We have nothing to lose but our chains!"

If we allow ourselves to be empowered and inspired by the testimonies and the struggles of our ancestors and elders, we will survive this terrible time in our history, and we will not be overwhelmed. Using the four healing questions of testimony therapy, we can remain clear about what happened to us. We can assess how what is happening to us is affecting our emotional and mental health and relationships. We can remind ourselves that despite these oppressive conditions, we resist and carry on, and we can collectively develop solutions for our healing toward the future. Through testimony approaches to decolonizing mental health, we will be able to agree with the defiant testimony of Frantz Fanon (2008), who wrote, "I am not a prisoner of history. I must not look for the meaning of my destiny in that direction. I must constantly remind myself that the real leap consists in introducing invention into existence. In the world I am heading for, I am endlessly creating myself" (p. 204).

Black people in America are not victims of history. We have a testimony filled with victorious moments, and we will continue to resist the domination of coloniality which seeks to imprison us in the Fact of our Blackness and distort our sense of collective and personal self. Through practices of healing grounded in the traditions of our ancestors as described in this book, I believe that we will be able to decolonize our lives as we continue to decolonize mental health work.

References

Aboriginal Health Council of South Australia. (1995). *Reclaiming our stories, reclaiming our lives. Dulwich Centre Newsletter, 1.*

Akbar, N. (1985). *The community of self* (Revised ed.) Mind Productions & Associates.

Akinyela, M. M. (1996). *Black families, cultural democracy and self-determination: An African-centered pedagogy.* (Doctoral dissertation) Emory University.

Akinyela, M. M. (2002). De-colonizing our lives: Divining a post-colonial therapy. *International Journal of Narrative Therapy and Community Work, 1*(2), 32–43.

Akinyela, M. M. (2025). *Culture, politics, spirituality and practice: A book of resistance and critical theory for disturbing times.* Dulwich Centre.

American Psychiatric Association. (2022). *Diagnostic and statistical manual of mental disorders* (5th ed., text rev.: DSM-5-TR). American Psychiatric Publishing.

Anderson, H. (2000). Supervision as a collaborative learning community. In *Readings in family therapy supervision* (pp. 8–11). American Association of Marriage and Family Therapy.

Aponte, H., & Kissil, K. (Eds.). (2004). *The person of the therapist: Training model.* Routledge.

Asante, M. (1989). *The Afrocentric idea.* Temple University Press.

Asante, M. K. (1998). *The Afrocentric idea* (rev. and expanded ed.). Temple University Press.

Atkinson, D. R., Brown, M. T., Parham, T. A., Matthews, L. G., Landrum-Brown, J., & Kim, A. U. (1996). African American client skin tone and clinical judgments of African American and European American psychologists. *Professional Psychology: Research and Practice, 27*(5), 500–505.

Barry, M. F. (2005). *My face is black is true: Callie House and the struggle for ex-slave reparations.* Knopf.

Bell, D. (1992). *Faces at the bottom of the well: The permanence of racism.* Basic Books.

Billingsley, A. (1994). *Climbing Jacob's Ladder: The enduring legacy of African American families.* Touchstone Press.

Boyd-Franklin, N. (1989). *Black families in therapy: A multisystems approach.* Guilford.

Boyd-Franklin, N. (2003). *Black families in therapy: Understanding the Black American experience*. Guilford.
Braverman, S. (1997) The use of genograms in supervision. In C. Todd & C. Storm (Eds.), *The complete systemic supervisor: Context, philosophy and pragmatics*. Allyn and Bacon.
Bulhan, H. A. (1985). *Frantz Fanon and the psychology of oppression*. Plenum Press, New York.
Breggin, P. R., & Breggin, G. R. (1998). *The war against children of color*. Common Courage Press.
Cauchi, E. D. (2025, February 21). *Justice Department shuts down federal law enforcement misconduct tracker*. CBS News. https://www.cbsnews.com/news/justice-department-shuts-down-federal-law-enforcement-misconduct-tracker
CCHR. (1995). *Creating racism: Psychiatry's betrayal*. Citizens Commission on Human Rights.
Cooper, A. J. (1892). *A voice from the South: A Black woman of the South*. Aldine Printing House.
Darder, A. (1991). *Culture and power in the classroom: Foundations for cultural education*. Bergin and Garvey.
Darder, A. (2024). *The student guide to Freire's pedagogy of the oppressed* (2nd ed.). Bloomsbury Academic.
Douglass, F. (1857, August 3). *If there is no struggle, there is no progress*. BlackPast.org. https://www.blackpast.org/african-american-history/1857-frederick-douglass-if-there-no-struggle-there-no-progress/
Du Bois, W. E. B. (1903). *The souls of black folk*. A. C. McClurg.
Duncan, B, Miller, S., Wampold, B. E., & Hubble, M. A. (2010). *The heart and soul of change: Delivering what works in therapy* (2nd ed.). American Psychological Association.
Fanon, F. (1963). *The wretched of the earth*. Grove.
Fanon, F. (1967). *A dying colonialism*. Grove.
Fanon, F. (2004). *The wretched of the earth*. Grove.
Fanon, F. (2008). *Black skin, white masks*. Grove.
Franklin, N. B. (2003). *Black families in therapy: Understanding the African American experience* (2nd ed.). Guilford.
Frazier, E. F. (1939). *The Negro family in the United States*. University of Chicago Press.
Freedman, J., & Combs, G. (1996). *Narrative therapy: The social construction of preferred realities*. Norton.
Freire, P. (1990). *pedagogy of the oppressed*. Continuum.
Freire, P. (2018). *Pedagogy of the oppressed* (50th anniv. ed.). Bloomsbury Academic.
Freire, P. (2021). *Education for critical consciousness*. Bloomsbury Academic.
Gates, H. L. (2014). *The signifying monkey: A theory of African-American literary criticism*. (25th anniv. ed.). Oxford University Press.
Givens, J. R. (2021). *Fugitive pedagogy: Carter G. Woodson and the art of Black teaching*. Harvard University Press.
Gordon, L. R. (2008). *An introduction to Africana philosophy*. Cambridge University Press.
Guttman, H. G. (1976). *The Black family in slavery and freedom, 1750–1925*. Vintage.
Hamer, F. L., (1964, December 20). I'm sick and tired of being sick and tired [Speech tran-

script]. *Women's Political Communication Archive.* https://awpc.cattcenter.iastate.edu/2019/08/09/im-sick-and-tired-of-being-sick-and-tired-dec-20-1964

Hardy, K. (1990). The theoretical myth of sameness: A critical issue in family therapy training and treatment. In G. Saba, B. Karrer, & K. Hardy (Eds.), *Minorities and family therapy* (pp. 17–33). Norton.

Herskovits, M. J. (1941). *The myth of the Negro past.* Harper and Brothers.

Hill, R. B. (1999). *The strengths of African American families: Twenty-five years later* (2nd ed.). University Press of America.

Hyde, L. (1998). *Trickster makes this world: Mischief, myth, and art.* Farrar, Straus and Giroux.

Hylton, A. (2024). *Madness: Race and insanity in a Jim Crow asylum.* Legacy Lit.

Jackson, V. (2002a). *In our own voice: Black-American stories of oppression, survival and recovery in mental health systems.* Center for the Study of Human Rights.

Jackson, V. (2002b). *Separate and unequal: The legacy of racially segregated psychiatric hospitals.* Healing Circles. http://www.healingcircles.org/uploads/2/1/4/8/2148953/sauweb.pdf

Jones, G. (1991). *Liberating voices: Oral tradition in Black American literature.* Harvard University Press.

Karenga, M. (1989). *The Black American holiday of Kwanzaa: A celebration of family, community and culture.* University of Sankore Press.

Karenga, M. (1993). *Introduction to Black studies* (2nd ed.). University of Sankore Press.

King, M. L., Jr. (1964). *Why we can't wait.* Harper & Row.

King, M. L., Jr. (1986). *A testament of hope: The essential writings and speeches of Martin Luther King, Jr.* (J. M. Washington, Ed.). HarperOne.

King, M. L., Jr. (2010). *Strength to love* (Gift ed.). Fortress Press. (Original work published 1963)

King, M. L., Jr. (2018). *Letter from Birmingham Jail.* Penguin Classics.

Kochman, A. J. (1981). *Black and white styles in conflict.* University of Chicago Press.

Leitch, L. (1992). Explicitly recognizing contextual influence broadens our scope of inquiry. *Supervision Bulletin, 5,* 6–7.

Libow, J. (1985). Training family therapist as feminists. In M. Ault-Riche (Ed.), *Women and family therapy* (pp. 16–24). Aspen.

Liddle, H. (1988). Systemic supervision: Conceptual overlays and pragmatic guidelines. In H. Liddle, D. Breunlin, & R. Schwartz (Eds.), *Handbook of family training and supervision* (pp. 153–171). Guilford.

Liddle, H., & Saba, G. (1983). On context replication: The isomorphic relationship of family therapy training. *Journal of Strategic and Systems Therapies, 2,* 3–11.

Madigan, S. (2019). *Narrative therapy* (2nd ed.). American Psychological Association.

Madigan, S., & Law, I. (Eds.) (1998). *Praxis: Situating discourse, feminism and politics in narrative therapies.* YaleTown Family Therapy.

Mbiti, J. S. (1969). *Black religions and philosophy.* Heinemann International Literature and Textbooks.

McGoldrick, M., & Gerson, R., & Petry, S. (1985/2008). *Genograms in family assessment.* Norton.

McGoldrick, M. (2016). *The genogram casebook: A clinical companion to genograms: Assessment and intervention*. Norton.

Memmi, A. (1965). *The colonizer and the colonized* (Expanded edition). Beacon Press.

Motivo Health. (2025, January 7). 2025 industry trends report: Bringing behavioral health & workforce into focus. *Motivo Health*. https://motivohealth.com/2025-trends-report

Moynihan, D. P. (1965). *The Negro family: The case for national action*. U.S. Department of Labor, Office of Policy Planning and Research.

Nobles, W. W. (1985). *Africanity in the Black family: The development of a theoretical model*. Institute for Advanced Study of Black Family Life and Culture.

Norris, L. (2025, June 6). The number of BIPOC therapists available in these major cities is . . . *CounselingPsychology.org*. Retrieved from https://www.counselingpsychology.org/availability-bipoc-therapists/

Ong, W. J. (1982). *Orality and literacy: Technologizing of the word*. Routledge.

Parry, A., & Doan, R. E. (1994). *Story re-visions: Narrative therapy in the postmodern world*. Guilford.

Peele, J. (Dir.). (2017). *Get out!* [Film]. Blumehouse Productions; QC Entertainment; Monkeypaw Productions.

Rabaka, R. (2009). *Africana critical theory: Reconstructing the Black radical tradition, from W. E. B. Du Bois and C. L. R. James to Frantz Fanon and Amilcar Cabral*. Lexington Books.

Raboteau, A. J. (2004). *Slave religion: The "invisible institution" in the antebellum South*. Oxford University Press.

Ramiriz, M., & Castaneda, A. (1974). *Cultural democracy, bicognative development and education*. Academic Press.

Rigazio-Digilio, S. A., Ivey, A. E., Kunkler-Peck, K. P., & Grady, L. T. (2005) *Community genograms: Using individual, family, and cultural narratives with clients*. Teachers College Press.

Scott, J. C. (1990). *Domination and the arts of resistance: Hidden transcripts*. Yale University Press.

Shakur, A. (1987). *Assata: An autobiography*. Lawrence Hill Books.

Sprenkle, D. H., Davis, S. D. & Lebow, J. L. (2009). *Common factors in couple and family therapy*. Guilford.

Storm, C. (1991). Placing gender in the heart of MFT masters programs. *Journal of Marital and Family Therapy, 17*, 45–52.

Sudarkasa, N. (1997). African American families and family values. In H. P. McAdoo (Ed.), *Black families* (3rd ed., pp. 9–40). Sage. Reprinted in modified form from N. Sudarkasa & L. A. Nwachuku (Eds.) (1996). *Exploring the African American Experience*. Lincoln University Press.

Sweet Honey in the Rock. (1993). *Still on the Journey.* [Album]. EarthBeat!

Thomas, A., & Sillen, S. (1979). *Racism and psychiatry*. Citadel Press.

Thompson, R. F. (1984). *Flash of the spirit: African and Afro-American art and philosophy*. Vintage.

Tomm, K. (2017). Preface to *A Galveston Declaration. Journal of Systemic Therapies, 36*(1), 1–3.

United Nations. (2001). *World Conference Against Racism, Racial Discrimination, Xenophobia, and Related Intolerance: Durban Declaration and Programme of Action.* https://www.ohchr.org/sites/default/files/Documents/Publications/Durban_text_en.pdf

U.S. Office of Personnel Management. (2023). Federal Equal Opportunity Recruitment Program (FEORP) Report: Fiscal Year 2020. https://www.opm.gov/about-us/reports-publications/fy-2020-feorp-report.pdf

Waldegrave, C., Tamasese, K., Tuhaka, F., & Campbell, W. (2003). *Just therapy—a journey: A collection of papers from the Just Therapy team of New Zealand.* Dulwich Centre.

Wampold, B. E., & Imel, Z. E. (2015). *The great psychotherapy debate: The evidence for what makes psychotherapy work.* Routledge.

Washington, H. A. (2006). *Medical apartheid: The dark history of medical experimentation on Black Americans from colonial times to the present.*

wa Thiong'o, N. (1993). *Moving the centre: The struggle for cultural freedom.* James Currey.

Wells, I. B. (1970). *Crusade for justice: The autobiography of Ida B. Wells* (A. D. Wells-Barnett, Ed.). University of Chicago Press.

Whiffen, R. (1982). The use of videotape in supervision. In R. Whiffen & J. Byng-Hall (Eds.), *Family therapy supervision: Recent developments in practice* (pp. 39–46). Grune and Stratton.

Whitaker, C., & Bumberry, W. (1988). *Dancing with the family: A symbolic-experiential approach.* Brunner/Mazel.

White, M., & Epston, D. (1990). *Narrative means to therapeutic ends.* Norton.

Williams, R. L. (Ed.) (1975). *Ebonics: The true language of Black folks.* The Institute of Black Studies.

Wilson, A. N. (1993). *The falsification of Afrikan consciousness: Eurocentric history, psychiatry and the politics of white supremacy.* Afrikan World Infosystems.

Wingard, B., & Lester, J. (2001). *Telling our stories in ways that make us stronger.* Dulwich Centre.

Wiredu, K. (1983). The Akan concept of mind. *Ibadan Journal of Humanistic Studies, 3*, 113–134.

Woodson, C. G. (2017). *The miseducation of the Negro* (T. Darnell, Ed.). Media Services.

Zirimu P., & Gurr, A. (Eds.). (1973). Oracy as a tool of development. In A. Gurr & P. Zirimu (Eds.), *Black aesthetics: Papers from a colloquium held at the University of Nairobi, June, 1971.* East African Literature Bureau.

Index

AALI therapists. *see* African, Asian, Latinx, or Indigenous (AALI) therapists
AAMFT-approved supervisors. *see* American Association for Marriage and Family Therapy (AAMFT)-approved supervisors
AAVE. *see* African American Vernacular English (AAVE)
Aboriginal children, Australian settler governments and removal of, 137
Aboriginal Health Council of South Australia, healing retreat at, purpose of, 130
Aboriginal people of Australia, oral storytelling and, 34–35
Aboriginal societies, in Australia, 136–37
ABPsi. *see* Association of Black Psychologists (ABPsi)
abuse, reparation and perpetrator of, 119
accent, ritual of Nommo and, 36
activist scholarship, second wave of, 25
Adorno, T., 8
Africa, colonization and exploitation of, 4
African, Asian, Latinx, or Indigenous (AALI) therapists
    mentorship and underrepresentation of, 98
    percentage of, licensed in U.S., 97
Africana critical theory, 69
    coloniality and, 8
    decolonizing mental health and, 17
    Fact of our Blackness and, 6–8
    person in the community in, 40–44

    teaching new therapists and, 100
African American Vernacular English (AAVE), 28–29
Africana (Black) studies, initiation of, as an academic discipline, 27
African-centered approach to mental health practice, mandate for, 24
African-centered institution building, detoxification and, 16
African-centered narratives, reparation movement and need for, 124
African Methodist Episcopal church, demand for reparations by, 118
African worldview, Cartesian dualism *vs.*, 41–42
Afrocentric methodology, Du Bois and, 8
agency
    determining, plotting stories across linear time and, 34
    discovery of, 74
    fostering, 79, 81–82, 83, 84
    lack of, asymmetrical social relationships and, 71
    lack of, Eurocentric version of Black history and, 125
agency policy, new therapists and, 113, 114
agreement form, for supervisees, 104, 108, 112, 114
Akan people, relationship in cultural perspective of, 42
Akbar, N., 61
alcoholism, Aboriginal people and, 139

Algeria, Fanon's work in, 11
Algerian freedom fighters, French colonialism and killing of, 20
Ali, M., 42
alienation, xviii, 7, 41, 123
  Black lived experience and impact of, recognizing, 29
  Blacks in America, institutional violence, and, 16
  coloniality and, 5
  contradicting oppressive messages tied to, 32
  countering with community building, 59
  cultural democracy and shedding centuries of, 160
  detoxifying, African-centered institution building and, 16
  indigenous therapists and challenging effects of, 136
  racialization and, 6
  Ubuntu and challenge to, 42
  from your own emotions, 63
Allende, I., 150
ambiguity
  being comfortable with, 103
  navigating, 79, 83, 84
American Association for Marriage and Family Therapy (AAMFT)-approved supervisors, 98
American Journal of Psychology, 121
American mental health profession, racist oppression and, 121–22
American Psychological Association, 121
Amnesty International, 139
Amo, A. W., 41
analogies
  in Colombian version of narrative, 149
  new therapists and use of, 106
  supervisees and sharing of, 103
  White's theories on, 33–34
  see also metaphors
ancestral kin networks, genogram work and, 61–62
ancestral knowledge, building on, 69
ancestral relationships, restoring harmony and balance in, 127–28
ancestry, honoring, 131–32

anger, testimony, emotional expression, and, 50
anti-Black MAGA extremism, rise of, 124
anti-Black sentiment in U.S., hardening of, xvii
anticolonialists, development of testimony therapy and, 56–58
anxiety, 123
apartheid in South Africa
  economic and psychological outcomes of, 152, 153
  ending of, 129
Argentina, truth and reconciliation restorative justice practices in, 129
artifact exploration, xix–xx, 59, 69, 84–88
  example, 85–88
  reflective process in, 84–85
arts therapy, in Rwandan healing practice, 145–46
Asians
  MAGA targeting of DEI policies and, 133
  scientific racism and oppression of, 20
asking questions, testifying and, 58–59
assessment, supervision and testimony therapy and, 112–15
Association of Black Psychologists (ABPsi), 27
assumptions, uncovering, 78–79, 81
asymmetrical social relationship, 70–71
Atkinson, D. R., 122
Auburn University, Marriage and Family Therapy program demographic report, 98
audience, in Black cultural tradition, 36
audio recordings, training new therapists and, 105
Australia
  Aboriginal societies in, 136–37
  realities of colonization and occupation in, 1
authenticity, 134
autonomy, fostering, 79, 81–82, 83, 84, *see also* agency

balance, restoring harmony and, 127–29
banking education, 57, 58

Index

Bantu-speaking people, of Zimbabwe, 151
barbershops
   alternative stories told in, 31
   testimonies of Black people in, 21
beat of therapeutic conversation
   new therapists and awareness of, 106
   paying attention to, 36–37, 48–49
   see also call-and-response interaction; rhythm
beauty parlors, alternative stories told in, 31
"because?" bridge, 77, 78–79
beliefs
   ancestral inheritance and, 62
   crossroads of choices and, 78
   social construction of ideas and, 40
Bell, D., 163
Biden, J., Executive Order 15074 signed by, 163
Billingsley, A., xii, xvii
binary choices, navigating, 78
biomedical mind/body paradigm, 41n
Black Americans
   colonization and enslavement of, 1
   family-in-community concept and, xii–xiii
Black bodies, medical experiments and use of, 20–21
Black children
   medical industry and targeting of, 122
   oppositional defiant disorder diagnosis and, 19
Black churches
   alternative stories told in, 31
   call-and-response interactions in, 30
   emotional liberation and, 50
   testimonies of Black people in, 21, 123
Black communities
   DOGE purge of federal workers and impact on, 162
   institutions as cultural organizing spaces, 16–17
   sympathy for Palestinian freedom in, 134–35
Black cultural tradition, "soul power" in, source of, 135
Black diaspora
   colonization and, 4
   scientific method, colonial oppression, and, 20
   trickster names throughout, 67
Black families
   African-centered focus on, background for, 27
   decolonized mental health practice for, 117
Black history, reclaiming, honoring ancestry and, 131–32
Black liberation, decolonizing mental health practice and, 27
Black Lives Matter, 162
Black matriarchy, Moynihan on rise of, 26–27
Black men
   demotion of, Moynihan on rise of Black matriarchy and, 27
   paranoid schizophrenia diagnosis and, 19
Black music, new therapist and listening to, 106
Blackness, lived experience of, 123. *see also* Fact of our Blackness
Black people
   alienated from other Black people, 6
   coloniality and impact on self-other relationships for, 18
   colorism and impact on, 109
   domination of the MAGA movement and, 161
   emotional expression and, 49–50
   fascist movements and impact on, 40–41
   First Nations peoples and, 71
   genocide practices against, 122
   Jim Crow and mental health conditions of, 120
   kin network and, 61
   MAGA targeting of DEI policies and, 133
   mental health support and avoidance by, 97
   psychiatry and oppression of, 121–22
   return to Africa movement, 118
   scientific method and colonial oppression of, 20
   storytelling by, 38–39
   whirlwind of MAGA shock and awe and, 163

Black Power Movement, Fanon's influence on, 10
Black pride, Ubuntu and, 43–44
Black prisoners in New Orleans, psychosurgery experiments on, 122
Black radical tradition, Africana critical theory within, 8
Blacks in America
  coloniality and cultural hegemony in lived experiences of, 4
  coloniality for, defining, 16
Black Skin, White Masks (Fanon), 11, 13
Black social and cultural studies, ongoing debate central to, 26–27
Black therapy for and by Black people, importance of, xiii
Black victimhood, countering doom-and-gloom narrative about, 22
Black welfare queen, Reagan presidency and myth of, 27
Black women
  borderline personality disorder diagnoses and, 19
  National Ex-Slave Mutual Relief Bounty and Pension Association led by, 118
blues music
  musicality in Black people's conversations and, 49
  new therapists and listening to, 106
  testifying or having a testimony in, 39
  trickster in, 31
body
  awareness of, 63–64
  beat of therapeutic conversation and, 36
  language and cultures grounded in orality and, 49
  new therapist and awareness of, 106, 110
  Obama's speeches and movement of, 37
  posture, context of therapeutic conversation and, 49
  ritual of Nommo and, 36
  storytelling in therapy room and role of, xix
borderline personality disorder, 19, 122
Boyd-Franklin, N., 65
branches, in tree of life approach, 158
Breggin, G. R., 122

Breggin, P. R., 122
Br'er Rabbit, 67
bridging questions, xix, 59, 77, 78
Brown children
  medical industry and targeting of, 122
  oppositional defiant disorder diagnosis and, 19
Brown people
  domination of the MAGA movement and, 161
  fascist movements and impact on, 40–41
Brown Shirt Nazi movement, MAGA's fascist violence and, 163
brush harbors, 123–24
  new therapists and, creating, 115
  self-defining testimonies of enslaved people in, 21
"but why?" technique, 77, 78

Cabral, A., 56
cadence, context of therapeutic conversation and, paying attention to, 49
call-and-response interaction, xix
  achieving spiritual release and, 51
  in Black storytelling, 30, 39
  at churches and political rallies, 29
  dialogue and, 70
  new therapist and, 106
  testifying and bearing witness and, 124
  in therapeutic conversation, 46–47
  see also beat of therapeutic conversation; rhythm
Canada, 138
  Indian school programs in, 137
  truth and reconciliation restorative justice practices in, 129
Caribbean region, colonization and, 4
Cartesian dualism
  African worldview *vs.*, 41–42
  traditional diagnostic psychotherapy and, 44
Cartwright, S., 121
case management, new therapists and, 113, 114
case presentation, focus on context in, 104
Catholic religion, indigenous people of Colombia and, 147

ceremonial work
    in Aboriginal narrative practice, 142
    in Rwandan healing practice, 146
    tree of life approach and, 159
check-in with emotions, daily, 63
Chile, truth and reconciliation restorative justice practices in, 129
choices
    crossroads of, 78, 81, 82
    problematizing questions and, 77, 78
churches. *see* Black churches
circle metaphor, in Black spirituality, 128
civil rights, MAGA and dismantling of, 133, 161
Civil Rights Act of 1964, 161
Civil War (U.S.), 116
    activist scholarship in wake of, 25
    "Negro insane asylums" developed after, 71
class
    accepting inequalities of, schooling and, 70
    hierarchy and privilege, mental health care system and, 19
    new therapists and issues of, discussing, 109
    supervisor/supervisee relationship and, 104
client, approaching with "an open hand," 66
client-centered tradition, testimony therapy and, 44
Clintons, the, view of Black youth, 125
closed-circuit video, 105
clothing as cultural expression, changes in, 23
codes
    creating, 88–91
    definition of, 90
    knotted, xx, 59
    presenting, 90–91
    unraveling, 69
code switching
    double consciousness and, 50
    in the therapy room, 99
cognitive behavioral therapy, 3
collaboration
    new therapists and modeling stance of, 107, 114, 115
    supervisees with some experience and, 103
collective pronouns, 42
Colombia, colonization and impact on, 146–47
colonialism
    dominance of Eurocentric world view and, 24
    sense of inferiority in the oppressed and, 14–15
coloniality, 126
    Aboriginal people and effects of, 138–39
    Black traditions and cultural resistance to, 22
    cultural democracy and people impacted by, 159
    definition of, 4, 17
    ethics, cultural responsibility, and, 3–4
    everyday lived experience of the colonized and, 18
    healing negative effects of, 29
    hidden power of, 8
    living with the Fact of our Blackness and, 7
    MAGA movement and enforcement of, 161
    social, cultural, and psychological impact of, 4–5
colonization, 40
    Aboriginal people and effects of, 138–39
    Colombia and impact of, 146–47, 148
    colorism and legacy of, 109
    education reproduced and shaped by, 70
    Eurocentric judgments and values and, 58
    purpose of, 4
    realities and experience of occupation and, 1–2
    restrained emotional expression and, 50, 51
    Rwanda and aftereffects of, 143–44, 146
    Rwanda's history before, 143
    South African peoples and effects of, 151–53
    surviving, kin network and, 61
    see also decolonization
colonized people, infra-politics of life for, 31–32

colonizer/colonized relationship, zone of nonbeing and, 14
color blindness and sameness, challenging ideas of, 28
color/caste
  new therapists and issues of, discussing, 109
  supervisor/supervisee relationship and, 104
"colored insane asylums," 122
colorism
  legacy of, 109
  new therapists and discussion of, 109–10
Coltrane, J., 76
Combs, G., 40
Common, 39
community
  building, critical pedagogy and, 57–58
  cultural authenticity and, 68
  kin network within, 61
  person in, 40–44, 61
  seeking feedback from, 64
  in tree of life approach, 158
community circles, reparations movement and, 125, 126
community cultural genograms, 61
community mental health work, in South Africa, 152–53
community of self, intersectional contexts and shaping of, 61
connectedness, African worldview and idea of, 41
context, supervisees and significance of, 104, 107–8, 113
contextual model, 29
continuity, strength-based assumption
  Herskovits and positing of, 26
  understanding Black family life and culture and, 27
Conyers, J., 116, 118
Cook, J., 138
Cooper, A. J., 25
Copeland, J., 39
cotherapists, nonintrusive, training new therapists and, 105
countertransference, new therapist and discussion of, 111

creative expression, connecting to your emotional self and, 64
critical consciousness, developing, 17
critical pedagogy, 57, 58, 59, 69, 70, 71, 88, 103
critical race theory, 41, 163–64
critical thinking, fostering, problematizing questions and, 84
crossroads
  in Black American folklore, 77
  of choices, 78, 81, 82
  trickster as guardian of, 31
cultural authenticity, nurturing, 68
cultural being, strengthening sens of, 17
cultural democracy, xx, xxi
  decolonizing practices and, 159–60
  indigenous therapists and, xv, 136
  multiculturalism *vs.*, xv–xvi
  vision of, building on, 159–60
cultural domination, occupation and, 2–3
cultural gathering places, self-defining testimonies of Black people in, 21–22
cultural humility, testimony therapy and, 32
cultural inferiority
  Blacks in America, institutional violence, and, 16
  detoxifying, African-centered institution building and, 16
culturally mediated ideas, 40
cultural purity and permanence, argument against notions of, 23–24
cultural responsibility, ethics and, 3–5
culture
  construction of, 22–24
  defining, viewpoints related to, 22–23
  dialectic of, 23
  ever-changing nature of, 32
  grounded in orality *vs.* in literacy, 35–36
Culture, Politics, Spirituality, and Practice (Akinyela), 161
curiosity, 45, 102, 111, 112

dance, 29, 36, 64
  achieving spiritual release through, 50
  as cultural expression, changes in, 23
Darder, A., 56, 69, 70
Davis, M., 67, 76

DC snipers, Ubuntu and stories told about, 43
decisions, crossroads as place of, 77
decoding questioning cycle
  sevenfold process in, 91–92
  testimony therapist's role in, 92–93
decoding questions
  define the benefits in the resolutions, 92
  define the problems with what is observed, 91, 94
  describe how the new situation might look, 92, 95–96
  describe what you see or hear, 91, 93–94
  example, 93–96
  question why there is a problem, 91–92, 94–95
  share similar experiences, 91, 94
  what can be done to resolve the problem, 92, 95
decolonization
  definition of, 5, 41
  example of, for an individual Black person, 5–6
  urgency of, 161–65
  see also future of decolonization
decolonizing mental health practice
  Africana critical theory and, 8
  alternative stories in, 31–32
  for Black families, need for, 117
  Black liberation and, 27
  call-and-response interaction and, 30
  challenging ideas of color blindness and sameness in, 28
  cultural democracy and, 159–60
  decentering Euro-Western assumptions and, 7
  decolonizing our lives and, 165
  developing critical consciousness and, 17
  Fanon's ideas and, five assumptions related to, 16–17
  future of, uncertainty with, 98–99
  helping people tell their story, 69–71
  indigenous therapists and, 136
  introducing idea of, with new therapists, 108
  new generations of therapists and, 99
  Palestinian therapists and, 134
  reclaiming our center and, 24–31
  shifting back to African-centered cultural worldview and, 27–28
  taking an emotional inventory, 62–69
  testimonies in, centrality and placement of, 6
  therapist's use of self and, 59–61, 111, 112
  training new therapists in, necessity of, 114–15
  see also Ubuntu
decolonizing our lives, respect and, xv
"De-colonizing Our Lives" (Akinyela), xv
deconstructionist therapies, 44
deeper inquiry, encouraging, 78, 80–81, 82–83
deficit-pathological view, Frazier and positing of, 26
DEI (diversity, equity, inclusion) policies and programs
  MAGA and targeting of, 133, 161, 162
  Trump administration's assault against, 118, 161–62
  weaponizing of, by the far right, 41
Democratic National Convention (2024), Nommo and Black communication styles at, 37–38
Denborough, D., xiv
Department of Education, Trump administration and elimination of, 162
depersonalization, 41
depression
  lived experience of Blackness and, 123
  sadness *vs.*, 54–55
Descartes, R., xviii, 41, 41n
despair, "the blues" and, 135
diabetes, Black people and, 139
diagnosis, medical model and, 18, 19
Diagnostic and Statistical Manual of Mental Disorders (*DSM*), 18, 19
dialectical engagement, in decolonizing mental health practice, 70
dialogical coding and decoding, in decolonized therapy room, 89–90
dialogue
  creating healthy relationships and, 69–71
  humanizing education through, 57
  monological conversations *vs.*, 70

dialogue (*continued*)
  reflective, in decoding questioning cycle, 91, 93–96
  solution-directed, communitarian values and, 90
disabled people, MAGA targeting of DEI policies and, 133
discursive therapies, 3
documentation for reparations movement, stories guided by healing questions and, 131
DOGE (Department of Government Efficiency), massive purge of federal workers and, 162
Domination and the Arts of Resistance (Scott), 31
Donaldson, L., 39
doom-and-gloom narrative, 33
  Black resistance to oppression *vs.*, 22
  construction of culture *vs.*, 23
  moving beyond, four healing questions and, 73, 77
  noticing victorious moments *vs.*, 44–48, 125
  opposing with unpredictability factor, 101
  reparations seeking and alternatives to, 123
  shifting, problematizing questions and, 83
double consciousness
  Blacks in America, institutional violence, and, 16
  coloniality and, 18
  contradicting oppressive messages tied to, 32
  cultural democracy and emerging from, 160
  detoxifying, African-centered institution building and, 16
  healing negative effects of, 29
  restrained emotional expression and, 50
  W. E. B. Du Bois and theory of, xviii, 8–10, 12, 29, 110
Douglass, F., 164
Drahm, T. M., 136–42
  Aboriginal ancestry of, 136–37
  dialogue and interview with, 137–42
  narrative therapy work of, 137, 139–42

drapetomania (runaway slave disorder), 19, 121
drawing, 64
drug cartels, indigenous population of Colombia and, 147
drumming, achieving spiritual release through, 50
DSM. see Diagnostic and Statistical Manual of Mental Disorders (DSM)
Du Bois, W. E. B., 25, 32
  double consciousness concept of, xviii, 8–10, 12, 29, 110
Dulwich Centre (Aboriginal Health Council of South Australia), xiv, 129
Dulwich Centre Master of Narrative Therapy program, 137
dysaesthesia aethiopica (oppositional slave disorder), 19, 121
Dying Colonialism, A (Fanon), 20

Ebonics, 28, 42
education
  asymmetrical social relationship in, 71
  limit situations and, 70
  problem-posing pedagogy, 69
  see also critical pedagogy; schooling
Education for Critical Consciousness (Freire), 69
elders in Black culture, honoring, 131
electroshock therapy, 20
Elegba, in West African cultural traditions, 30
emotional choices, broadening client's sense of, 52–53
emotional force, spiritual release and, 50
emotional inventory, 62–69
emotional journaling, 64
emotional liberation, focus on, 49–51, 68
emotional naming, 51, 63
emotional self, attentiveness and reconnecting to, 63, 65
emotional vocabulary, providing, in testimony therapy, 55
emotions
  alienation from, 63
  empathizing and naming of, 51
  new therapist and awareness of, 106
  Rwandan understanding of, 145

emotion wheel, 63
empirically supported treatments (ESTs), 29
empowerment, problematizing questions and, 84
engagement
    dialectical, 70
    of testimony therapist, 65
English language, as "official" language of the U.S., 162
Enlightenment, the, scientific method and rationalism of, 19
enslavement
    coming to terms with history of, 119–20, 129
    Jim Crow apartheid in aftermath of, 117, 120
    reparations to repair effects of, 116
    taking responsibility for ongoing impact of, 118
    see also reparations movement; slavery
Epston, D., 33, 34, 35, 38, 56, 140
Equal Employment Opportunity rule, Trump and rescinding of, 161
Eshu, 67
ESTs. *see* empirically supported treatments (ESTs)
Esu, in West African Cultural traditions, 30
ethics, cultural responsibility and, 3–5
ethnicity, supervisor/supervisee relationship and, 104
Euro-American social settings, emotional restraint in, 49, 50
Eurocentric domination, cultural democracy *vs.*, 159, 160
Eurocentric training, questioning in decolonizing mental health practice, 28–29
Eurocentric world view, colonialism and dominance of, 24
Europe, far-right fascist movements in, 40
European organizations, abuse of Blacks in U.S. sanctioned by, 119
Euro-Western assumptions, decentering in decolonizing mental health, 7
evaluation, ongoing, skill development and, 112
evangelical fundamentalist white Christians, MAGA movement and, 161

Evans, C., 39
evidence-based therapeutic approach, medical model and, 18, 19
"expert knowledge" orientation, new therapists and, 100
exploring artifacts. *see* artifact exploration
externalizing language, 46, 48

facial expressions
    beat of therapeutic conversation and, 36
    new therapist and awareness of, 106
Fact of our Blackness
    Africana critical theory and, 6–8
    double consciousness and, 9
    MAGA's impact and, 163
    medical experimentation history and, 21
    resistance and, 165
    zone of nonbeing and, 14
FALN (Algerian National Liberation Front), 11
family
    in Black American cultural context, xvii–xviii
    extended, kin network and, 61
family gatherings
    alternative stories told in, 31
    testimonies of Black people shared at, 21
family genogram exploration, 61–62
family-in-community concept, xii–xiii, xvii
family therapy
    key purposes of, 58
    narrative therapy and, xii
    new therapists trained in, 100
    significant transitions in, xi
    term for, questioning, xii
Fanon, F., xviii, 32, 56, 165
    Black Skin, White Masks, 11, 13
    culture and resistance and, 16–17
    A Dying Colonialism, 20
    life and work of, 10–11
    as a mental health worker, understanding, 11–15
    on racialized inferiority complex, 15
    reclaiming, 10–17
    work with Algerian freedom fighters, 11, 16
    The Wretched of the Earth, 10

Fanon, F. (*continued*)
  zone of nonbeing concept of, xviii, 13, 14, 110, 163
fascism
  MAGA and encouragement of fascist violence, 163
  normalization of Black and Brown inferiority and, 40–41
faux kin, 61
federal workers, massive layoffs of, 133, 162
feedback
  community, seeking, 64
  supervision and testimony therapy and, 104, 112–15
First Amendment, MAGA movement and dismantling of, 161
first do no harm model, new therapists and, 105
First Nations (Native American) tradition, three healing questions from, 71
food as cultural expression, changes in, 23
forest, in tree of life approach, 158
40 acres promise, rescinding of, 116, 118
four healing questions, xix, 59, 69, 71–77, 164
  empowerment and, 77
  evolution of, three healing questions and, 71–72
  example, 74–77
  "how does what happened to you affect you today?," 72, 73, 75
  "what do you need to heal?," 72, 74, 76–77
  "what gives you the strength to carry on?," 72, 73–74, 76
  "what happened to you?," 72, 75
Fourteenth Amendment, MAGA movement and dismantling of, 161
Frankfurt School of critical theory, 8
Franklin, N. B., 21–22
Frazier, E. F., deficit-pathological view posited by, 25–26
Freedman, J., 40
freedom, pedagogy of, 57
Freire, P.
  codes created by, 88–89
  critical pedagogy of, 56, 57–58, 59, 69, 70, 71, 88
  dialogical teaching methodology of, 57–58
  Education for Critical Consciousness, 69
  on limit situations, 70
  pedagogy of freedom and, 57
Freud, S., psychoanalytic/psychodynamic theory of, 28
fugitive pedagogy, building on tradition of, 99
future of decolonization, 133–60
  "a hundred flowers blooming" metaphor and, 160
  dialogues with indigenous therapists and, 136–59
  vision of, xx–xxi

Gacaca courts (Rwanda), reconciliation efforts through, 143
Gaza
  Israel's war in, 134–35
  realities of colonization and occupation in, 1
gender
  accepting inequalities of, schooling and, 70
  new therapists and issues of, discussing, 109
  supervisor/supervisee relationship and, 104
gender hierarchy and privilege, mental health care system and, 19
gender policies, Trump administration and redefining of, 162
generational mapping, in Aboriginal narrative practice, 142
genocide
  Australian settler governments and, 137
  Black people's mental health and story of, 123
  indigenous population of Colombia and, 147
  Native Americans and, 119
  of Ndebele by Shona people of Zimbabwe, 152
  of Tutsi community of Rwanda, 129, 142, 143, 144, 146
genograms
  building, 61–62
  supervisees and use of, 104, 109, 111

gestures and gesticulation
    beat of therapeutic conversation and, 36
    language and cultures grounded in orality and, 49
    Obama's speeches and use of, 37
Get Out! (film), "sunken place" idea and, 13
Givens, J. R., 99
"giving testimony," exploring meaning of, xix. *see also* testimony
Gordon, L. R., 40, 41
gospel music, 28
    new therapist and listening to, 106
    testifying or having a testimony in, 39
Great Barrier Reef, 137
Great Zimbabwe, trading empire of, 151
grief, testimony, emotional expression, and, 50
ground, in tree of life approach, 158
Gukurahundi (Shona term), loose translation of, 152n
gynecology, enslaved Black women and medical experiments in, 21

Habermas, J., 8
Hall, G. S., 121
Hamas, Israelis killed and taken hostage by, 134
Hamer, F. L., 164
hand movements, new therapist and awareness of, 106
harmony, restoring balance and, 127–29
Harris, K., 37
healer/witness, stance of, 126
healing
    community building and, 59
    emotional freedom and, 50
    family genogram exploration and, 61
    honoring ancestry and, 131–32
    indigenous resources for, 135
    national, examples of, 128–29
    processes of reparation and, 119
    Rwandan approach to, 145–46
    testimony reparations groups and, 124
    see also four healing questions
healing spaces, intentional, reparations movement and, 117, 118

health insurance industry, medicalization of mental health work by, 100, 115
Heath, R., 122
Hegel, G. W. F., "master-slave" dialectic of, 13
hermeneutics
    decolonizing therapeutic conversations and, 30
    definition of, 31
Hermes, 31
Herskovits, M., continuity, strength-based assumption posited by, 26
hidden testimonies, supervision and, 103
High John the Conqueror, 67
Hill, R., 61
hip-hop, 29
    cypher circles, 39
    musicality in Black people's conversations and, 49
    new therapist and listening to, 106
    testifying or having a testimony in, 39
Hitler, A., Brown Shirt Nazi movement and, 163
HIV/AIDS crisis, in South Africa, 154
    tree of life approach and, 155–57
    working with women and children, 151
homosexuality, 20
honesty, 103
hope and hopefulness
    "carrying on" and sense of, 74
    eliciting testimonies of, 50
    new therapists and encouraging sense of, 101
    nurturing, identifying victorious moments and, 44–48
    testimony therapist and, 67–68
    see also future of decolonization
hope-focused mental health practice, testimony therapy and, 32
HR 40 (reparations bill), history behind, 116, 118
human rights abuses, American mental health profession and, 121–22
humility, 32, 66, 103
humor
    new therapists and use of, 106, 113
    opposing doom-and-gloom narrative and, 101

Hutu community of Rwanda
  colonization and effect on, 143
  genocide against Tutsi community by, 142, 143, 144
Hylton, A. A., 122
hyperbolic language, opposing doom-and-gloom narrative and, 101
hysterectomy, 20

ideas, social construction of, 40. *see also* meaning
imbeleko practice, in African cultures, 157
immigrants
  attacks on, 98
  undocumented, deportation of, 133
indigenous narrative practices, creating, ethical responsibility related to, 4
indigenous people
  of Colombia, genocide against, 147
  MAGA targeting of DEI policies and, 133
indigenous therapists
  Chaste Uwihoreye, 142–46
  cultural democracy and, xv
  developing in our cultural communities, 135
  Marcela Polanco, 146–50
  Ncazelo Ncube-Mlilo, 151–59
  Tileah M. Drahm, 136–42
individualism, Western theory of personhood and, 41
inequality, South Africa and issues of, 153, 154
infallible therapist myth, challenging, 107
inferiority of Black and Brown people
  far-right fascist movements and idea of, 40–41
  white supremacist racism and sense of, 14–15
inferiorization, indigenous therapists and challenging effects of, 136
infra-politics of everyday life, for colonized people, 31–32
internal commentary, checking in with, 65
internalized racism, xviii, xix
internal state psychology, 3
  Cartesian, Black sense of personhood *vs.*, xviii
  individualistic, challenging, xix

International Journal of Narrative Therapy and Community Work, xv
interpretation
  decolonizing therapeutic conversations and, 30
  thin telling of stories and, 44–45
intersectional contexts
  community of self and, 61
  new therapists' sense of self and, 60
intimate partner violence
  code and dialogue with client about, 90
  South African men and issue of, 151
Israel, war in Palestinian Gaza, 134–35

Jackson, V., 71, 72, 122
jazz, 28
  musicality in Black people's conversations and, 49
  new therapist and listening to, 106
  testifying or having a testimony in, 39
Jim Crow, 4, 14, 25, 117, 120, 123, 124, 129
Johnson, A., Field Order 15 rescinded by, 116
Johnson, L. B., 26
journaling, emotional, 64
Journal of Systemic Therapy, xii
joy, testimony, emotional expression, and, 50
Joyner, F., 42
Jung, C., 41
justice
  honoring ancestry and, 131–32
  reparations and struggle for, 117
  restorative, 129
  spiritual component to, 127
Just Therapy, xiv

Kemet (Egypt), temple of Karnak, self-knowledge inscription at, 59, 65, 69
Kentucky, LSD experiments on Black prisoners in, 122
Khoisan people, Western Cape area, South Africa, 151
King, M. L., Jr.
  assassination of, 27
  "inescapable network of mutuality," 160

"Letter from Birmingham Jail," 41n
Testament of Hope, 164
kin network/family
    Black people and, 61
    Ubuntu concept and, xvii–xviii
kin network genograms, 61
kinship structure, Aboriginal narrative practice and, 141–42
Kinyarwanda language, in Rwanda, 143, 145
knotted codes, creating, xx, 59
Kochman, A. J., 50, 51
Kulilli people, Australia, 136
Kwanzaa
    pouring libations tradition and, 127
    Seven Principles of Kawaida and, 42

language, cultures grounded in orality and, 49
Latin American people, *testimonios* and, 150
Latinx people
    MAGA targeting of DEI policies and, 133
    scientific racism and oppression of, 20
learning, social nature of, 105
leaves, in tree of life approach, 158
legacy story, testimony and, xiii
"Letter from Birmingham Jail" (King, Jr.), 41n
letters, in narrative therapy, 34
LGBTQ+ people
    MAGA targeting of DEI policies and, 133, 161
    massive resistance of, 20
libations, pouring of, as African tradition, 127–28
libation statements, 127–28
liberals, Black people's problems as seen by, 125–26
liberating testimony, four healing questions and, 72–74
liberation psychology, 11
liberatory teaching attitudes, new therapists and, 100
licensure, barriers to, reasons for, 98, 115
life terrain map, creating, 73
limit situations, 70
Lincoln, A., assassination of, 116

linear time, plotting stories across, 34
literacy
    culture grounded in orality *vs.* in, 35–36
    privileging of, over orality and orature, 35, 40
literary cultures, "truth" in, 36
literary metaphors, xix, 3
Louisiana state prison, LSD experiments on Black inmates in, 122
love, fear of, therapeutic conversation example, 51–55
LSD experiments, conducted on Black inmates in Louisiana state prison, 122

Maat, Kemetic (Egyptian) notion of, 127
Madigan, S., xiv
MAGA movement, 133
    fascist racism and rise of, 162
    fascist violence against oppressed people and, 163
    normalization of Black and Brown inferiority and, 40
    white supremacist domination of, 161
magical realism, Colombian version of narrative and, 150
Malcolm X, 118
Malvo, L. B., 43
Mapungubwe kingdom, trading empire of, 151
Marcuse, H., 8
marginalization, 123
    of AAMFT-approved supervisors, 98
    new therapists and, discussing, 108
Márquez, G. G., 150
Maslow, A., humanistic psychology of, 28
"master-slave" dialectic (Hegel), 13
Mbiti, J., xviii
meaning
    crossroads and cocreation of, 31
    determining, plotting stories across linear time and, 34
    finding in musical parts, new therapists and, 106
    identifying victorious moments and, 44–45
    interpreting, decolonizing therapeutic conversations and, 30–31

meanin (*continued*) g
  living stories with plot lines and, 33
  making, artifact exploration and, 84, 85
  rhythm and beat of therapeutic conversation and, 37, 48–49
  in ritual of Nommo, 36
  social construction of ideas and, 40
Medical Apartheid (Washington), 20–21
medical experiments
  healthy paranoia of Black people and, 48
  use of Black bodies in, 20–21
medicalization of mental health work, by health insurance industry, 100, 115
medical model
  empirically supported treatments and, 29
  mental health care system and, 18–19
  training, new therapists and, 100–101
medications
  medical model and prescribing of, 18–19
  side effects of, 19
medicine, Black people and distrust in, source of, 21
Memmi, A., 56
mental health care system, medical model and, 18–19
mental health problems in Colombia, rethinking, 147–48
mental health workers of color, barriers to licensure of, 98
mental self, awareness of, 65
mentorship, Black, lack of for new Black therapists, 98
metaphorical mapping, 73
metaphors, 135
  in Aboriginal culture, 141
  of "a hundred flowers blooming," 160
  in Colombian version of narrative, 149
  cultural democracy and, 160
  culturally mediated, xv
  Eurocentric training and, 27
  literary, xix, 3
  of resistance and defiance, 48
  Rwandan healing approach to, 145
  supervisees and sharing of, 103
  testimony therapy and, 29
  in tree of life approach, 157–59

victorious moments and use of, 47, 48
  see also analogies; meaning
microaggressions, xviii
  racist, xvii
  zone of nonbeing and, 14
Middle Passage, 123
militia groups, normalization and protection of, 133
mingos, in Rwandan healing practice, creating, 146
monological conversations, dialogue *vs.,* 70
Montgomery, Alabama dock brawl (2023), Ubuntu and stories told about, 43–44
Moore, A., 118
Motivo Health, 98
Moving the Centre (Thiong'o), 160
Moynihan, D., 125
  The Negro Family: The Case for National Action, 26–27
Muhammad, E., 118
Muhammad, J. A., 43
Muisca people, of Colombia, 146
multiculturalism, cultural democracy *vs.,* xv, 159
music, 36
  as cultural expression, changes in, 23
  new therapist and listening to, 106
  Rwandan approach to, 145
  testimony therapy akin to, 35
musicality, in Black people's conversations, 48, 49
Musk, E., 162

NABSW. *see* National Association of Black Social Workers (NABSW)
naming, of emotions, 51, 63
narrative assessment, providing to new therapist, 114
narrative determinism, definition of, 101
Narrative Means to Therapeutic Ends (White & Epston), 33
narrative therapy, xii, 44
  analogized as text, 34
  Colombian experience and, 149
  externalizing problems in, 48
  literary metaphors assumptions in, 3

testimony therapy as, xiii–xiv, 33
testimony therapy *vs.*, 35
Narrative Therapy and Community Work conference (Adelaide, Australia), xiv
National Association of Black Social Workers (NABSW), 27
National Coalition of Blacks for Reparations in America (N'COBRA), 118
National Ex-Slave Mutual Relief Bounty and Pension Association, 118
national healing, promoting, examples of, 128–29
National Law Enforcement Accountability Database (NLEAD), Trump administration and dismantling of, 162–63
Nation of Islam, demand for reparations and, 118
Native Americans
  broken treaties between U. S. and, 116
  genocide against, 119
Native indigenous peoples, scientific racism and oppression of, 20
N'COBRA. *see* National Coalition of Blacks for Reparations in America (N'COBRA)
Ncube-Mlilo, N., 151–59
  dialogue and interview with, 151–59
  mental health healer journey of, 154–55
Ndebele people
  massacre of, Gukurahundi story about, 152
  tribalism between Shona people and, 151–52
  of Zimbabwe, 151
Negritude (Negro skin coloration disorder), 19
Negro Family, The: The Case for National Action (Moynihan), 26–27
"Negroid" racial group, scientific racism and, 20
"Negro insane asylums," 71
new therapists
  challenges related to decolonization work and, 100
  "expert knowledge" orientation of, 100
  family and life experience conversations with, 111–12

"first do no harm" model and, 105
focusing on the now moment with, 102
medical model training of, 100–101
sharpening skills of, 115
see also supervision and testimony therapy; training new therapists
New Zealand, Māori, Samoan, and Pākehā culture and history of, xiv
Nguzo Saba, in Ujima principle, 128
Nietzsche, F., 41
NLEAD. *see* National Law Enforcement Accountability Database (NLEAD)
Nommo, 59
  creative power of the spoken word and, 36, 39, 42
  Democratic National Convention (2024) and use of, 37–38
  helping people tell their story and, 69
  musical nature of, 48
  testimony reparations groups and power of, 124, 126
norms, social construction of ideas and, 40
note taking, new therapists and, 113
not knowing
  artifact exploration and state of, 85
  dialogical coding and decoding and, 89
now moment, supervision and focus on, 102
nuclear radiation, medical experiments on Black people exposed to, 21

Obama, B., 37
objectifying distance, new therapists and, 100
occupation
  cultural domination and, 2–3
  Israeli, Palestinian resistance and, 134, 135
  realities and experience of colonization and, 1–2
  see also colonialism; coloniality; oppression; resistance
Ong, W.
  on how writing structures consciousness, 35
  on orality, 36
"open hand" attitude, approaching each client with, 66

openness of therapist, testimony therapy and, 32
oppositional defiant disorder, 19
oppositional slave disorder (dysaesthesia aethiopica), 19, 121
oppression
  Black people's mental health and story of, 123
  critical theory and analysis of, 8
  doom-and-gloom narrative vs. Black resistance to, 22
  emotional disconnection and, 51
  limit situations and, 70
  lived realities of colonization and occupation and, 1–2, 4
  medical model and role in, 19
  psychiatric, 71
  psychological, history of, 119, 121–27
  scientific method and, 20
  self-determination and resistance to, 16
  structural, 117
  see also colonialism; coloniality; occupation; resistance
orality
  call-and-response interactions and, 30
  language and cultures grounded in, 49
  musical nature of, 48
  privileging of text and literacy over, 35, 40
  storytelling with a focus on, xix
  testimony and notion of, xiii
  testimony reparations groups and, 124
  testimony therapy and, 35–38
oral tradition
  in Aboriginal culture, 141
  Black storytelling grounded in, 38
  new therapists and grounding in, 106
orature
  oral literature vs., 35
  privileging of text and literacy over, 35, 40
Outraged methodology (South Africa), prevention of gender-based violence and, 152–53

Pacific Islands, realities of colonization and occupation in, 1
painting, 64
Pākehā, meaning of, xiv

Palestine, occupation and resistance to occupation in, 1
Palestinian Gaza and West Bank, ongoing tragedy in, 134–35
paradox
  new therapists and use of, 106
  opposing doom-and-gloom narrative and, 101
paranoid schizophrenia, 19
pedagogy of freedom, 57
Peele, J., 12, 13
person, communitarian sense of, 40–44, 61
personhood and identity
  social/relational idea of Black sense of, xviii
  Western theory of, 41
Peterson, J. B., 139
physical self
  new therapist and awareness of, 106, 110–11
  reflective awareness of, 65
physical sensations, tuning into, 63–64
Pinochet, A., 129
Polanco, Marcela, 146–50
  background and family therapy focus of, 146, 148–49
  dialogue and interview with, 147–50
police abuse, 117, 118
police accountability program, Trump administration and dismantling of, 163
positivist approach, new therapists and, 100
postcolonialism, Fanon as founder of, 11
post-structuralist therapists, 56
posture, new therapist and awareness of, 106
poverty, 126
power, negotiating, construction of culture and, 23
practical paranoia, 22
Pressley, A., 116, 118
problematizing questions, xx, 59, 77–84
  "because?" bridge, 77, 78–79
  breaking stagnation, 79, 81, 82
  "but why" technique, 77, 78
  codes and, 89
  crossroads of choices, 78, 81, 82
  encouraging deeper inquiry, 78, 80–81, 82–83

example, 79–84
fostering autonomy and agency, 79, 81–82, 83, 84
interpretation and, 30
navigating ambiguity, 79, 83, 84
supervisees and use of, 103–4, 113, 115
uncovering assumptions, 78–79, 81
problem-focused approaches, Cartesian dualism and, 44
problem posing, problem solving *vs.*, 92
problem-posing pedagogy, horizontal approach in, 69
problem-posing therapy, decoding questioning cycle and, 91
problem solving, problem posing *vs.*, 92
problem story, Aboriginal people and, 139
process and content issues, new therapists and, 112
progress, struggle and, 164
pronouns, collective, 42
Proud Boys, normalization and protection of, 133
proverbs, Rwandan healing approach to, 145
psychiatry, oppression of Black people and, 71, 121–22
psychoanalytic theory, 3
psychological oppression, history of, 119, 121–27
psychology, Black people and source of distrust in, 21, 48, 121
psychotropic drugs, control of Black children and, 122

quantum physics, unpredictability concept in, 66
questions
asking, testifying and, 58–59
bridging, 59
curious, 107
decoding, 91–96
in decoding questioning cycle, 91–93
four healing questions, 59, 69, 71–77, 164
for genogram work, 62
problematizing, 59, 77–84, 89
therapist's use of self and, 60–61
three healing questions, 71–72

race
accepting inequalities of, schooling and, 70
new therapists and issues of, discussing, 109
racial capitalism, economic superexploitation via, 117
racial dissociation, 12
racial hatred, internalized, coloniality and, 4
racial hierarchy and privilege, mental health care system and, 19
racialization, alienation and, 6
racialized inferiority complex, basis of and treatment for, 15
racial trauma, recognizing Black lived experience and impact of, 29
racism, 126, 127, 128
Get Out! and horror of, 13
internalized, xviii, xix
Jim Crow, 4, 14, 25, 117, 120, 123, 124, 129
new therapists and, discussing, 108
practical paranoia and, 22
scientific, 20
structural, xviii, 4, 16
systemic, xv, 4
zone of nonbeing and, 14
racist inferiorization, coloniality and, 18
racist microaggressions, xvii
racist slave control diseases, end of, 20
rap battles, hip-hop cypher circles and, 39
rascality, 121
R&B, 29
musicality in Black people's conversations and, 49
new therapist and listening to, 106
testifying or having a testimony in, 39
trickster in, 31
Reagan administration, hyperracist policies of, 27
re-authoring of lives and relationships, narrative therapy and, 34
reciprocity, Black communities and attention paid to, 128
reconciliation efforts
in Rwanda, 143
in South Africa, 129
truth telling and testifying and, 121

recorded therapy sessions, 105–6, 113
redlining, 118
Reeves, D., 39
reflection paper, supervisees and, 108, 112, 113, 114
relationship(s)
　Akan people and perspective on, 42
　codes and reinforcing power of, 89
　cultural authenticity and, 68
　healthy, dialogue and, 69–71
　restoring harmony and balance in, 127–29
　therapeutic, asymmetrical social relationship in, 71
　Ubuntu and sense of, 42
　see also community
religious practice as cultural expression, changes in, 23
remembrance rituals, reparations movement and, 125
repairing realm (healing realm), reparation and, 127
reparations, xx
　cost of a human soul and, 117
　healing and processes of, 119
　international law standards and, 119
　reciprocity and, 128
　repairing realm and, 127
　repayment realm and, 127
　seeking, honoring ancestry and, 131–32
　testimony approaches and, 124
reparations bill (HR 40), history behind, 116, 118
reparations movement
　healing testimony and success of, 131
　history behind, 117–18
　intentional healing spaces and, 117, 118
　sacred spaces within, organizing, 130–31
　as soul healing, 128
　testimony in, creating space for, 120
repayment realm (economic realm), reparation and, 127
resilience
　restoring, in Rwandan healing practice, 146
　sources of strength and, 76
　see also victorious moments

resistance, 1—3
　infra-politics of everyday life for colonized people and, 31
　metaphors of, 48
　occupation in Gaza and, 134
　reclaiming our center and, 25
　see also occupation; oppression
resourcefulness, identifying in victorious moments, 46–47, 48
respect, decolonizing our lives and, xv
restorative justice, 129
revolutionary praxis, 70
rhythm
　in Black storytelling, 39
　of a conversation in Black orature, 36
　new therapists and awareness of, 106
　in therapeutic conversation, paying attention to, 36, 37
　see also beat; call-and-response interaction
right-wing politicians, Black people's problems as seen by, 125
Ritalin, control of Black children and, 122
Rogers, C., humanistic psychology of, 28
roots, in tree of life approach, 157–58
runaway slave disorder (drapetomania), 19, 121
Rwanda ("Land of a Thousand Hills")
　artificial ethnic divisions created in, 143, 144
　colonization and mental health challenges in, 144
　genocide of Tutsi community of, 142, 143, 144, 146
　pre-colonization history of, 143
　truth and reconciliation restorative justice practices in, 129

sacred spaces and places
　alternative stories told in, 31
　crossroads as, 31
　gravesites of enslaved people as, 131–32
　in reparations movement, organizing, 130–31
　self-defining testimonies of enslaved people in, 21
　see also safe spaces

sadness
  depression *vs.*, 54–55
  witnessing, 53–54
safe spaces
  brush harbors as, 21, 115, 123
  struggle for reparations in, 118
  in supervision and testimony therapy, creating, 115
  see also sacred spaces and places
San people, of Zimbabwe, 151
schooling, traditional Western, limit situations and, 70. *see also* critical pedagogy; education
scientific method, colonial oppression of Black people and, 20
scientific racism, 20
Scott, J., 31
segregation, Jim Crow, ongoing effects of, 120
self
  African-centered relational idea of, xviii
  communitarian sense of, 40–44
  intersectional aspects of, exploring, 61
  of the therapist, using, 59–61, 105, 110, 111
self-determination
  resistance to oppression and, 16
  victorious moments and, 47
self-discovery, problematizing questions and, 79, 84
self-doubt, xviii, 7
self-knowledge, testimony therapist and, 64–65, 69, 105, 111
self-other relationships, coloniality and inability to enjoy, 18
self-reflection
  artifact exploration and, 85
  problematizing questions and, 78
self-reliance, victorious moments and, 47
Seven Principles of Kawaida, 42
sexism, 126
sexual hierarchy and privilege, mental health care system and, 19
sexuality, accepting inequalities of, schooling and, 70
Shakur, A., 164
Sherman, W. T., 116

Shona people
  tribalism between Ndebele people and, 151–52
  of Zimbabwe, 151
Sierra Leone, truth and reconciliation restorative justice practices in, 129
signification
  new therapists and use of, 106
  opposing doom-and-gloom narrative and, 101–2
signifying monkey, 67
silences, context of therapeutic conversation and, paying attention to, 49
Skinner, B. F., behaviorism of, 28
skin tones, privilege and, 109
slavery, 4, 123
  colorism and legacy of, 109
  Frazier's research on, 26
  Jim Crow apartheid in aftermath of, 117, 120
  legacy of the brush harbor after era of, 21
  racist haze of miseducation about, 25
  surviving, kin network and, 61
  zone of nonbeing and, 14
  see also enslavement; reparations movement
social activism, Colombian *testimonios* and performance of, 150
social constructionist therapies, 3
social construction of ideas, 40
social groups, production and reproduction of culture and, 23
social marginalization, xviii
social pyramid, medical model and, 19
social safety nets, dismantling of, 98–99
solidarity, therapy of, Colombian version of narrative and, 149
solution-focused therapy, 44
songs, achieving spiritual release through, 50
Sotho-Tswana people, South Africa, 151
soul food, 28
soul healing, reparations movement and, 128
"soul power," in Black cultural tradition, source of, 135

South Africa
  Bantu migrations and role in, 151
  colonization and mental health problems of people in, 151–53
  HIV/AIDS crisis in, 151, 154
  mental health and social justice in, 153
South African Truth and Reconciliation process, 129
South America, realities of colonization and occupation in, 1
Southern Reconstruction period, 117
Spain, Colombia colonized by, 146
speaker, in Black cultural tradition, 36
spiritual damage, pondering reparations issues and, 117
spiritual/energetic self, paying attention to, 65
spirituality, justice and, 127
spiritual release, achieving, three elements in, 50, 51
spirituals, musicality in Black people's conversations and, 49
spoken word, Nommo and creative power of, 36, 39, 42
stagnation, breaking, 79, 81, 82
stance
  of healer/witness, 126
  of supervisor, 103
stories
  empowering, victorious moments and, 125
  against the grain, 31–32
  healing questions, reparations movement, and, 131
  interrogating meaning in, 30
  meaning making and, 124–25
  plotting across linear time, 34
  reconstructing, honoring ancestry and, 131–32
  social construction of, xiv–xv
  thickening, in sacred spaces, 124
  thin telling of, 44
  in tree of life approach, thickening of, 158
  see also meaning; storytelling; testimony
storms of life, in tree of life approach, 159
storytelling
  in Aboriginal culture, 141
  by Black folk, 38–39
  Black people's culture in U.S. and, 30
  indigenous therapists and, 135, 136
  problem-laden, contradicting, 44, 45
  Rwandan approach to, 145
  see also meaning; stories; testimony
storytelling therapy, testimony therapy as, xiii–xiv
strengths-based approach, new therapists and, 101
strengths of supervisees, focusing on, 102, 104, 113
structural racism, xviii, 4, 16
struggle, progress and, 164
suicide, in Colombia, community approach to, 148
supervisees
  agreement form for, 104, 108, 112, 114
  critical pedagogy principles and, 103
  encouraging, 104
  genograms and, 104, 109, 111
  reflection paper for, 108, 112, 113, 114
  strengths of, focusing on, 102, 104, 113
  values and goals questionnaire for, 104, 108, 113, 114
supervision and testimony therapy, xx, 97–115
  collaborative work and, 103, 114, 115
  context and, focus in, 104
  "expert knowledge" orientation and, 100
  feedback and assessment, 112–15
  first do no harm, 105–7
  problematizing questions and, 103–4, 113, 115
  supervisor's role in, 102
  working with a new therapist, example, 107–12
  see also training new therapists
supervisors
  AAMFT-approved, 98
  reflections of, new therapist observations and, 113
  stance of, 103
  testimony therapy supervision and role of, 102
Sweet Honey in the Rock, 67
systemic racism, xv, 4

Tairona people, of Colombia, 146
Tamasese, K., xiv
technology, training new therapists and use of, 105
tellers
  in Black storytelling, 39
  call-and-response interactions and, 30
Testament of Hope (King, Jr.), 164
testifying, xvii
  asking questions and, 58–59
  in Black cultural spiritual tradition, 38
  collective story of triumph and, 123–24
  meaning of, for Black people, xiii
  reconciliation process and, 121
  see also testimony
testimonios, Colombian culture and context for, 150
testimony
  as an African-centered theory, 33–55
  in Black cultural tradition, 30
  emotional nature of, 50
  healing, construction of, 51
  in reparations movement, creating space for, 120
  supervisees and sharing of, 103
  see also stories; storytelling; testifying
testimony therapists
  artifact exploration and "not knowing" state of, 85
  in Black orature, 36
  cultural authenticity nurtured by, 68
  decoding questioning cycle and role of, 92–93
  engagement of, 65–66
  goal of, 50–51
  hopefulness nurtured by, 67–68
  oral tradition and values privileged by, 38
  as organizer, role of, 125
  reparations seeking and role of, 123
  self-knowledge and, 64–65, 69, 105, 111
  therapeutic humility and, 66
  unpredictability and, expecting and respecting, 66–67
  use of self, 59–61, 105, 110, 111
testimony therapy, xvii, 17
  client-centered tradition and, 44
  community construction of preferred story in, 39
  cultural humility and openness and, 32
  definition of, 29
  development of, background story on, 56–58
  emotional force and, 50
  ethics, cultural responsibility, and, 3–4
  focus of, 29–30
  international narrative therapy community and, xv
  likening to music, 35
  multiple awarenesses in, 65
  naming of, xiii
  as a narrative therapy, xiii–xiv, 33
  orality and, 35–38
  social justice and possibilities of, 117
  teaching new therapists and, 100
  Western narrative therapy *vs.,* 35
  see also narrative therapy; supervision and testimony therapy
testimony therapy in practice, 56–96
  asking questions and testifying, 58–59
  creating codes, 88–91
  decoding questioning cycle, 91–93
  decoding questions example, 93–96
  dialogue and creating healthy relationships, 69–71
  emotional inventory, 62–69
  exploring artifacts, 84–85
  exploring artifacts example, 85–88
  four healing questions, 71–74
  four healing questions example, 74–77
  genogram work, 61–62
  problematizing questions, 77–79
  problematizing questions example, 79–84
  therapist's use of self, 59–61
text, privileging of, over orality and orature, 35, 40
text-based storytelling, linear nature of, 36
textual analogy, privileging, White & Epston's focus on, 34
theory, discussing with new therapists, 109, 114. *see also* Africana critical theory
therapeutic change, empowering of, elements related to, 29

therapeutic circle, bringing unspoken issues into, 102
therapeutic conversations
  afraid to love, case example, 51–55
  analogy of therapy as text and, 34
  ancestral contemplation in, 62
  beat of, paying attention to, 36–37, 48–49
  rhythm of, paying attention to, 36, 48–49
Therapeutic Conversations conference (Toronto), xiv
therapeutic decolonization and liberation, assumptions underlying, xvi
therapeutic humility, 66
therapeutic posture, Aboriginal narrative practice and, 141
therapeutic process, importance of ideas of freedom in, 57
therapeutic relationships, asymmetrical social relationship in, 71
therapists
  AALI in U.S., underrepresentation of, 97
  crossroads and role of, 31
  encounter with testimony therapy, feelings about, 99
  see also new therapists; testimony therapists
therapy room, noticing "vibes" in, 65
thin telling, of stories, 44
Thiong'o, N. W., 160
Thirteenth Amendment, MAGA movement and dismantling of, 161
three healing questions, First Nations tradition and, 71
time, Aboriginal culture and stretching of, 141
Tomm, K., xii
tone
  context of therapeutic conversation and, paying attention to, 49
  ritual of Nommo and, 36
Torres Strait Islander children, Australian settler governments and removal of, 137
Tosquelles, F., 11
training new therapists
  critical pedagogy and, 103
  in decolonized mental health practice, necessity of, 114–15

documents related to, 104
feedback and assessment and, 112–15
problematizing question and, 103–4
recorded therapy sessions and, 105–6
supervisor's role in, 102
teaching decolonizing stance, 100
working with a new therapist example, 107–12
see also new therapists; supervision and testimony therapy
transparency, cultural authenticity and, 68
trauma, addressing, four healing questions and, 71–74
tree of life approach
  description of, 157–59
  HIV/AIDS crisis in South Africa and origins of, 155–57
tree of life certificate, awarding, 159
trickster(s)
  in Black/African culture, 31
  crossroads and encounter with, 31, 77
  names for, throughout the Black diaspora, 67
Trump, D., 37, 98, 161
  assault against DEI programs and, 118
  second presidency of, 98, 116, 133
trunk, in tree of life approach, 158
trust issues, new therapists and, 100
"truth," in literary cultures, 36
truth telling, reconciliation process and, 121
Tulane University, 122
Turner, H. M., 118
Tutsi community of Rwanda
  colonization and effect on, 143
  genocide of, 129, 142, 143, 144, 146
Tutu, D., 129
Twa people of Rwanda, 143
two-way mirrors, live supervision and use of, 105, 107

Ubuntu, xx
  Black pride and, 43–44
  communitarian sense of person and self and, 42
  community collective shame and, 43

kin network/family and influence of, xvii–xviii
understanding, importance of, xix
Ujamaa family circles, 56. *see also* testimony therapy
Ujima, translation of, 42
Ujima principle, Nguzo Saba in, 128
undocumented immigrants, deportation of, 133
unemployment
   in Black communities, DOGE purge of federal workers and, 162
   in South Africa, 153
United Nations World Conference Against Racism (Durban, South Africa), 119
United States, 138
   Africanizing of European culture in, 24
   broken treaties between Native Americans and, 116
   emerging crisis for Black and Brown people in, 135, 161
   English language as "official" language in, 162
   Indian school programs in, 137
   MAGA movement in, 40, 133, 161
unpredictability
   expecting and respecting, 66–67
   new therapist and factor of, 101
   the trickster and cultural expectation of, 67
urban Black life, Moynihan's scholarly research on, 26–27
U.S. Capitol, January 6th terrorist attack on, 163
using the self of the therapist, 59–61, 105, 110, 111
us-ness, Black cultural ethos and, 39
Uwihoreye, Chaste, 142–46
   context and professional background of, 142–43
   dialogue and interview with, 143–46
   mental health practice journey of, 144–45

values
   ancestral inheritance and, 62
   crossroads of choices and, 78
   social construction of ideas and, 40

values and goals questionnaire, for supervisees, 104, 108, 113, 114
Veterans Administration, 45
victim blaming, challenging practice of, 126
victimization of Black people, racist domination story about, 120
victorious moments, 59
   Black people and testimony filled with, 165
   community power and, 126
   empowering stories and, 125
   highlighting, life terrain map and, 73
   lives defined by, 33
   recalling, breaking stagnation and, 81
   resilience of client and, 73–74
   see also resilience
victorious moments, identifying, 44–47
   nurturing hopefulness and, 44–45
   reflection on, 47–48
   rhythm and beat of the conversation and, 48–49
   Shabaka, case example, 45–47
video recordings, training new therapists and, 105, 107
violence initiative, inner-city children and, 122

Waldegrave, C., xiv
Washington, H. A., *Medical Apartheid*, 20
Watson, J. B., behaviorism of, 28
Wells, I. B., 25
West Bank, realities of colonization and occupation in, 1
Western ideas and practices, belief in superiority of, 2, 3
Western schooling, limit situations and, 70
White, M., xiv, 33, 34, 35, 38, 56, 130, 140, 141
"white gaze, the," Fanon and concept of, 12
white guilt, doom-and-gloom narrative and, 22
white nationalist sentiment, hardening of, in U.S., xvii
white supremacy, 7, 10, 40, 126, 127
   MAGA movement and, 161
   negating of Black history and, 131
   surviving, kin network and, 61

wholism, African worldview and idea of, 41
Wilhelm, A., 41
Wilson, A., 32
Winans, the, 39
Wingard, B., 140
Wiredu, K., 42
witnesses
    in Black storytelling, 39
    call-and-response interactions and, 30
    mental health workers as, 128
    testimony therapists as, 48, 49
witnessing, 30
    in collective story of triumph, 124, 126
    presence, supervisor's role in cultivating, 102
women, working-class, MAGA targeting of DEI policies and, 133
Wonder, S., 39
Woodson, C. G., 25

Wretched of the Earth, The (Fanon), 10
writing, structuring of consciousness and, 35

Xhosa people, South Africa, 151

yarning, Aboriginal culture and, 141
Yidinji people, Australia, 136, 137–38

Zimbabwe
    ethnic and national groups in, 151, 152
    genocide of Ndbele by Shona people in, 152
Zirimu, P., 35
zone of nonbeing
    cultural democracy and emerging from, 160
    Fanon's ideas on, xviii, 13, 14, 110, 163
Zulu kingdom, founding of, 151

About the Author

Makungu M. Akinyela, PhD, LMFT, is a leading authority on cultural democracy, narrative practice, anti-racist resistance, and mental health, and a professor of Africana Studies at Georgia State University. He is the author of *Culture, Politics, Spirituality, and Practice: A Book of Resistance and Critical Theory for Disturbing Times.* Dr. Akinyela is a lifelong committed social justice organizer with a focus on struggles for human rights and justice for Black people in the United States and the African diaspora. His research and writing include such subjects as cultural democracy and mental health care, cultural domination and therapeutic resistance, reparations and the role of mental health workers in repairing oppressions wounds, and African-centered family therapy. He is a clinical fellow and an approved supervisor of the American Association of Marriage and Family Therapy (AAMFT).